soul
friendship

Other books by Ray Simpson published by
Hodder & Stoughton

Exploring Celtic Spirituality: Historic Roots for our Future
Celtic Worship Through the Year
Celtic Blessings for Everyday Life

Chic Lidstone

SOUL FRIENDSHIP

CELTIC INSIGHTS INTO SPIRITUAL MENTORING

RAY SIMPSON

Hodder & Stoughton
LONDON SYDNEY AUCKLAND

British Library Cataloguing in Publication Data
A record for this book is available from the British Library

ISBN 0 340 73548 1

Typeset by Avon Dataset Ltd, Bidford-on-Avon, Warks

Printed and bound in Great Britain by
The Guernsey Press Co. Ltd, Channel Isles

Hodder & Stoughton
A Division of Hodder Headline Ltd
338 Euston Road
London NW1 3BH

DEDICATION

I dedicate this book to those who, through their friendship, their writings, their challenge, their teaching, or their counsel, have helped me move through painful struggles towards my 'place of resurrection'.

Among these are Stuart Burns, Eric Hutchison, Gert and Siri Kratzmeier, Frank Lake, Russ Parker, Sally Simpson.

These people have also helped me through their story or their writings: Aidan, Brigid, Columba, Cuthbert, David of Wales, Frank Buchman, Francis de Sales, Brother Klaus, Thomas Merton, Leanne Payne, Brother Roger of Taizé, Father Seraphim, Gilbert Shaw, Ruth Stapleton Carter, Thérèse of Lisieux.

I also thank Brother Ramon SSF for his call for a new lay vocation of soul friendship, and for his advice on the Form of Commissioning of a Soul Friend which is printed as the first appendix.

Ray Simpson
Lindisfarne Retreat
Holy Island
Berwick-upon-Tweed
TD15 2SD
UK
website: http://www.ndirect.co.uk/~raysimpson

CONTENTS

Introduction

Part 1 The need

Part 2 Soul friendship in the Celtic tradition

Part 3 A beginner's guide to finding and becoming a soul friend

INTRODUCTION

Life is a journey

For some people life is a dead end. They are going nowhere. Others realise that life is a journey. But what is the journey about? Thoughtful people have offered different answers, yet perhaps there is a common thread.

Life is a journey:

* From being unreal to being real
* From not knowing myself to knowing myself
* From being split into pieces to being all of a piece
* From being lost in a maze to finding an inner compass
* From being alienated from love to being enfolded in love
* From being ego-centred to being Other-centred
* From compulsion to contemplation
* From being addicted to being free
* From idolatry to worship.

The journey of life is

* Developing a healthy personality
* Plumbing the depths of life
* Finding our centre
* Stripping away the things that are false in our lives

* Learning to make good relationships
* Allowing into our consciousness all there is to be aware of
* Getting to know our own past
* Travelling through anguish, boredom, terror to a light beyond
* Getting fit for eternal life.

Different traditions have different names for aspects of this journey

* Enlightenment
* Conversion
* Actualisation
* Transcendence
* Individuation
* Death and resurrection.

Yet these traditions all see the journey as one of movement from

* Fear to trust
* Dark to light
* Despair to hope
* Division to unity
* Hate to love.

The journey of life is full of troughs as well as triumphs. For some people life seems to be a cul-de-sac or a downward spiral. Such persons add their voice to the chorus 'Stop the world, I want to get off!'

In order to find and remain on a route that takes us towards eternal reality we need people to accompany us who have experience of this journey. This book will explore the journey and how enabling companions can come alongside us.

The special friend who accompanies a person through life's journey is more precious than gold. Such a friend is one who has gone through troughs, who has been stripped to bare essentials, who experiences divine wisdom and love as a constant resource, and who is called to travel alongside and share this with another.

This special friend, who is a companion on the journey, is known by different names:

- Mentor
- Prayer partner
- Companion on the way
- Guru
- Spiritual director
- Guide
- Growth buddy
- Co-discerner
- Spiritual father or mother
- Listener
- Spiritual midwife
- Confessor
- Sponsor
- Tutor
- Co-counsellor.

The Irish of the early centuries of the Christian Era had a heart-warming name for this person, the *anamchara*. *Anam* is the Gaelic word for soul; *cara* is the word for friend. *Anamchara* literally means 'friend of the soul'. The 'soul' in Celtic, as in biblical thinking, refers to the total self. It does not refer to a bit of a person, a spiritual bit, as in Greek thinking which splits the spiritual from the material. The 'soul' refers to the whole personality: body, mind and spirit. The *anamchara* was a person with whom you could talk through practical matters, reveal hidden intimacies, and break through the barriers of convention and egotism to an eternal unity of your soul. Irish soul friendships were graced with affection. We will learn from them, and from others, some secrets of a friendship so true that it reaches parts other friendships do not reach.

In this book we shall use the term 'soul friend', and we shall use the word 'seeker' to describe the person who invites a soul friend to help them discover their soul and their path. This book is written for people who are soul friends or who wonder if they might become one, and also for those who would like to have a soul friend and want to find out more of what this means.

At the end of each chapter there is a summary, and some exercises and suggestions for further reading. To be a soul friend one must practise spiritual exercises oneself before advising others. To be a seeker who invites someone to be their soul friend is to begin a journey oneself; an inner spiritual journey which requires us to leave behind ways that hold us back. Both soul friend and seeker are on the journey, though the soul friend has been journeying longer, or has been given grace to travel further. Therefore the insights and exercises in this book will help everyone who has started out on the inner journey, including the general reader who has not yet found a soul friend to accompany them.

The art of soul friendship is like a pyramid; its base coincides with that of ordinary friendship. So some of the secrets and treasures of ordinary friendship are also woven into the book.

A soul friend is like

Water for a picked flower, or
Gentle rain on seedlings;

The warmth of eiderdown, or
A fire to a cold hearth;

A lighthouse in the dark, or
An anchor to a blown ship;

Play after hours of toil,
And the lightness of thistledown;

A window on a new world, or
Secateurs to an overgrown rose;

Clear air in a smoky room,
Or a guiding star for a journey.

Such friends are freeing as Love,
With the healing touch of Jesus.

So is Christ to you –
So may you be for many more.

HEULWEN CARRIER[1]

Why not walk into the third millennium with a soul friend?

Why not begin the process of becoming a soul friend yourself?

PART 1

The need

CHAPTER 1

WHY THE REVIVED INTEREST IN SOUL FRIENDSHIP?

This chapter explains why there is such a need for people to become soul friends.

A person without a soul friend is like a body without a head.

Brigid of Kildare

Everyone needs friends. We need friends who share similar interests, difficulties or places, but we also need friends who will be there for us regardless. We need friends who will celebrate with us, but we also need friends who can understand us and share our pain. We need at least one friend who will accompany us as we try to find our true path, and who will help us move on in our journey through life. We need, in other words, a soul friend. People from all walks of life are showing increasing interest in such a person, however that person is named.

Here are ten reasons why soul friendship is a good idea whose time has come.

1. The yearning for friendship due to the breakdown of community and family life

As world crises multiply and our global village becomes more pressurised, people become fearful and confused, and cry out for wise and trusted guides. Many people now realise that the years of materialistic self-sufficiency did not satisfy our deepest human needs. 'There is no such thing as society,' said Margaret Thatcher in the 1980s. 'A contemporary family is an arrangement of beds around a fridge,' says a social observer.

This creed of self-sufficiency is a delusion. It does not accord with the way things are in reality. The world is an organism that grows out of intimate interlinkings. We are made for one another. The loss of the bonds of affection and support that used to be normal in communities and families has led to an unquenchable yearning for deep friendship that has to find other ways of being requited.

This yearning for deep friendship comes out in many pop songs, as in these echoes of two songs that I jotted down:

> *We all stand in the bin*
> *Everybody needs a friend*
> *Let me tell you about mine*
> *He's my forever friend.*

Or this:

> *When you're on your own*
> *You could go to the grave.*
> *You need your friend*
> *Someone who'll let you talk when you want to talk.*

Young people need to have older friends they can admire and learn from. Many young people are crying out in a world where no one will listen to them. Who will listen to these cries?

* 'I want to fly like a white bird . . .'
* 'I want to be friends even when I'm not on Ecstasy . . .'
* 'I want to be a man who's allowed to cry . . .'
* 'I want a warm cuddly family . . .'
* 'I just want some peace. . . '
* 'I want to know the connections between me and the rest of the world.'

Adults, too, need to be able to share their soul with someone else. Many unemployed adults, or adults in employment who suffer from stress or burn-out, feel that they have no one to turn to. Even people in churches expend their energy on task-oriented programmes which strain rather than enrich their relationships, and which deflect their attention from their own inner journey.

2. The widespread new interest in spirituality

From the 1990s onwards there has been large-scale interest in spirituality among people outside the churches. People look for it in nature, primal religions, New Age movements, Eastern philosophies, mythology, music and meditation centres. Many church people, too, are awakening to an interest in spirituality, which they have not found in their churches. Often this quest for spirituality is ill-defined. This questing generation looks for wise people, well founded in their tradition, yet who enable a seeker to grow spiritually in a way that is true for them.

3. The pace of life and the number of choices available has increased the need to check things out

The massive increase in technology, data, mobility and choice means that we have more opportunities available to us for good or ill than ever before. We have to make more and quicker decisions. We can easily make bad decisions through lack of a wise friend with whom we can talk things through.

4. Many needs are best met through one-to-one guidance

Schools now have arrangements for counselling pupils and parents in the event of an accident. Increasingly, doctors recognise that many patients need a listening ear more than a pill.

Within Christianity, 'cell churches' are being established in which each new member has a mentor. Evangelical churches encourage members to have prayer partners. Anglican and Roman Catholic churches are restoring the catechumenate – in which each new Christian is personally guided for at least a year by a more experienced church member.

In business and service professions, the value of a mentor is becoming widely recognised. The mentor – variously described as a role model, a guide, a coach, a tutor, a confidante – is looked upon as a valuable tool for the development of the trainee. It is often recognised that this role helps the mentor to develop as well as the trainee. David Clutterbuck's book *Everyone Needs a Mentor*[1] lists some benefits of mentoring:

* an improved sense of self-worth
* learning about the values and ways of the company
* improved communication skills
* identifying key decision-makers and the rules of the game
* gaining insight into the management process.

Mentoring is even proving successful with young people who have serious behaviour problems. The president of the USA-based Points of Light Foundation wrote about a programme named 'Big Brothers Big Sisters', that provides juniors with adult mentors: 'The most notable effects are the deterrent effect on initiation of drug and alcohol use, and the overall positive effects on academic performance.'[2]

The London *Times* called for a human form of memorial to Diana, Princess of Wales, to harness the idealism that her death brought to the surface, and suggested a massive programme to use volunteers to do person-to-person work in schools and to provide mentors to disabled teenagers.

A good mentoring relationship is built on mutual respect, recognition of the need for development, and clarity about where the two people involved both want to go. A good mentoring programme is expected to help people recognise their abilities and limitations, and help them seize opportunities and come to terms with the realities of their situation.

5. Past and present societies recognise the need for special enlightened helpers

Examples are the shaman of primitive tribes, the guru of the Hindus, the Zen master of the Buddhists, the rabbi of the Jews, the astrologer of today's New Agers. In Russia the name *staretz* has been given to the holy hermit, committed to the people of his neighbourhood, whom local people turn to for counsel.

The Greeks had philosophers who recognised the supreme importance of friendship.

> Of all the gifts that a Wise Providence grants us to make a life full
> and happy, friendship is the most beautiful.
>
> *Epicurus*

All I myself can do is to urge you to place friendship above every other human concern that can be imagined! Nothing else in the whole world is so completely in harmony with nature, and nothing is so utterly right, in prosperity and adversity alike. But one point I particularly want to make is this, friendship is only possible between good people.

Cicero

Two friends, one soul.

Euripides

I can only truly know myself through the other.
Jean-Paul Sartre, a twentieth-century philosopher

6. Soul friends reach parts that other helpers can't

Although there is some overlap between soul friendship and mentoring or counselling, there is a vital difference. We mostly use a mentor to develop aptitudes and attitudes that will improve our performance or advance our career. We mostly use a therapist or a counsellor to help solve a problem, or to function better within our existing values. We use a tutor mostly to increase our knowledge. These helpers are used for a part of our life. A soul friend, however, is used for the whole of our life.

The soul friend may use some of the tools of the counsellor or of the mentor, but for a different purpose. In soul befriending your main aim is not to solve problems (though you may need to do that 'on the way'); your aim is to achieve wholeness. Often counsellors are trained not to let a client get to them, whereas a soul friend might, on appropriate occasions, share something of their own vulnerabilities in order to encourage a seeker to unlock theirs. The model of wholeness that a Christian soul friend uses is Jesus Christ, not the latest theory of this or that psychologist.

The purpose of the soul friend is to help the seeker discover where they are, and what should be their next steps in their journey through life, in the light of eternity. A third person is always invited to be a full partner; that third person is the Holy Spirit of God.

The benefits of Christian soul befriending relate to much more than a person's career. They relate to the whole person – body, mind and spirit. They relate both to practical matters of the present and to a person's eternal destiny. Only if we can know ourselves and be known by another can we grow into the likeness of God, which is our destiny.

In his book *Conferences* about the early desert Christians, John Cassian says of the indissoluble bond between friends: 'This, I say, is what is broken by no chances, what no interval of time or space can sever or destroy, and what even death itself cannot part.'[3] Brigid of Kildare told a young minister whose elderly soul friend had died, and who had not bothered to find another one, 'A person without a soul friend is like a body without a head.' Our lives need reference points. We need people to whom we can pour out our immediate problems, yes, but also with whom we can explore the meaning of our soul's anguish and aspirations.

7. Christian history witnesses to the value of soul friendship

The early Christian communities in Ireland placed a very high value on soul friendship. The Rule of St Comgall, founder of the monastery at Bangor, who died in 602 contains these wise words: 'Though you may think you are very solid it is not good to be your own guide.' St Brigid told a young priest in fifth-century Ireland that just as the water in a well full of lime was good for nothing, so was a person without a soul friend. 'Go off and don't eat until you get a soul friend,' she told him.[4]

The holy Celtic theologian St Morgan wrote letters about the value of soul befriending. In his letter to Demetrius he writes: 'People cannot grow in virtue on their own. We each need companions to guide and direct us on the way of righteousness; without such companions we are liable to stray from the firm path, and then sink into the mud of despair.'

Aelred, who was born at Hexham in 1109, wrote in his treatise *Spiritual Friendship:*

> Friendship is nothing else but wisdom, and the person who abides in friendship abides in God, and God in them ... He is entirely alone who is without a friend. But what happiness, what security, what joy to have someone to whom you dare to speak on terms of equality as to another self; one to whom you can unblushingly make known what progress you have made in the spiritual life; one to whom you can entrust all the secrets of your heart and before whom you can place all your plans.[5]

8. Spiritual direction, as practised in recent times, has become too narrow

In recent centuries certain streams within Christianity have encouraged the use of a spiritual director. 'Spiritual direction' is a term that was much used in Anglican and Roman Catholic churches, and the novels of Susan Howatch have introduced this to a new public.

One aspect of traditional spiritual direction is formal confession of sins. The penitent Christian asks to see a priest. This may be in a confessional cubicle in a church, or in a room at the priest's house. The penitent may bring a list of sins which they have committed since the last confession; these they may have written down or rehearsed in their mind. They may skate round things ('I had bad thoughts towards someone,' 'I have cheated. . . ') or they may call a spade a spade ('I had sex with so-and-so,' 'I hit my spouse'). Sometimes, a person may be so overwhelmed by a problem that they simply blurt out that one thing: 'I have been unfaithful to my wife.'

It is customary, after a prayer, Scripture or silence, for the penitent to kneel, and say words such as 'Father, I have sinned before heaven . . .' and to repeat the list of sins. The priest then lays a hand on the penitent's head and pronounces the forgiveness of sins. The priest may then give the penitent a penance or a task: 'Don't go to a pub for two weeks' (if the penitent has confessed to drunken brawling); 'fast on Friday until your next confession' (if the penitent has confessed to gluttony) and so on.

This ancient approach has its value and is not to be belittled, but we have to recognise that, for many, it has become too mechanical. A sign of this is a sharp decline in the number of formal confessions.[6] Many penitents are now as well educated as the priest, and they do not wish for a paternalistic relationship. New insights of psychology and human development lead people to focus more on the growth of their humanity. Since the Second Vatican Council the Roman Catholic as well as other churches have recognised that spiritual direction is a process of mutual discernment, but many parish priests are too busy to be fully available in this way to more than a limited number of persons.

There is a need to restore a more equal relationship with the spiritual director. We don't want to be directed from on high; we want to feel we are not strangers to each other, but human beings who are pilgrims together. It is not necessary that a soul friend who can provide such discernment be a priest. A seeker who has a lay soul friend is also free to confess sins to a priest.

In previous generations it was assumed that the clergy had a particular authority as spiritual directors by virtue of their training and their authorisation by the church. Now that information is made public about the scandals and unmet needs of clergy, people are less sure that they *per se* are the right people to entrust with their deepest needs. In previous generations it was assumed that the most learned persons were the natural spiritual directors. Nowadays the term 'academic' has a gained a bad name; it conjures up an image of a person who lacks both street wisdom and balance of body, mind and spirit. Advances in research show that there can be depths of spirituality and wisdom in people regardless of their age, background or accreditation by any formal authority. So there is a need to expand our understanding of who is acceptable as a soul friend.

9. New Christians don't know how to find a soul friend

As soon as my book *Exploring Celtic Spirituality: Historic Roots for our Future* was published,[7] I began to receive letters from people who had read in it the *Way of Life* of the Community of Aidan and Hilda, a network of Christians from many churches and walks of life. A typical letter, addressed to me as the Guardian, was this: 'I have read the *Way of Life*. I feel that at last I belong, I have come home. I want to explore this way. But please will you find me a soul friend? I don't know anyone in my church or elsewhere who understands about soul friendship, and my minister is not interested.' Pleas such as this became a pattern, and underscored the need for many more people to learn how to become soul friends.

10. Traditional spiritual directors are being drawn to the Celtic way

Finally, I also received letters such as this from a Catholic sister who had long been a skilled spiritual director in another tradition: 'Please can you tell me how I can learn spiritual direction in the Celtic tradition?' It became clear to me that we had to address the need of those who are already spiritual guides to become familiar with the ways of the Celtic soul friends.

So on all sides there is the rise of new aspiration. From many quarters we see a need to discover more about soul friendship. In the years following my first book I have tried to respond to these needs in a humble way, and this book is a small contribution to that end. It is not a book for experts; it is a book for beginners. In order for a few people to climb a Mount Everest, many people have to learn to walk the foothills. This book is about the foothills of spiritual guidance, by a soul friend who has himself only begun the ascent. That is as it should be. For soul friendship, which has long been a treasured tradition for a few, now needs to become part of the good life of the many.

Summary

The gap left by the breakdown of community, the new interest in spirituality, the confusion caused by the multiplication of choice, the leisure now available to explore 'inner space', the record of civilisations, the incomplete nature of helping agencies, the witness of Christian history, and the narrow framework of traditional spiritual direction, have contributed to a mass yearning for soul friendship. This, and the frustration of many Christians who are unable to find a soul friend, requires us to find ways to respond.

Exercises

These are for readers who are not a soul friend; the first two are for readers who do not have a soul friend either.

1. 'I want to be . . .' What are the deepest things you want to be that you would like to share with a soul friend?

2. Name three things in your life that you'd like to check out with a wise person whom you trust.

3. Would you like to be a soul friend to someone? If so, what do you think you need to learn before this becomes appropriate?

CHAPTER 2

BECOMING A SOUL FRIEND – A NEW CALLING?

In this chapter, which is mainly for readers who are not yet soul friends, we shall clarify what is the role of a soul friend, how we may know if we are not at present suited to this role, how not to let false images of ourselves or of a soul friend deter us, and how to explore the possibility of becoming one.

> World crises multiply and everybody deplores the shortage, or even total lack, of 'wise' men and women, unselfish leaders, trustworthy counsellors etc. It is hardly rational to expect such qualities from people who have never done any inner work and would not even understand what is meant by the words.
>
> *E.F. Schumacher*[1]

Yearning for soul friendship is increasing, but the demand for soul friends far outstrips the supply. We may recognise that a soul friend is more precious than gold, but such friends are also rarer than gold. Soul friends do not grow on trees; they cannot be manufactured by marketing exercises or be nurtured by a frenetic and dysfunctional society, for soul friendship grows out of a lived spirituality.

Yes, the crisis is real, but could these words of William Waldo

Emerson (1803–82) point towards a solution: 'The only way to have a friend is to be one'? Could it be that you, the reader, could become such a friend? In the process of becoming one, you yourself would also be enriched. For this will motivate you to practise spiritual disciplines, to reflect more deeply, to observe more carefully, and to experience the blessings of deepening friendship, mutual gratitude and esteem.

Why should I become a soul friend?

Turn the question around, so that it echoes the words of US President John F. Kennedy: 'Some dream of what people could do to create a better world and ask "Why me?" Some dream likewise and ask "Why not me?" ' Why not become a soul friend? If your answer is that you have neither the desire nor the time to be one, that is sufficient reason. But if your answer is that you lack knowledge, or confidence, or opportunity, that is a reason to explore the possibility further.

The role of a soul friend – some commonly asked questions

What is a soul friend?

A soul friend is not the same as a soul mate. That term is used of someone with whom there is a rapport, but it does not involve joint commitment to change. A newspaper reported in 1998 that Rod Steiger and Elizabeth Taylor had become soul mates. It explained that they had much in common, including Taylor's eight and Steiger's four marriages, replacement hips, unhappy childhoods, weight problems, depression, alcoholism and ill health. (Taylor has had a brain tumour and Steiger two heart bypasses.) 'I always say it's like two famous gun fighters meeting,' says Steiger.[2]

A soul friend is not the same as a pastor. A pastor may visit or offer care within the framework of a church; the soul friend accompanies the other person in the framework of their inner journey.

The exact definition of a soul friend will vary according to the perspective of different streams within Christianity. Here is one group's definition:

> The soul friend is chosen by the individual to provide a listening ear, and to help the individual find and follow their true life journey. The soul friend is a person of spiritual discernment, with compassion, understanding, and a non-judgmental attitude, whose role is one of service. The relationship is confidential.

The *Dictionary of Christian Spirituality* defines the spiritual director as 'one who seeks to diagnose the condition of the soul with its graces and ills and to assist it in the way of growth ... The most positive use of spiritual direction is in two specific areas: under-standing ourselves in the light of God, and growth in the light of faith and prayer.'[3]

There are varieties of soul friend. Some people restrict their soul friendship to a limited number of formal sessions, others become informal soul friends for life; some specialise in being a soul friend to the unchurched, or to students or other common interest groups, or to contemplatives.[4] Some famous soul friends have done most of their work through letters.

How many seekers does a soul friend have?
Often just one, if soul friendship is not their primary calling. Some people have more, even though they are busy people, and find it useful to put a limit on the number of people they accept as seekers, following the example of Jesus who shared so much of himself with just twelve apostles. More than this can be too emotionally draining. However, it has been known for monasteries to appoint one gifted monk or nun to be the spiritual director to many people who seek guidance. They can do this because they have the boundaries and resources of the monastery to support them in this ministry, and in

the USA some people do this for a living.

As with most things in life, there are some notable exceptions. The French Curé of Ars and the Russian Staretz Seraphim, after long mystical deepening, saw hundreds of people in a short time, since they read their thoughts before they arrived, or while they queued, and gave them instant advice! If any reader was called to such a ministry, it would be a gift of God and they would know. They would not desire it, for it would require extreme sacrifice.

How equal is the relationship between a soul friend and a seeker?

The seeker expects to receive listening and guidance from the soul friend, not vice versa. The soul friend is not, however, paternalistic, and is willing, if this is helpful to the seeker, to share themselves.

Can an ordinary friendship develop into soul friendship?

It is possible, but not all that likely. Often seekers find it more helpful to go to someone who has no preconceptions about them, who can ask difficult questions, and who, because they don't socialise with mutual friends, won't be worrying about what was or was not confidential. If a seeker does ask an existing friend to become their soul friend, it is important to have a clear understanding about the nature of the soul friendship meetings, and about what is confidential.

Would a seeker expect a Christmas or birthday card from a soul friend?

Not necessarily, especially if they had only met a few times, or if the soul friend was, say, a monk or nun who had a large number of seekers. But where a rapport has developed that overflows the boundaries of mere advice they might well send cards.

Why can't a spouse be a soul friend?

There *are* examples of spouses making brilliant soul friends, but these seem to be exceptions to the rule. Each partner has a unique journey to make, at a distinctive pace. There are pressures, blocks or blind spots in most marriages which need to be clarified with a skilled person outside the situation, in order for them to be prayed through by the partners together. For this reason, also, it is not usually wise for both spouses to visit the same soul friend at the same time. That does not preclude doing this on appropriate occasions.

How formal is the relationship, e.g. in terms of payment?

It is important (see Chapter 17) to have a clear understanding of the nature and frequency of meetings. This is usually verbal, but it can be written down if this is what both parties find most helpful. Some people prefer the arrangement to be more *ad hoc*, and just to contact a soul friend when they feel the need; the danger of this is that they fail to grow in discipline or accountability.

There are conflicting views about payment. Traditional churches often insist that spiritual directors must not charge. They argue that ordained soul friends already receive a stipend to enable them to do this work, and soul friends from religious communities hand any donations to their community; they believe that the voluntary nature of this ministry is of its essence. In the USA it is often thought to be unprofessional if charges are *not* made. Now that so many more people seek out soul friends (just as they do counsellors, or homoeo-pathists, etc.), it means that many soul friends (including the increasing number of non-stipendiary clergy) who do this work do not receive sufficient other income. A middle way is for the soul friend to suggest donations, or to charge on a sliding scale, so that the poorest can still benefit from a soul friend.

How much advice and support does a soul friend give on non-spiritual areas?

Every soul friend should focus on the deepest things of the heart and spirit. In our busy, multi-resourced world, that may be all that is appropriate. However, in the Celtic tradition, soul friends helped seekers apply their wisdom to the whole of life; the spiritual was not divorced from the practical. That is a sound principle. To apply this principle today can take many forms. It is more likely today that a soul friend will have a *feel* for how to apply spirituality to every part of life, and will then suggest ways in which the seeker can do this. To take some random examples: the soul friend might suggest programmes for physical fitness, money management, skill training, personality indicators, theology or ecology provided by other agencies. The soul friend should look out for imbalances between body, mind and spirit, between work and recreation, being and doing, relationship and solitude, and suggest practical exercises, or mundane routines, which help to correct any such imbalance.

How do I know if I am not meant to be a soul friend?

We need to be honest with ourselves about our reasons for wishing to become a soul friend. Many people covet any 'helping' role in order to shore up their own fragile egos. If anyone wants to become a soul friend because they have nothing else to do, or because they think it is easy, they should pursue anything *except* soul befriending! For soul befriending is far from easy; in fact, it is a sacrificial service, and if we are not willing for it to be costly, it will come to nothing.

If we think we 'ought' to be a soul friend, because of our position in a church, perhaps, we have not understood what this is about. If you feel like this, repeat the prayer 'Lord, deliver us from "oughtery"' until the compulsion to be a soul friend departs! Some other wrong reasons for wanting to be a soul friend are the desire to prove something to ourselves or to others, to assuage loneliness, or to possess another person.

A group which explored this question of who should and should not become a soul friend came up with the following list:

Don't become a soul friend if you can't

* listen
* be flexible
* relate to life as a journey
* value different ways of praying
* understand different temperaments
* welcome being known as you really are

* love people regardless of what you 'get' out of them
* enjoy giving quality time to soul befriending sessions
* get to know yourself and areas that are out of proportion
* refrain from projecting your own experience on to others
* be earthed (be real about money, sex and power)
* take 'shocking' revelations in your stride
* accept spiritual direction for yourself
* accept silences and plateaux
* be at home with your body
* refrain from being bossy
* keep confidences
* meditate

Do not be discouraged by what has been written. All of us, at some time or other, are partly motivated by our own unmet needs. This has been true of myself. If this is true of you, it suggests that you should focus on your own process of inner healing for a time. There is work to be done to bring your own fragile, hurt or bitter ego towards a greater wholeness. Learn to pray for yourself and nurture your own inner child. Find yourself a soul friend with whom you can work through these things.

The real 'you' is the you that has no hidden agendas to be needed, to be noticed, to have influence or to control. The real 'you' is the you that is not seduced by inhibitions caused by poor conditioning. Only when you have faced these inhibitions will you know whether God is calling you in this, or in some quite different direction. It may even be that the time is not now right for you to become a soul friend, but later it will be.

There are, of course, other valid reasons why a person should not become a soul friend. Here are three of them.

You have not grown wiser as you have grown older. Cassian, in his *Conferences*, warns against confusing grey hair with wisdom: 'The hoary headed old men whose sole merit is derived from their number of years are not necessarily the ones whose footsteps should be followed nor whose doctrine and counsels should be accepted unquestionably.'[5]

You are a task-oriented personality. There is nothing wrong with being a task-oriented person. But the person-oriented person is more likely to be suited to the role of soul friend.

Your priorities do not permit you the space needed for this ministry. Perhaps you are responsible for a demanding family in its formative stage, or for paid or voluntary work that, to do it justice, requires your primary energy. Those are good reasons to say no to other callings. It is possible for a soul friend to be a busy person, but not if there is insufficient emotional space.

False objections to becoming a soul friend

Some of us have such a low self-image that we write ourselves off. This is not God's will for us. 'I could never be a soul friend,' you say? Who says so? Neither God nor other people may agree with you. The question you should answer honestly is, 'Would you *like* to become a soul friend?'

'I'm not good enough,' says someone else. Who is 'good enough'? You don't cease to be a brother, sister or parent because you are 'not good enough'. The question is whether you are called to this, not whether you are good enough.

'I'm not educated enough.' Some soul friends have much education, some have little. The willingness to learn from everyday experience and the wisdom of a humble heart are more important than a string of university degrees.

'This is all very well, but I have no experience of soul friendship,' another voice pipes up. Nobody had experience of anything before they began. As a matter of fact, all of us have begun in one sense. We have daily experiences of relationships of varying kinds. It is possible to reflect upon and learn from these as a preparation for any formal soul friendship.

'I could never be like so-and-so who is such a good spiritual director,' objects a fifth person. No, but you can be true to yourself and let the friendship that *is* within you unfold.

'I don't have the sort of influence that others have.' No, but you do have a circle within which you are called to share what you have.

'It's only for priests or pastors.' Lay people can be deterred from offering themselves because they think this ministry is only for priests or professionals. In fact, as we have seen, there are different kinds of spiritual direction, and many people feel more at home with a soul friend who is not a priest or pastor.

'It's only for specialists.' Others are deterred because they think this is a ministry only for specialists. It is true that soul friends can be expected to give advice, about how to discover the will of God, how to pray, how to grow in virtue or understanding. It is expected of some soul friends that they are aware of the work of writers of spiritual classics. The important point is that one soul friend is called to specialise in one area, a second in a different area, and a third soul friend may be called to be content to share their earthy wisdom that no book-learning could provide. The wisdom of the desert was something that an unlettered person could acquire, and such a person who acquired this would be sought after.

> The learned Father Arsenius went to an old Egyptian and asked him to give him some counsel. Another person, who was watching, asked him: 'Father Arsenius, how can you, having received such a fine Greek and Roman education, speak to this country bumpkin?' Arsenius replied: 'It is true I have received a Greek and Roman education, but I do not even have the basics of the knowledge this peasant has.'
>
> *Sayings of the Desert Fathers*

Arsenius knew that the Holy Spirit was speaking through the peasant, and he had the humility to learn. This has an important truth for soul friends today. There has been a danger that the ethos of spiritual direction networks would make uneducated people feel it is not for them. It is! Soul friends have tended to come from too narrow a background. It is not necessary to be a specialist in order to be a soul friend. I know someone who can barely read, but she often instantly senses what is in a person, and has a clear insight into what is needed for their healing.

'It's only for retreat conductors.' Retreat centres often offer guided retreats in the Ignatian tradition. The client gets spiritual direction on a one-to-one basis for, say, a week. These retreats are popular, and this is one helpful approach; it may be that you will wish to learn more about this. But it is not the only approach, and in any case, people who go on these retreats often need to continue this approach on a long-term basis, and for this they need to find a soul friend. That soul friend could be you.

So let us beware of putting others on pedestals. To reject the possibility of becoming a soul friend because one does not fit into this or that stereotype is not a good thing. Do not hold back the precious personality and experience that is yours alone to give.

Motivating a new calling to soul friendship

In his book *The Heart of Prayer*, the Welsh Franciscan Brother Ramon envisages the emergence of a vocation to soul friendship among lay folk. He writes:

> This is already happening, for there are men and women of all the main line Christian churches, who are increasingly aware of who they are, of what the soul friendship tradition consists, and who have the communicative ability and love of their brothers and sisters to give themselves as channels of the Holy Spirit within the sustaining network of the Church of God. They are not ordained, professional or hierarchic, though a form of recognition and laying-on of hands would be appropriate. This would be a wider recognition of their validity and authority for such a task, making them responsible to the wider network, and would weed out the many

> people who would 'covet' any counselling role in order to shore
> up their own fragile egos.[6]

As Brother Ramon perceives, there are many unnoticed members of churches who could make excellent soul friends. Yet this huge pool of potential soul friends lies largely dormant. They need a vision of how ordinary people can be used in this way. They need church leaders who discern and encourage them in this motivation. They need opportunities to explore this calling in safe contexts. They need training. They need to read this book!

It is true that to become a soul friend you need to be emotionally literate, and that millions of people go through our education system without learning to be emotionally literate; they have no vocabulary to describe what goes on in their own or another's inner being. They need to be taught listening, speaking and mediating skills. Yet it is also true that in places this need is being addressed. For example, St John's Roman Catholic School, Gravesend, Kent, has introduced into the lower sixth form a peer ministry course on befriending. Another Catholic school gives sixth-formers a badge if they complete a course in listening skills. Some who complete the course offer themselves to listen to people from their congregations after the church liturgy, or go on to become catechists.

Churches as well as schools now offer resources that develop emotional and spiritual literacy. There are prayer groups based on listening attentively to each person in turn and then praying for them. I have heard of churches that facilitate 'spiritual conversations'. There are Christian Listeners training programmes. There is a movement of prayer guidance teams: those who complete the training live in a parish for a week and meet each day on a one-to-one basis. Emmaus walks takes this concept further. Two people think deeply during a walk to some special spot, and walk back silently reflecting, only speaking if God reveals something to them for the other person. So, despite our frenetic culture, there are seedbeds from which new soul friends can, and will, emerge. And you, the reader, can learn these skills, too. The second part of this book will help you to do this.

There are very many Christians in and beyond both traditional and new churches who have never been part of the tradition of spiritual direction, but who now see the value of soul friendship. Since there is such a need for, yet such a shortage of, soul friends, we need to take a fresh look at soul befriending. The practice of soul friendship is meant to embrace a wide spectrum, from the trained soul friend who is also a confessor, to the friend who is a good listener and a willing learner.

How does one become a soul friend?

The general view in Britain, though not in the USA, is that soul friends are discovered. You do not become a soul friend by putting yourself forward, completing a training course, or answering an advertisement. Who you are, not what you have done is the key. Soul friends emerge from that invisible community of people who daily seek to be better friends of God and of God's creatures, and who are themselves journeying through life with a soul friend.

That does not mean that nothing can be done to respond to the world's need for a new crop of soul friends. For there are many members of that invisible community who already seek daily to be better friends of God and of others, and who could take some further steps. They need to be assured that there is not one group of experts who 'have it all' and the rest who 'don't have it': all of us are involved in a continual process of conversion, reflection and growth.

In the following chapters we shall explore Celtic, desert and modern insights into soul friendship. A reader who has worked through this book, and still feels a nudge in this direction should first pursue their inner journey with a soul friend. They might then ask friends to pray about these nudges. They might find out through clergy or through resource networks listed in Appendix 2 some suitable training they could undertake. They will be alert to respond to people who ask them to listen to them. If this recurs, they might talk through with a priest or pastor how God might be leading them.

It is important that the clergy recognise this sense of call, and do not sidetrack you by asking you to do other, less appropriate jobs. Show your priest or pastor the suggestions in Appendix 1, and explore whether they would be willing to pray for your exploratory ministry in a public church service, or to write a commendation, or to have a commissioning.

Summary

If you have the desire to become a soul friend, first get clear about the role, and whether you are able or mature enough to focus on the other person's true needs. Identify and reject false objections. Take next steps towards growing in spiritual discernment.

Exercises
To help a seeker discover if they should become a soul friend

Place a tick in the square if the answer is yes, a cross if the answer is no, and leave it blank if you are not sure. Be completely honest and immediate in your response. Any of these three responses might be the right one.

☐   Do you 'engage' with people and with life?

☐   Do you engender trust?

☐   Have you suffered and not been cowed or embittered by it?

☐   Have you experienced failure?

☐   Are you at ease with yourself when alone and when in company?

☐   Would you describe your attitude as more contemplative than activist?

☐   Do you monitor how well you listen to people?

☐   Are you self-confident enough to ask questions and make contributions in a group?

☐   Do you accept people's strong emotions more than you avoid them?

☐   Are you aware of what your body is saying to you right now?

☐   Have you meditated on the Bible in the past week?

☐   Do you try and understand why the people nearest to you react in the way they do?

Remember, even the best soul friends have faults and blind spots. If you have ticked less than seven, seek out a soul friend, work on your own journey, but do not yet make plans to become a soul friend. If you have ticked more than seven, explore possibilities of becoming a soul friend. Whatever your score, work through some of these issues.

Further reading
Barry, William A. and Connolly, William J., *The Practice of Spiritual Direction* (Harper & Row, 1991), especially Chapter 8, 'Becoming a Spiritual Director.'

PART 2

Soul friendship in the Celtic tradition

These chapters inform existing spiritual directors and the general reader about the Celtic tradition of soul friendship. They present the story of soul friendship in historical order. Those who hope to become soul friends, however, should not apply the lessons in the same order. They may prefer to work through the beginner's guide presented in Part 3 first and then come back to this section.

CHAPTER 3

RAPPORT – JOHN AND BIBLICAL INSIGHTS INTO SOUL FRIENDSHIP

The first century, during and after Christ's life on earth

This chapter throws light on how a specific soul friendship can emerge out of an ordinary friendship that is growing in depth, as in the case of Jesus and John. We can learn timeless secrets of friendship from them and from other Bible personalities, even though in our frenetic society some soul friendships may have to be more programmed.

John, the foster-brother of Christ.

Carmina Gadelica

eltic Christians were soaked in the Bible, which teaches about friendship at the deepest level. They loved the Gospel of John, which portrays John as a soul friend to Jesus. Although the word *anamchara* is not used, John is described as 'the loved disciple'. Celtic Christians regarded John as their spiritual father. In The *Carmina Gadelica*, the prayers and poems of the Western Isles of Scotland collected in the nineteenth century by Alexander

Carmichael, John is sometimes referred to as 'John of love', 'foster-son of Mary' or 'foster-brother of Christ'.

The fact that Jesus chose John as a soul friend should encourage us, because when they first met, John must have seemed unsuitable. John and his brother James demanded 'top places' when Jesus, as they expected, swept to power (Mark 10:35–45). They wanted to curse a village that refused to welcome Jesus by calling down a violent thunderstorm upon it (Luke 9:54). Jesus nicknamed these tempestuous brothers 'Sons of Thunder'.

Jesus, however, could spot a person's potential. Soon, John's temper mellowed into tenderness. The secret, it seems, was the unconditional love that Jesus offered him. John responded to this love deeply and appropriately, and ever afterwards he thought of himself not as a threatened, unwanted person but as the loved disciple. John became sensitive to the heartbeat of Jesus, and Jesus shared intimately with him.

John became one of Jesus's most intimate circle of three. At the final Passover meal which Jesus shared with his team the evening before his arrest, John leant across him, and Jesus confided in him. John and two others stayed with Jesus during three hours of foreboding (Mark 14:33). After more than two hours in agony nailed to a wooden crossbeam, Jesus gasped out his dying wishes for the two people who were dearest to him. He asked his mother, 'Take John to be your son'; he asked John, 'Take her to be your mother.' Ever afterwards people would be able to wander into places of Christian worship and see portrayed on the altar, on either side of the crucified Jesus, his mother and his adopted brother. The arms of Jesus outstretched in welcome seem to say, 'Come to me and you come also into my family.'

Tradition gave John the name *paranymphos* ('friend of the bride'). Through Mary, John became like Jesus's foster-brother to succeeding generations of believers. Tradition says that John suffered under the persecution of the Roman Emperor Domitian. He barely escaped being plunged in a cauldron of boiling water, and he suffered exile on the Isle of Patmos. John survived these trials and lived into old age at Ephesus, where he penned his three New Testament letters. Jerome records how, when John was dying, his friends asked him if he had any last message for them. 'Little children, love one another,' he repeated, once again, as he had repeated in his letters. They asked him if that was all he had to say. 'It is enough,' he said, 'for it is the Lord's command.' Love was the essence of John's friendship. He became a spiritual father to many, and to Celtic Christians John was their spiritual father, too.

John as a soul friend

A story told by Eusebius helps us to see why Celtic Christians, who had passionate natures and compassionate soul friendships, drew such inspiration from John. John visited a Christian community near Ephesus, and he was drawn to an exceptionally fine-looking young man. John turned to the leader of the community and said, 'I commit this young man into your care, and I call the whole community to witness that I have done so.' The church leader took the young man into his household, discipled and baptised him. But afterwards this man fell in with a gang of criminals and, when his crime was discovered, fled with them to the mountains. When John made a return visit he was distraught to learn what had happened. He decided to go to the mountains and allow himself to be captured by the criminals, so he would be brought to the young man, who was now their leader. The young man felt so ashamed when he saw John that he tried to run away from him. John, despite his age, ran after him.

'My son,' he cried, 'are you running away from your father? I am old and frail, pity me, do not let fear rule you, there is hope for you that you can be saved. I will stand for you before the Lord Christ. If need be, I will gladly die for you as he died for me. Stop, stay, trust! It is Christ who has sent me to you.' John's appeal broke the heart of the young man; he threw away his weapons and wept. Side by side, as father and son, they came down the mountain, and the man was restored to the church and to the Christian way.

In his old age John met with other church leaders to compile meditations on the life of Jesus which would help Christians advance along their journey of faith. In these pages (which we know as John's Gospel) he reveals intimate moments in Jesus's friendships. He records Jesus's friend Mary anointing his feet with costly perfume, and drying them with her hair (John 12:3). John, more than any other Gospel-writer, delights in the fragrance of intimacy expressed with all the senses.

John recalls Jesus saying to his apostles, 'I no longer call you servants, from now on I call you friends' (John 15:15). Why? Because servants are not taken into the confidence of an employer; friends are. Jesus had shared with those disciples everything his Father had imparted to him. It is as if Jesus is saying to them, 'Before I introduced a new way of friendship, your relationships were on the basis of what you could get out of another person. In that way of living people are servants, customers or clients; people relate to them because of what they provide, not because of who they are. I bring in a new way of relating.'

The quality of rapport which we sense between biblical soul friends such as Jesus and John did not perish with them. There existed between Patrick and Brigid, according to the eighth-century Book of the Angel 'so great a friendship of charity that they were of one heart and one mind'.[1]

We, who are an 'orphaned' generation, have much to learn from John. Men especially seem unable to make deep but non-possessive relationships with other men. Recent movements of God's Spirit have tried to rekindle the experience of this among Christian men.

The Trinity as the source of friendship

John helps us to understand that the source of the love that makes soul friendship possible is the limitless love of the Three Persons in God. He portrays the Trinity as an eternal flow of friendship. Friendship is the nature of God. God is one love expressed as three eternally loving selves. 'The Father loved me from before the world's beginning,' said Jesus (John 17:24). 'The Helper will come – whom I will send to you from the Father ... the Helper will give me glory' (John 15:26; 16:14). Jesus told his friends, 'I love you just as the Father loves me' (John 15:9). That is why Jesus laid down his life for the people, because the Three Divine Selves had been eternally laying down their lives for one another. In his Gospel John presents the Creator as a Father friend (14:1–11), the Son as a woundable friend (15:18–23), and the Holy Spirit as a helping friend (14:16–17). He uses the Greek word *parakletos* for the Holy Spirit, which means someone who comes alongside you, who is linked with you and who stands with you.

Friendship in the Bible

The value of soul friendship has been recognised from early biblical times. Moses and Joshua, David and Jonathan, Ruth and Naomi, Barnabus and Saul, Paul and Timothy, and women such as Huldah (2 Kings 22:14) are examples of it in Scripture. Its value is recognised in biblical sayings:

A faithful friend is the medicine of life.

Ecclesiasticus 6:16

Some friends are more loyal than brothers.

Proverbs 18:24

In both Hebrew and Greek (the original languages in which the Bible was written) two common words for 'friend' are related to words for 'love'. *Ahab* (Hebrew) means 'loved one'. *Philos* (Greek) means 'dear one' or 'loved one', as in Galatians 6:1–2 or James 5:16–20. So in the Bible friendship is a form of love. A friend is someone you appreciate and trust, someone to whom you commit yourself and with whom you share yourself. A friend is someone you want to do things for and give things to.

Another aspect of Christlike friendship is mutual giving and

41

receiving. St Paul urges Christians to 'encourage one another and build each other up' (1 Thessalonians 5:11), 'to bear one another's burdens' (Galatians 6:2) and 'to admonish one another' (Romans 15:14). Soul friendship in the Celtic style always has this sense of a mutual sharing of two people on a journey.

Is soul friendship specifically recognised as a calling in the New Testament? Paul likens the Christian journey to a race run by an athlete (2 Timothy 2:5), and it was understood then, as now, that athletes need coaches. Perhaps Paul had soul friends in mind when he referred to those who have ability to 'succour, or mutually give to another' (1 Corinthians 12:28).[2]

The wisdom of friendship

We do well, before we leave the subject of soul friendship in the Bible, to note what the Bible has to say about one other aspect of friendship: it needs to be earthed in wisdom. The book of Ecclesiasticus, in the Apocrypha, warns us against telling what is on our mind to all comers, and it advises us never to discuss our plans with a fool, for the fool cannot keep a confidence (Ecclesiasticus 8:19, 17). It encourages us to actively cultivate wisdom, for it is not like 'an instant buy':

> Come to Wisdom wholeheartedly and keep to her ways with all your might. Follow her track and she will make herself known to you.
>
> *Ecclesiasticus 6:22, 26*

In order to cultivate wisdom we are encouraged to learn from mature people of experience and learning:

> If you really want to, you can be trained ... When you stand among your elders decide who is wise and join them ... If you discover a wise person, rise early to visit them.
>
> *Ecclesiasticus 6:32, 36*

Friendship is rooted in God's love

At the beginning of the Bible we learn that God decided, 'Now we will make human beings who will resemble us' (Genesis 1:26). Human beings are meant to resemble God in reflecting love. That is why, when Jesus was asked to select the greatest of the laws that God had given to Moses, he selected these two from the book of Deuteronomy: 'The most important one is "Love the Lord your God with all your heart, with all your soul, with all your mind, and with all your strength"; the second most important commandment is this: "Love your neighbour as yourself" ' (Mark 12:29–31).

You love God with mind, feelings and action, says Deuteronomy because that is what love involves. Our love is a reflection of God's, and God's is like that. God appreciates us, enjoys spending time with us, is glad to see us, finds us interesting, trusts us, makes a commitment to us, shares intimate secrets with us. All that applies to human relations . . . Like love between us and God, it is of the essence that this is two-way. It would not work if only one of two people wanted that kind of friendship.

So what is the point of taking the risk and expending the energy? Why not hide from other people? One reason is the way our friends change us. As in marriage, which is a form of friendship if you are lucky, our friends may decide that they themselves want to change us, and they may succeed in some respects, though these changes are likely to be external.

The more profound changes come about when people are not trying. Perhaps we like something about a friend and find ourselves thinking the same way as they do. We may conclude that if they reckon a particular thing is important or interesting or worthwhile, there must be something in it. We end up changing our thinking, our attitudes, our lives . . . because of our friendship.

There is also an obverse process, because all this is mutual. Aspects of what you are will seem off-the-wall to your friends. They ask why you think or act in a certain way, and you have to work it out as you may not have done before. By that process friends help us discover things about ourselves . . .

There is indeed risk. God takes risks in entrusting intimate secrets with us, in sharing the ministry of the Godhead in the world with us, instead of just getting on with it. We take risks with God in opening up our lives to heavenly scrutiny and looking at ourselves through God's eyes, in saying we will do what God wants and go where God wants. We take risks in sharing our secrets with each other, too, the risk of looking stupid and sinful and proud and narrow, to the other person and thus to ourselves.

Like our love for God, our love for someone else as a person like ourselves tends to develop gradually. The whole of God is not focussed on us at once, and we do not give all of ourselves to God at once. Friendship, too, happens gradually, and happens because both sides subconsciously take the risk of letting it happen, stage by stage.[3]

Summary
Jesus had a deep rapport with God the Father. As John matured he developed a deep rapport with Jesus which was mutually strengthening. As a result John developed a deep rapport with Father, Son and Spirit. This is the source of friendship. We, too, can develop this rapport with God and with other human beings. To begin to do this is a precondition of being a good soul friend.

Exercises
The first three relate to general friendship, the last to soul friendship

1. Slowly read John 14 and 15. Repeat Jesus's words as if you were in his shoes. Allow the feelings of rapport which he had with his Father and with his friends to flow through you. Now review your relationships in the light of this meditation.

2. Focus your imagination on your favourite football team or music band. The best teams and bands have a rapport that flows. What bits

of your life flow? Who with? What stops the flow? Visualise in prayer what would happen if nothing stopped the flow. Begin to live what you envisage.

3. It seems that insecurity turned into love in the apostle John. Reflect on places of insecurity within yourself, and bring these, one by one, to the unconditional love of Jesus.

4. Think of yourself as a soul friend relating to someone you know who might become a seeker. Dedicate yourself to offer unconditional love as Jesus did to John. What might this mean for you?

Further reading
The Gospel and the Epistles of John.

Newell, Philip, *Listening for the Heartbeat of God* (SPCK, 1997).

CHAPTER 4

DETACHMENT – DESERT
INSIGHTS INTO SOUL
FRIENDSHIP

The third to fifth centuries after Christ

Since the practice of seeking out a specific experienced guide as a soul friend began in the third to fifth century deserts, we shall learn about the rigorous disciplines of the desert first. But if we are beginners it is best not to start with these disciplines, since we do not live in desert conditions. To do this would be like jumping in at the deep end of a swimming pool when we are learning to swim; it is probably better to wade in from the shallow end. This chapter will give us information which helps us build up a background picture; we need to start to carry out the desert disciplines only when we are ready.

A teacher ought to be a stranger to the love of domination and a foreigner to vainglory.

Amma Theodora

In 313 the Roman emperor made Christianity a favoured religion. Whereas in earlier centuries to be a Christian was a sacrifice, now it was a social advantage. Christians became attached to comfort, buildings, status and the trappings of power. Often their faith became second-hand, their morals became lax and their clergy became career-minded.

What were Christians who were hungry for God, and who wanted to learn to live like Jesus, to do? A few of them had already emigrated to the deserts of Egypt, Syria or Palestine to live as hermits, basing their lives on the 'beautiful attitudes' that Jesus taught (Matthew 5:1–12). Now many more joined them. They realised that to advance in the true way of life they had to be free of the distractions of their old way; that time, space and a soul friend were essential if they were to be stripped of self-will, and to grow in holiness.

This may seem extreme to us, yet the underlying dynamics are surely still with us. Young people in our society, not knowing about this Christian tradition, visit Buddhist monasteries in order to learn how to overcome selfish desires and to acquire inner wellbeing. People in some churches seem to carry too much 'baggage' to attend to the inner path. Once when I was becoming too busy as a parish priest my soul friend said to me: 'Working on your inner life is like trying to repair an aeroplane while it is in flight.' So, although we would not wish to adopt some of the more bizarre practices of those desert Christians (for we now know more about developmental processes that engender wholeness), we can recognise them as an amazing laboratory from which we have much to learn.

Christians in Celtic lands were inspired by the desert Christians' example even though they themselves lived in different conditions. They formed their own solitary places which they named their 'deserts'. Christians today are doing the same, and creating 'desert' days, weeks or places.

The first desert Christians lived as hermits far from anyone else; but in time some lived near to others or formed communities. The desert became a training ground of the spirit. Those who found it too difficult returned to the towns, or coped by becoming weird. But many moved forward with God, and these became known as athletes of the Spirit. The older, wiser ones were called 'abbas' or 'ammas'; these were affectionate terms of respect, such as the words 'poppa' or 'mama' might convey in parts of the world. These were sought out as soul friends.

Although the lives of these desert Christians were anchored in solitude, this was not contrary to friendship. In fact, the cultivation of silence released a greater capacity for a friendship that did not depend upon trivia. John Cassian observed that the desert was pervaded by a deep spirit of friendship which was made up of people being joined together in spirit rather than by being in one place. Cassian called this indissoluble bond the 'common dwelling'.[1]

News of these spiritual fathers and mothers stirred the imagination of sincere Christians in the towns, and they began to seek out desert fathers and mothers as guides. Young people would test out whether they, too, could live this way, by choosing an amma or abba to be their soul friend. They would share the work, the prayers, the silence and the cell, and learn from the life as much as from the words of the older Christian. So soul friends, in their origin, were cell mates.[2]

Busy town Christians would make journeys to some wise old desert Christian and ask him or her to be their soul friend for a weekend. Desert hermits would pay visits to one another, and those with the clearest spiritual discernment would bring to light hindrances to spiritual growth in others that needed attention. When Abba Helle was staying with some brothers, they so trusted him that 'When he revealed the secret counsels of each of them, saying that one was troubled by fornication, another by vanity, another by self-indulgence, and another by anger, they could only respond, "Yes, what you say is true." '

Gradually collections were made of the sayings of the ammas and abbas. This was one of their sayings:

Let us each give his heart to the other, carrying the Cross of Christ.

Abba Theodore[3]

Visitors to churches in the Celtic lands brought news of these desert fathers and mothers for whom spiritual direction was part of the pursuit of holiness. Writings about them by Cassian and Athanasius were read in monastery libraries. John Cassian for a time shared a desert cell with his friend Germanus in Bethlehem. The desert spirituality caught the imagination of Celtic Christians, with their single-minded passion for God, and they applied it to their own society.

The hermits Paul and Antony

Two figures often depicted at the top of large, tenth-century, ornamented stone crosses in Ireland are the desert hermits Paul and Antony who, at the end of many solitary years, were joined together as soul friends. Jerome records a beautiful story of their soul friendship:

> For a hundred and thirteen years Blessed Paul, the first known Christian hermit of the Egyptian desert, lived the life of heaven upon earth, while in another part of the desert lived Antony, an old man of ninety years. At first Antony assumed that no better monk than he lived in that vast desert, but once, as he lay quiet at night, it was revealed to him that there was, deep in the desert, another better by far than he, and that he must make haste to find him.
>
> Although he was frail and he had no indications of the other's whereabouts, Antony set out saying 'I believe in my God that he will show me His servant as He promised.' He followed the trail of a wolf seeking water by a cave, and saw a light. Paul locked his door when he knew another man was outside, but the tears and entreaties of Antony eventually convinced him that this visitor was a friend, not a foe. He opened wide the door, and they embraced and greeted one another by name. 'Look at me, the man you have searched for,' said Paul, 'and you look at a man who is soon to become dust.' Nevertheless, Jerome records, 'for love's sake' they

conversed much, and spoke about the state of the world they had forsaken.

As they talked, a crow which had flown with a large chunk of bread in its mouth from some hospitable place, flew down and gently deposited this before them. They understood this to be God's blessing on their meeting. 'At your coming Christ has doubled his soldier's rations,' Paul told Antony. They then knew that their friendship was something to celebrate, in a way which, for lack of such food, would not have been possible for any other happening. They together drank water from the spring, sang praises to God, and passed the night in vigil.

As day dawned Paul confided to Antony 'For a long time, brother, I have known that you lived in the desert, and long ago God told me that you, my fellow servant, would come to me. But since my time on earth has now come, and since I desire that my body be dissolved so that I can be with Christ, it is clear that you have been sent in order to cover my body as it returns earth to earth.' Antony wept. He could not bear the thought that this priceless friendship should be snatched from him so quickly. He pleaded that Paul would not leave him, but take him with him on his journey to heaven. 'You must not seek your own, but another's good,' said Paul. 'It is good for you to follow the Lamb of God, but it is good for the brothers who have come to live in the desert that they have you to model the life of Christ for them.' Paul wished to spare his friend the pain of his dying, so he added: 'Go back to your cell and bring the cloak that Athanasius gave to you so that it can cover my dead body.'

Amazement fell upon Antony that Paul, who had lived in silence all these years, could have known, no doubt by some inner revelation, of Athanasius, let alone of his gift to him of his cloak. He dared not answer Paul, for he saw and worshipped Christ within him. He silently kissed Paul's hands and his eyes and set out on the five-day return journey to his cell. So overwhelmed was Antony by this extraordinary once in a lifetime soul friendship, that he spoke no word to his disciples at his cell, and took no food for the return journey; he was athirst to see his friend again. He feared that his friend would have returned his spirit to God before his return. His fears proved to be true, for before he reached Paul's cave Antony saw a host of angels, companies of prophets and apostles, and Paul, climbing the steeps of heaven, shining white as snow.[4]

The relationship between a seeker and a desert soul friend

One of the first things Antony did after his conversion was to go to a neighboring village and seek advice from an old man who had practised the solitary life from his youth. Antony himself became a soul friend to many. Jerome, who wrote much about these desert Christians, advised a friend not to set out into the unknown without a guide. Why was the relationship between an abba or amma and the disciple who came to learn the hermit life so fundamental? Few people were prepared to undertake the desert life without such direction, for without it they were unlikely to survive the desert's ravages of body, mind and spirit. A teacher was needed who could see into the heart of the beginner and discern the appropriate course for them. They had to learn the difference between running away from and running towards responsibilities; between rushing into false heroics, and making steady progress in self-mastery; the difference between delusion and true temptation. The novice's growth in the Christian life was manifested primarily by the alacrity with which he renounced his own will, and allowed himself to be guided by his father in God. Two things were necessary if this relationship was to work. The soul friend had to teach by example as well as by advice, and the seeker had to be willing to obey without question. 'Be an example, not a lawgiver' was a saying that circulated widely. Cassian records some advice from Abba Moses:

> True discretion is impossible without humility. And the first proof of humility is to submit to the judgement of the seniors not only

51

what we propose to do, but even what we think, so that by
agreement with their decisions in everything we may know what is
right and what is wrong. In this way the young man will be taught
to keep on the straight path and will be preserved from Satan's
tricks and snares. For deception is impossible in the case of him
who directs his life, not according to his own judgement, but
according to that of his seniors ... The bad thought shrivels up
the moment it is made public, and even before the senior has had
time to pronounce his wise verdict the horrid serpent (dragged by
confession into the light from his gloomy underground cave)
scurries off as best he can and with a lively sense of confusion. In
fact his suggestions have the upper hand only as long as they are
hidden in the heart.[5]

The cell

The first focus of the desert fathers and mothers, and of their
disciples, was the cell. This alone gave them the 'soul space' in
which wisdom and holiness could grow.

Go to your cell and your cell will teach you everything.

A famous desert maxim

Being with a desert father or mother was more important even than
listening to them. Therefore to share the soul space of their cell was
a privilege the soul friend guarded with care and the seeker
cherished. The desert Christians believed that this soul space should
be used either for silence or for the opening up of one's heart to the
other in a way that leads to peace and serenity. This mutual opening
up was known as *exagoreusis*, and the serenity it led to was known
as *hesychia*.

Their second rule was hospitality. Some cells had a window
through which seekers could receive advice at certain times. Other
cells had two rooms, with space for a guest to sleep. As younger
people sought out abbas as spiritual guides these would share with

them their lives: their cell, the silences, the prayer, the work, the meals, and occasionally their conversation.

Detachment

The purpose of soul friendship, and of the desert experience, was to strip away all inessentials, so that only love remained. Physical comforts had been left behind at the outset, but what about the emotional baggage every person carries with them? We hang on to pride, prejudice and possessiveness for as long as we can, but whereas in the busyness of urban life we can hide from these sins, in the desert they are shown up for what they are.

The collections of sayings and stories from the desert[6] portray soul friendship within the framework of renunciation of possessions, parents, sexual activity and society. The soul friend (sometimes simply referred to as 'the old man') is involved with the struggles of their disciple, but in a way which does not destroy their own detachment.

Soul friends help us to face up to the fact that we all have things inside us which are substitutes for reality. Some things we moderns need to be detached from are

* resentment
* status
* shopping
* virtual reality
* favouritism
* possessions
* clutching relationships
* sexual compulsion
* over-busyness.

The value of detachment is a theme common to classic Christian spirituality, though in the desert, where people are freed from so many distractions, it has a better chance to 'take'. Many modern

53

Christians, however, dislike or disagree with the concept, because they think it will make them distant from people. In the Celtic tradition, detachment does not mean detachment from what makes us human, but from what prevents us being fully human. We detach ourselves from anything that is not love, in order that love alone may reign in us. Detachment does not stifle spontaneity; it sets us free to be like Adam and Eve who walked intimately with God in the garden, unashamed. When the pattern of control by which we seek to cover up what is false in us is laid aside, then what is true and beautiful, what we love deeply and what really belongs to us comes into its own.

Nor does detachment mean abdication of any true responsibility; though it does mean renouncing possessiveness, and letting go of the many things that we are not meant to waste our energy on. The following story illustrates this.

A Seeker asked to join a desert Father and use his spare cell. He told him that he wanted to renounce the world and become a monk. 'You cannot' the Father told him; 'I can' the Seeker replied. 'If you want to do this, go and renounce the world and then come back here and sit in your cell', the older man told him. The young man departed and gave away half of his money, keeping a hundred coins for himself, and returned to the monk. 'Go and sit in your cell' he advised him. While the Seeker was sitting there his thoughts said to him, 'That old door needs replacing.' Later the monk told him that he had not renounced the world. 'Go and do that, and then come back here.' The young man gave away ninety coins and hid ten for himself. On his return he informed the old man 'Look, this time I have really renounced the world.' 'Go and sit in your cell,' said the older man. As he sat, his thoughts said to him, 'The roof is old and wants replacing.' In due course he told the old man what his thoughts were saying. 'Go away and renounce the world' the old man told him. He went away again, gave away his last ten coins, and returned. Again he sat in his cell. This time his thoughts said to him 'Everything here is old, and a lion is coming to eat me up.' He told these thoughts to the old man. The old man said to him, 'I expect everything to come down on top of me, and the lion to come and eat me up so that I may be set free. Go, sit in your cell and pray to God.'[7]

The negative passions

To the desert mothers and fathers, the human heart is the most important battleground. There the opposing forces are the positive qualities which they called the virtues, and the destructive qualities which they called the passions. By the passions they did not mean strong drives *per se*, for they believed in being passionate for good; they meant drives that are destructive and enslaving. Their concept of the passions offers us a useful tool with which to learn to love better.

To be made in God's image means to see each person and thing as they truly are, as God sees them, through the lens of love. It follows that to truly love we must be able to see God, others and ourselves as more than an extension of our own needs. The passions obscure this way of seeing in love. They also rob us of the freedom to make real choices and act on them. The fear of abandonment and the compulsive need for approval that many of us carry over from childhood rob us of our freedom to choose the way of love.

A fourth-century monastic teacher, Evagrius Ponticus, warned people about eight passions: gluttony (that is, never being satisfied with what we have), lust for other people's bodily parts, acquisitiveness, depression, anger, restless boredom, love of flattery and pride.[8] He regards anger as 'the most fierce passion', and describes it as 'a boiling and stirring up of wrath against one who has given injury – or is thought to have done so. It constantly irritates the soul and above all at the time of prayer it seizes the mind and flashes the picture of the offensive person before one's eyes.' The angry person is not responsible for the origins of their anger, but can nevertheless choose to nurse that anger to the point where it controls them – 'for both anger and hatred increase' – or can fight against it and refuse to let it reach the point of becoming destructive.

All the desert guides felt that these passions must be wrestled against and mastered. Father Ammonas told someone that he had spent fourteen years in Scetis asking God night and day to give him the victory over anger. Tools that were commonly used to tackle these passions were fasting, silence and abstinence from sleep, sex and ownership.

The positive virtues

Detachment and wrestling against the passions are not ends in themselves; they are the preconditions for the flowering of the virtues. These are the opposite qualities to the destructive passions, for example: self-control, chastity, generosity, gentleness, peaceableness, contentment, appreciativeness, humility. 'Virtue', taught one desert father, 'leads to God and unites us with one another.' Father Dorotheus taught that we are made in God's image, so God has sown the virtues like seeds within us. We are called to resemble God, as Jesus taught: 'Be merciful for your Father is merciful.'

One of the fathers taught that three particular virtues should be honoured: the fellowship of Holy Communion, the fellowship of a shared meal, and the washing of another person's feet. Antony taught people to make a conscious pursuit of one virtue at a time: 'Whoever hammers a lump of iron first decides what he is going to make of it, a scythe, a sword or an axe. Even so we ought to make up our minds what sort of virtue we want to forge or we labour in vain.'

After monasteries came into being, Antony wrote letters to help the monks grow in the virtues. 'I, as your elder, will share what I know and the fruits of my experience,' he wrote.[9] In his first letter he describes how our bodies from top to bottom – the tongue, the hands, the belly, the genitals, the feet – may be integrated into God's love. He repeats to his disciples that he has a love towards them which is not limited to the body, but which is of the spirit.

Antony soon realised that even many desert Christians had no idea of the different kinds of will which act in human lives. He urged them to distinguish between these three wills: God's all-perfect and saving will, our own human will, which, even if it is not destructive is not saving, and the devil's will which is wholly destructive. He might have added a fourth will for town-dwellers, the will which other people lay upon us.

Entering a personal desert with a soul friend

Without an environment of 'space', one form of which is to live in a desert, we are unlikely to get to know either ourselves or God, or to accumulate 'the wisdom of the desert'. Without purity of heart, spiritual direction is a waste of time. And without a willingness to get to know every part of ourselves, including our earthy and our disguised parts, we cannot enter into the reality which is God's will for us.

Yet it is no light matter to enter any form of desert. A physical desert has no water, trees or beauty to hand, and nor does an inner desert; we cannot truly enter an inner desert if we are trying to fit it into other things. To enter a desert we have to leave behind other things, and be prepared for things to get worse before they get better.

> In the desert our spirit travels blindly in directions that seem to lead away from vision, away from God, away from all fulfilment and joy. It may become impossible to believe that this road goes anywhere at all except to a desolation full of dry bones – the ruin of all our hopes and good intentions.
>
> *Thomas Merton*[10]

Most of us are attached to things that prevent us from journeying to the place where there is nothing. Some people attach themselves to superficial or flattering talk in order to hide from a feeling that their inner core is hollow. Their need is to be detached from these false defences, and to walk into the desert with the pain of their feelings. The role of a soul friend is to give them space and gentle encouragement to get in touch with these feelings, to discuss how they can dialogue with God about them. The soul friend is there with them as they journey, but should not play God by giving superficial palliatives, and should beware of going down sidetracks.

Other people fear that their centre is a seething mass that is out of control. So they button everything up by successfully organising themselves and others. If they allow themselves to have a soul friend at all, they will want the soul friend to propose tasks which they can accomplish and tick off as achievements. A soul friend may, at first, use this approach, but should steer it towards the inner life. For example, the task could be to pay attention to the times during the day when the stomach is most taut, and to note down the things that triggered this. Then, when they next meet, they might discuss the feelings that accompanied this. Gradually, the seeker may explore their body and their feelings, and in the process allow their vulnerability to come to the surface.

A third type of person may despair of sustaining a true relationship, so they cocoon themselves to avoid interacting with others, or they pour their emotions into idealising the future or the past, in order to avoid the disharmony of the present. In order to become detached from these defences they need to acknowledge their raw emotions. A soul friend needs to face them with the here and now.

These three examples correspond to Enneagram types 2, 3 and 4. The Enneagram is a method of classifying human beings into nine categories of personality, each of which has distinctive traits and defence mechanisms. Different personality types tend to put up particular barriers which prevent them from entering the 'desert' where they will find reality.

Some people, however, are already in a desert. They may have come to a standstill, assume that this is failure, and want their soul friend to suggest ways of moving on. The soul friend needs to find out if this standstill is caused by wilful refusal to heed inner promptings. If it is not, the soul friend needs to say: 'Do not run away from this darkness. Do not torture yourself. Keep still, open, trusting in One who is greater than this aridity.'

So we see that spiritual direction in this tradition does not beat about the bush; the starting point is that God needs to have his way. As seekers allow themselves to enter the desert something will seep into their soul that is deeper than darkness or definition. They will be purified. They will get that indefinable satisfaction that, while the outer self of the senses is unsatisfied, the deeper core of self is in the will of God.

Summary

The hermits Paul and Antony discovered soul friendship in the desert. When many Christians followed after them, the whole desert was pervaded by a spirit of friendship. The method of a desert soul friend was to share their cell with a seeker for a short or long period. The purpose of this discipline was, through ceaseless prayer, to strip away negative, self-centred habits, and to let God's qualities within them such as patience, gentleness and love come to flower.

Exercises
For soul friends and seekers

1. Whether you are a soul friend or a seeker, make a list of the negative passions which hijack true love in your life, and number them in order of their hold over you. Decide what tool you will use to combat the passion at the top of your list.

2. Whether you are a soul friend or a seeker, make lists of examples of the four types of will (God's, yours, others, evil) which seek to control your life at the present time.

3. Whether you are a soul friend or a seeker, make a list of the virtues you most desire, and number them in order of priority. Decide what steps you will take to practise the number one virtue.

4. Imagine you are soul friend to a seeker who can only see you once a year after a long journey. How will you arrange your house,

your schedule, your heart and your mind so that the seeker experiences *exagoreusis* and *hesychia*?

Further reading
The Wisdom of the Desert Fathers, translated by Sister Benedicta Ward of the Fairacres Community, contains a selection of systematic sayings from the desert fathers and mothers. Available from SLG Press, Fairacres, Oxford OX4 1TB. A companion volume, *The World of the Desert Fathers*, contains further stories and sayings translated by Columba Steward OSB.

A helpful book which explains the different types of personality that the Enneagram brings to light, the defences each type tends to put up, and how soul friends can work with them to become real is by Suzanne Zuercher OSB, *Enneagram Companions: Growing In Relationships and Spiritual Direction* (Ave Maria Press, Notre Dame, IN, 1993).

CHAPTER 5

ENVISIONING –
PRE-CHRISTIAN INSIGHTS
INTO SOUL FRIENDSHIP

From before Christ to the sixth century after Christ

Tony Blair, Britain's prime minister at the turn of the millennium, has a mentor, and members of Britain's royal family have spiritual directors. Although few soul friends will have a national leader as their seeker, we should remember that in the society that Celtic Christians inherited it was normal for rulers to employ soul friends, and we should be ready to respond to the need of public figures for soul friends today. Christian soul friends discarded those methods of the pagan spiritual guides which lacked integrity or truth, such as fortune-telling, casting spells, or conjuring up psychic or spirit powers that were not God-centred, yet they recognised the value of the roles of the spiritual guides in envisioning the people, passing on the wisdom of nature and the memory of their heritage. An understanding of the druids' role in shaping the people may help us to explore the soul friend's role in developing vision for others as well as to see the importance of soul friends for national leaders and for communities.

Where there is no vision the people perish.

Proverbs 11:14

rue friendship releases the power of possibility. Although Celtic soul friends drew their primary inspiration from the Gospels and from the Christian fathers and mothers of the desert, they inherited from their pre-Christian society the tradition of envisioners such as druids, bards and shamans. Local rulers employed and consulted druids, and doubtless others did too. Celtic saints such as Patrick, Columba and Brigid were taught by druids when they were young. Druids were the pagan equivalents to a soul friend. They can be thought of as holistic advisors to top people, and soul friends to the community as a whole. Although they lacked the Christian understanding of sin, forgiveness and eternal life in Christ, they were steeped in the wisdom of nature, folklore and philosophy.

The justice of the king consists in having wise counsellors.

Seventh-century saying

The word 'pagan' became a term of abuse during the Enlightenment centuries, but we should remember that before Christianity came to Britain there were some good as well as evil pagans, who followed the highest wisdom that they knew. It was good that their society valued people whose job was to raise people's sights.

Celtic Christians drew from, sifted and transformed this heritage. They introduced pagans to a Person who was the Source of what was good, and who changed what was bad in their society. They were secure enough in their faith not to feel threatened by the people's existing guides, to confront them when necessary, and to learn from them when possible.

The role of druids, bards and shapers

Some scholars think the root of the word 'druid' means 'knowledge of the oak', while others think it means 'those whose knowledge is great'.[1] Since druids passed on everything from memory, and wrote nothing down, much of what we know about them comes from biased Roman writers who belittled them. Scholars argue as to the exact nature of their practices. Some allege that they once offered humans as sacrifices, but there is no evidence of this in sixth-century Britain. Julius Caesar tells us that druids acted as arbiters in all private and public matters, as well as officiating at rituals and sacrifices; and Pliny describes them as doctors as well as magicians. Pomponius Mela (first century CE) describes the druids as: 'teachers of wisdom, who profess to know the greatness and shape of the earth and the universe, and the motion of the heavens and of the stars and what is the will of the gods ... They teach many things to the nobles of the race in sequestered and remote places during twenty years.'[2] It took twenty years' education to become a druid; the entire body of folklore had to be committed to memory; nothing was written. Saints Clement and Cyril of Alexandria saw druids as enlightened philosophers who believed in the immortality of the soul.

In Ireland the social system could be broken into three groups. The third, small but influential group were known as the *aes dana* – the people of learning or poetry. They included poets, historians, lawyers, doctors, skilled craftspeople and the storytellers. Some of these acted as druids. Their moral authority was sometimes equal to that of the ruler, and they all had the privilege of travelling anywhere as honoured guests. This group of people were the purveyors of the tribe's values, the advisors to its rulers, the communicators to the people.

The bards, especially, wandered from place to place, where they would be invited to speak or sing. These envisioners provided a 'hitchiker's guide' to the past and the present, to the worlds of nature and of the spirits, which linked everyone in an all-embracing friendship.

The poets, or bards, were as influential in Britain as in Ireland. Merlin, of the sixth-century Arthurian legends, was the bard of the British King Gwenddlau. Taliesin was the bard of Urien, King of Rheged, the major kingdom in north-west Britain.

A bard who was asked whence he came replied:

> *I move along the columns of age*
> *Along the streams of inspiration*
> *Along the fair land of knowledge*
> *The bright country of the sun*
> *Along the hidden land which by day the moon inhabits*
> *Along the first beginnings of life.*[3]

As Amergin Whiteknee, a chief bard and shaman of the mythical Milesian invaders of prehistory, greeted the land of Ireland from his ship, he believed he could remember many transmigrations:

> *I am a hawk on a cliff*
> *I am a tear of the sun*
> *I am a turning in a maze*
> *I am a boar in valour.*[4]

Caitlin Matthews comments:

> In Amergin's mystical identification with all things, he becomes one of the physicians of the soul, reweaving the scattered elements of life into a new wholeness. This is the task of the Celtic poet, whose skill is to bring the soul to the point of vision, rest, and stillness. The music of their healing skill is known by three strains: the laugh strain which raises the spirits; the sorrow strain, which causes the release of tears; and the sleep strain, which brings rest to troubled souls.

In the stories of the pagan Celts[5] the heroes frequently changed their shapes and became birds or animals. Sometimes shamans were prophetic. For example, it is recorded that when Fedlimid's pregnant wife issued a primal scream, a shaman named Cathbad predicted that her child would be a tall, lovely long-haired woman, but that she would also be a source of contention and slaughter. It seems he predicted correctly! The origin of shape-shifting may have been in the need ancient hunters felt to protect themselves from the angry spirits of animals they had killed. So the shaman emerged – a person who could clothe himself with parts of the animal, go into a trance or out of the body, and so gain a rapport with and an influence over the spirits. Shamans then evolved to become clairvoyant guides to humans, who could put spells upon people, either through hypnotism or the channelling of psychic or spirit forces, or with the use of drugs.[6]

What Christians rejected from the pagan guides

Christian Celts rejected the use of psychic forces to control others and the practice of shamanism, but they believed that God as revealed in Christ could use them to shape people's lives by freeing them from fear and other evils. They renounced the use of magic, drugs and spiritism, but Christian soul friends sought to be people whom the population would feel able to consult as much as they consulted the shamans. They gave up the shape-shifting that shamans went into trances to achieve, yet they did not give up the idea of shaping people according to their true image of God.

The prayer known as 'St Patrick's Breastplate', which scholars believe to be from seventh- or eighth-century Ireland, pinpoints some key elements in the pagan heritage that Christians rejected:

> *This day I call upon ... the might of Heaven ...*
> *to protect me*
> *from snares of the demons*
> *from evil enticements*

from failings of nature
from one man or many
that seek to destroy me
nearby or afar
against false prophesyings
against pagan devisings
against spells cast by women
by blacksmiths, by druids
against knowledge unlawful
that injures the body,
that injures the spirit.

What Celtic Christians refashioned from the pagan guides

Christian soul friends emerged who respected the integrity of those they sought to shape. They gradually replaced the shamans, taking on some of their roles in a new way. They said to them, in effect: 'We are grateful that our society has people to envision it, but have you noticed how sometimes this goes wrong? Envisoners can build castles in the air or, though seeing accurately, use this to inflate their own ego or to gain control over others. Moreover, it is not always helpful for a person to be told what will happen to them; it is like taking someone into a minefield. Yes, there is gold to be found there, but mines can explode and destroy them and then the gold is useless. Nor is everything in the unseen world good (spirits can be deceitful and malevolent), so we should only seek to enter it through the Lord of that world, whom we now know is God's Son, Jesus Christ. We admire, and indeed emulate your well-honed intuition, but intuition can be wrong; it needs to be accountable to a higher power, the High King of the universe. It is also a fact that the psychic powers that one has can go to one's head; power corrupts and one can easily believe what one wants to, or become a manipulator rather than a servant of others.

The Celtic Christians introduced the pagan guides to the God who had revealed truth through Christ. Their own vision and hearts needed to be purified; that is why they prayed, 'Be Thou my vision, Thou Lord of my heart.' But they continued to guide people; they did not leave the whole area of envisioning to the pagans. Rather, purified by penance and humbled by service of the poor, they allowed the Lord of seen and unseen powers to pour out his gifts of seeing, wisdom and poetry as he willed. Always these were tested by Scripture, and always their purpose was to build up souls to the glory of the High King of all creation.

Pagan guides were replaced by Christian soul friends who retained the envisioning role of the old guides. The Christian *anamcharas* came to have a variety of roles: some, such as Patrick, Brigid and Columba, were healers, seers and spiritual guides to rulers and ordinary people. Many, such as Aidan, Hilda and David, were tutors both to younger students and to adults. Some were mystics like Samthann of Clonbroney and Maedoc of Ferns.

What can we learn from the envisioners?

The pagan envisioners do show the value of having soul friends to communities. Christian envisioners provide for the continuity of Christian memory, draw from and sift the wisdom of contemporary guides, and win over people in the pagan or New Age scene.

The druids, bards and shamans shaped the people by guarding and passing on the folk memory; by introducing the next world into this world, and by receiving visions of the future and calling forth its potential. People today need to be shaped in these ways too.

In the Old Testament we learn of seers. These were a tiny minority of the population who could see clearly what was going to happen to a person or a people, because they could see into their spiritual condition and could discern, through the law of cause and effect, what their spiritual condition would lead to. Later came the prophets. Some of these were false. They had psychic gifts and sharp intuition, but these were not dedicated to God and his good purposes, so their psychic world became confused and manipulative. The Scriptures suggest that a key question to ask, in order to find out whether a prophet is true or false, is: 'What does the prophet get out of it?' If he has a track record of showing neither fear nor favour, he is honest, though he might still be blind. So a second test is: 'Has he a track record of prophecies that prove to be true?' People looked forward to the promised time of the Messiah, when spiritual discernment would be possible for all people (Jeremiah 31:33, 34).

Here are seven specific things we can learn from envisioners.

1. To know the whole story

We are unlikely to be whole if we do not know our own story as a member of a family or of a people. The shapers who passed on folk memory helped their students know that their lives were not meaningless incidents, but were related to those who were before them and around them. The role of the *anamchara* is also to pass on the living memory, and that should include the story of the inspired people who have helped to shape one's land. The soul friend, even if they are of another race, should aim to see the whole picture and to pass this on to the seeker.

Perhaps the soul friend senses that something in the seeker is not quite as it should be. The seeker seems to be banging their head against walls. The soul friend realises that the seeker's life is like a piece in a jigsaw puzzle. The soul friend glimpses something of the whole picture, but the seeker is not even aware that there is one. This causes a sense of futility, if not panic. So the soul friend begins to fill in some of the missing pieces. The soul friend may introduce the seeker to other contexts, ways of thinking, types of temperament, to the past as well as to the present. The seeker begins to realise that they have been blinkered, taut, trying to fit everything round their own little space. Now, the seeker begins to breathe more freely, to look around, to see how their own piece of life can harmonise with other pieces, to go with the flow, to become whole.

2. To bring the spiritual realm to bear on this world

The Roman writer Mela wrote that the druids claimed to know the will of the gods. Lucan, in a rhetorical address to the druids declaims: 'You assure us that with a new body the spirit reigns in another world – if we understand your hymns, death is halfway through a long life.' Stories of the otherworld gripped the imagination of the people, and gave them something to aspire to.

The Celtic Christians rejected as untrue the stories of gods and of earthly heroes who had transmigrated into the otherworld. Yet they did not let the otherworld become a no-go area for the devil to take over. Rather, they held up Jesus as a door into heaven, which was peopled by angels and saints. Sometimes they were vouchsafed visions of these, which generated excitement. They taught people Scriptures and prayers about these things; in their liturgies they re-enacted heavenly realities, and in their soul befriending they freely focussed upon saints, angels, the triumphant dying of friends and the place of resurrection to which a seeker could aspire.

Our lives are so easily dominated by immediate pressures that we fail to live in the perspective of eternity. Yet we are destined for eternal life, and the purpose of our short stay on earth is to learn to reflect heaven on earth. This short-termism impoverishes us, even if we do not realise it, for a person who has not prepared for death has hardly begun to live. So an important function of a soul friend is to help us reflect upon everyday experience in the light of heaven. A contemporary soul friend might encourage a seeker to journey to the borderlands between earth and heaven; suggest meditations on death, resurrection or angels; ways of celebrating saints days; or help the seeker become aware of 'heaven in the ordinary'. As the seeker becomes acquainted with the wonder of the invisible world, hidden fears of losing control melt away, and daily thought and action begin to flow out of a life in God. The grace of heaven and the poise of eternity gradually replace empty worldliness in the seeker.

3. To call forth the potential in people

Soul has a fluency and energy which is not to be caged within any fixed form.

John O'Donohue

We can learn from Celtic Christians how to envision others, rather than let envisioning be monopolised by non-Christian guides. Certainly Celtic Christians armed themselves and their protégés against shamanic spells. Patrick rebuked shape-shifters, yet Patrick himself disappeared from the sight of the officers the High King of Ireland had sent to ambush him. All they saw was a herd of deer passing by. This gave rise to the belief that the Lord had confused their sight. That is why the prayer known as 'St Patrick's Breastplate' is also known as 'The Deer's Cry'. This experience surely echoes that of the Old Testament prophet Elisha who asked the Lord to blind the eyes of enemy troops who had come to capture him. The Lord answered that prayer, too (2 Kings 6:18).

Although Celtic Christian leaders confronted false shamanism, they refused to allow a no-go area to develop. They took an offensive in the realm of Spirit-filled prophecy. Whereas shamans used a created force to make a person be or do something alien to their God-given selves, Christian envisoners leapt across the parameters of fear, small-mindedness, group prejudice, low self-esteem and poor conditioning to give the real person God-sight. Having been granted a glimpse of the essence of the person, the true potential of that person was by faith called forth. Their potential began to be actualised, the oak began to grow out of the acorn. Examples of such prophetic prayer are given in Chapter 10.

A soul friend who has helped a seeker work through more immediate issues may sense that a time has come when it is appropriate to pray with a seeker along similar lines, so that the seeker's potential is not stunted.

4. To value soul friends to the community

Some people are called to be soul friend to a gathered community, a neighbourhood or even a people. John Paul II seems to have envisaged the role of the pope as a soul friend to a whole church. In *Man from a Far Country*,[7] Mary Craig quotes his poem entitled 'Marble Floor'. He contemplates the stones of St Peter's Square, Rome, which seem to him to symbolise the role of the pope at the heart of the church:

> Our feet meet the earth in this place;
> there are so many walls, so many colonnades,
> yet we are not lost. If we find meaning and oneness,
> it is the floor that guides us. It joins the spaces
> of this great edifice, and joins
> the spaces within us,
> who walk aware of our weakness and defeat.
> Peter, you are the floor, that others
> may walk over you (not knowing
> where they go). You guide their steps
> so that spaces can be one in their eyes,
> and that from them thought is born.
> You want to serve their feet that pass
> as rock serves the hooves of sheep.
> The rock is a gigantic temple floor, the cross a pasture.

5. To sustain a Christian memory

We can learn this important lesson from the druids: A tradition knows more than it can make explicit in words, which is why people have to learn that tradition by apprenticeship to it under a master. That is why a break in a living tradition of a land or a faith can kill it in a single generation. Many of our countries are in grave danger of such a break today. This truth is brilliantly expounded by Michael Polanyi in his masterpiece, *Personal Knowledge*.[8] Because we are in a world dominated by instant technology and surface distractions, young generations are losing contact with folk or church memory. They throw the baby out with the bath water. They do not know the story of their people, or of their spiritual formation. They do not know how they have come to be as they are. They do not know how to relate to what is around them in a way that leads to wholeness. They lose the skills of listening to the wisdom of the ages.

Perhaps only a large-scale acceleration of soul friendship as a mentoring in the tradition of our Christian birthright can avert such a disaster. Not all soul friends will feel this is their role, but those who have some learning should not shy away from passing on what they know, in any capacity that is open to them.

6. To draw from and sift the insights of our society's guides
Celtic Christians imbibed wisdom from envisioners in their society, and Christians rightly do the same in ours. We can learn from the insights of guides such as Carl Gustav Jung. Christopher Bryant, in his books *Jung and the Christian Way* and *The River Within*[9] draws deeply upon Jung's insights in helping Christians discover their true journey. In his *Modern Man in Search of a Soul*,[10] Jung helps us to see how the rhythms of our soul are meant to fit in with the larger rhythms of creation.

However, Dr Jeoffrey Satinova warns us against a new form of 'gnosis', the idea that certain psychic forces are infallible guides and may be followed unconditionally. Satinova reminds us that all our psychic forces, even the self which Jung distinguishes from the ego, need a Redeemer; we should should not abandon ourselves unconditionally to any of them, for they are all fallen in some way.[11]

7. To win over the neo-pagan scene
The origin of shamanism may be attributed to ignorance, fear or evil.[12] So why include this information in a book about spiritual direction? First, because shamanism was a case of spiritual *mis*direction, and it is now gaining currency again in the West, albeit in newfangled forms. Noted world leaders consult astrologers and mediums, and it is claimed that there are now more of these in Britain than there are Christian clergy. This area of influence is

sometimes called 'the alternative scene'.

If we are to have Christian guides who are credible to people in the alternative scene, we need the humility to accept there is much that we do not know, the patience to focus on the long walk on wisdom's way, sensitivity to know what and when to confront, the vision to adapt our approaches to the needs of a new generation, and the winsomeness which marked the Irish saints.

Storytelling

Storytelling played an important role in the shaping of the Celtic people. One version of *The Voyage of Bran* states that a local ruler named Mongan (d. *c.* 625) was told a story by his poet (*fili*) every winter night from Samhain to Beltane. It is generally assumed that storytellers memorised the outlines of the tale and filled in details in an extempore way. That is no doubt why, when these tales came to be transcribed from the seventh century onwards, there were various versions of most of them. Most surviving manuscripts date from the twelfth century, by which time they had accumulated many errors and had a second-hand feel about them. These include *The Book of Leinster* (*c.* 1160), *The Yellow Book of Lecan* (fourteenth century) and *Egerton 1782*, which includes *The Dream of Oengus* and is dated 1419. The earliest of the surviving manuscripts is *The Book of Dun Cow* (*Lebor na Luidre*), so called after a famous cow that belonged to that great soul friend and saint, Ciaran of Clonmacnoise. The half of the manuscript that survives contains thirty-seven stories. The chief scribe was a monk at Clonmacnoise monastery named Mael Muire, who was killed by raiders in 1106.[13] So we see that storytelling was thought to be important far into the Christian centuries.

The ancient's art of storytelling has never quite died in Scotland and Ireland, and stories are part of the ceilidhs. Now the Bible Society of England and Wales has introduced storytelling as part of its work, and English Heritage employs a full-time storyteller to visit its historic sites and relate to schools.[14] Of course, the love of storytelling continues in the TV 'soaps'; but these have limited horizons. Those few soul friends who relate to a seeker as a general guide do well to become acquainted with the storytelling genre, and some may use storytelling as one of the tools of their trade.

Conclusion

Some readers may feel intimidated by this chapter. Do not let it deter you from becoming a soul friend. I have little doubt that in Celtic days ordinary people had soul friends who knew little of the world of the leaders, philosophers or community advisors. So, today, many will carry on soul befriending who are removed from the world of philosophers, poets or historians. That is as it should be. Soul friends who come from that part of the spectrum, however, do have a valuable part to play, and that, too, is as it should be.

Summary
Celtic Christians rejected the manipulation of people through occult forces and inaccurate perceptions of the spirit world, but they recognised that under Christianity there was a continuing need for envisioners to help the people picture God's hand in their past, present and future, and to use imagination to release the potential in individuals.

Exercises
For anybody

1. When you next travel by car, bus or foot, bless everything your eye sees – the energy of motors, humans, hedges; sorrow for what spoils them, for mindless rush or pollution. Practise trying to see as God sees, not projecting the distorting demands of your ego on to places or people.

2. Create a flow chart, drawing or naming the significant stages in the life of your family, your community or your nation. What gaps in the story are you aware of? Plan how to fill in the gaps.

3. Write your own obituary which views your life from the point of view of eternity. What was most significant in it from eternity's point of view?

4. Choose an episode from the life of your favourite Celtic saint which has lessons for a seeker or someone else you know. Try writing down the story in your own words, or recording it on a dictaphone. Rework it to give it more flow and human interest. Rework it again, so that the material builds up to and does not detract from the main point.

Further reading

O'Donohue, John, *Anam Cara: Spiritual Wisdom from the Celtic World* (Bantam, 1997). Beautifully written by an Irish poet and scholar, this book reconnects the reader with the treasures of wisdom, both Christian and pre-Christian, that lie within the Irish soul.

Lofmark, Carl, *Bards and Heroes* (Llanerch, 1989).

Madden, Eric, *A Teacher's Guide to Storytelling at Historic Sites* (English Heritage, 1992).

DISCERNMENT: ST MORGAN'S INSIGHTS INTO SOUL FRIENDSHIP

The fourth and fifth centuries after Christ

Nowadays a soul friend is sometimes called a co-discerner. Once, when priests just pronounced absolution of sins and prescribed penances or rules according to a set formula, self-discernment did not come into the matter. Now, it is recognised that a soul friend's role is to help the seeker to develop their own discernment.

> At each moment of decision, you must sincerely seek to discern the will of God.
>
> *St Morgan*

Discernment is fundamental to soul friendship and to each person's spiritual journey. The Oxford Dictionary traces the root of the word 'discernment' to the old French word *discernier*, which means to separate out as distinct. Spiritual discernment is to separate distinctly that which is authentic from that which is false. As the Scripture says: 'Solid food is for adults who, through practice, are able to distinguish between good and evil' (Hebrews 5:14).

Discernment is also the art of finding God's will in the concrete decisions which face us in the maze of life. It is the process by which we examine, in the light of our faith and our experience of God's love, what draws us away from God and what does not. As Christians interact with Scripture, church, circumstances, creation, and inner conviction, they gradually discover what are the indicators of the divine will.

Jesus brought the art of discernment to its perfection: 'The Son only does what he sees his Father doing' (John 5:19). This was not an instant or easy discernment for Jesus, of a sort that we could not aspire to. Even Jesus needed to go through a process of sorting out which of his compelling thoughts were from God and which were from an evil source.

How did Jesus discern:

* what shape his mission should take?
* what his priorities should be?
* what persons he should choose for his task force?
* which requests he should say 'yes' or 'no' to?
* who wanted him for himself, rather than for what they could get out of him?
* who among the top people secretly wanted to do right by him?

Jesus knew the pull of ambition and the temptation to speed things up in order to avoid heartache, as the stories of his temptations in the desert reveal (Luke 4:1–13). Before he chose the twelve apostles he needed to spend a night alone on a mountain. How can we learn to discern the Father's will as did Jesus?

Morgan was an esteemed Celtic soul friend, whose letters of spiritual direction offer us some pertinent guidance. Born somewhere in Britain not long after 350, this lay monk had an educated mind, a wrestler's frame and a holy heart. In the early eighties he went to

Rome, where he was known by the Latin form of his name, Pelagius. There he acquired a reputation as an eloquent teacher. Morgan was horrified to discover the extent of moral laxity and confusion among Christians in Rome, and that this was buttressed by Augustine's new teachings about predestination and the incurable sinfulness of everyone. This produced an 'anything goes' mentality, and people said there was nothing they could do about sin. Morgan opposed such views. He taught that God gave each person the ability to choose between good and evil, and that each had a responsibility to discern and follow right callings and conduct.[1]

He gathered around himself an influential group from Rome's Christianised aristocracy who had been drawn to study the Bible and pursue holy lives. Morgan became their esteemed teacher and guide. Several of his writings and several of his letters as a soul friend have been preserved.[2] After Rome was conquered by Alaric in 410 Morgan made his way to Palestine and Africa, continuing to write his letters of spiritual guidance, and he died there not long after 418.

What does Morgan teach are the foundations of discernment?

1. Learn God's general will from Christ's life and teaching

In the teachings and example of Jesus Christ we learn the general principles of behaviour that please God.

Morgan

The record in Matthew 5–7 of the teachings Jesus gave on a mountain are a summary of this teaching. This has itself been summarised as four absolute standards of honesty, purity, unselfishness and love. These provide a good standard against which to test our every thought and action. Many thoughts or actions can be eliminated as not God's will because they are not absolutely honest, pure, unselfish or loving.

St Paul provides a useful summary of Jesus's teachings in his lists of the fruits of God's Spirit and the fruits of the bad that is in us (Galatians 5:19–23). If something is of God it will produce fruits such as love, joy, peace, patience, kindness, goodness, faithfulness, humility, self-control. Something is not of God if it spawns immorality, worship of created or occult things, jealousy, temper, division, drunken or disorderly behaviour.

> We must be honest with ourselves, recognising clearly those areas
> of our lives that we have not yielded to Christ.
>
> *Morgan*

Absolute honesty is an aspect of light which Scripture regards as an important test of what is in the will of God (see, for example, John 1:5; 1 John 3:24; 4:13). If we do not wish things about a projected step to come out into the light, it is probably not of God. Morgan says that these requirements are not optional. Nor is it acceptable to embrace some sacrifice that is optional, such as celibacy, and to imagine that then gives you a right to follow selfish desires.

2. Use reason to weight up good and bad consequences

> At each moment of choice we must apply those principles in practice. To do this God has given us two vital tools. The first is reason: we can use reason to work out how God's spiritual law applies in each and every situation.
>
> *Morgan: to Demetrias*

Morgan recommends that a person weighs up the good and bad consequences they anticipate are likely to result from each course of action. To do this it helps to draw up two lists: On the first you write down what will be the likely consequences if you follow plan A; on the second list you note the likely consequences if you do not follow plan A. Then another two lists may be drawn up for plan B and so on.

3. Pray about your provisional intentions

The second is prayer: we can talk to God, asking him to guide our thoughts. We can be sure that, if we consider every choice carefully, and if we seek divine guidance, our decisions will please God.

Morgan: to Demetrias

The desire to do God's will is a precondition of finding it. A childlike attitude that brings everything out in the open before God, makes discernment possible.

4. Sense whether your actions bring peace or unease

Listen to your conscience ... It works by inducing guilt when you do wrong, and by inducing feelings of peace when you do right. Confess your sins by describing precisely, within your own mind, those actions which induced guilt during the previous day. Equally note carefully those actions which induced peace and tranquillity.

Morgan: to Celantia

If we have embarked on a course of action in good faith but we find that the actions it entails do not bring us peace, then it is a sign that we need to go back to square one; we have not heard the Lord aright.

Thus for Morgan the soul friend did not foster dependency but liberated discernment in the seeker. In his writings to Demetrias he says, in effect: Don't ask me. Listen to what is deepest in your heart. Then write it out. If it does not accord with Christ, listen again. Morgan believed that Christ frees us to become truly ourselves.

Four things that hinder discernment

We should not be surprised that discernment is a long, hard process, and that we can so easily get it wrong. Morgan warns of four strategies of the devil which distort discernment. These can be presented in the following way.

Sin binds

We get tempted, and assume that we won't be able to keep to the path of God's will; we dread failure, so we 'stop the journey'. Morgan calls this depression. He seems to recognise, as does modern medicine, that we may not be responsible for our depression; but he asserts that we are responsible for the way we respond to it. Much depression is, nevertheless, linked with what we feed our unconscious minds upon. Once we feed our bodies, minds or emotions upon something that is a substitute for God, we become addicted. In order to feel better about this we tell ourselves that this addictive living is normal, and that a God-centred way of life is abnormal. We reach out to others who are addictive, and this forms a narcissistic web. When we are bound in this way, how can we discern? Jesus had to use shock language to free people from this: 'If your eye offend you, pull it out. It is better to go into the kingdom of God with one eye than not at all.'

In order to overcome this hurdle we have to be radical and cut through the web. Whether our black cloud is of our making or not, we do well to follow Morgan's advice; this is to be open about it before God.

Sin multiplies

Morgan regards speed as the great enemy of discernment. Much of our society is pressurised and driven. We may rush through life because we fear to face what lies under the surface. We rush to acquire or prove more than we are meant to. Thus we take short cuts and are economical with the truth. I tell a little white lie; in order to sustain this I have to tell another one, and another. I upset someone, or a group, because of an impatient or negligent approach.

This causes criticism, and leads to more hurts, which breeds more misunderstandings. Then more psychic energy has to be spent coping with the multiplying grievances.

> Little fleas have bigger fleas on their backs to bite them; bigger fleas have larger fleas, and so on ad infinitum.
>
> *Anon.*

Jesus knew it was vital to break this vicious spiral. That is why he told the crowds, 'Blest are the pure in heart, for they shall see God.' Morgan urges us to take prime time to mull and pray slowly over decisions.

Sin blinds

Morgan calls this complacency. When this sets in we no longer see people as they really are. We look out upon the world as if our ego is its centre, so we view everything with a distorting lens. The British call it the 'I'm all right, Jack' attitude. As far as we are concerned, the world can go by, so long as we get what we want.

> As the cost of loving escalates many of us grow weary and settle for much less than we had dreamed of.
>
> *Thomas H. Green*

The maps that the Chinese used to publish had China as the one civilised country in the centre of the world, and all the other nations were lumped together as barbarians. That serves as a parable for the way we tend to view others. It reminds me of the old Devon man's words to his wife: 'All the world's queer except thee and me, and even thee's a bit queer.' Jesus had to use shock language to wrench people out of this distorted way of seeing: 'Before you can remove the speck that is in your brother's eye you need to remove the log that is in your own' (Matthew 7:4). In order to overcome this hurdle to discernment we do well to pray:

O wad some Pow'r the giftie gie us
to see oursels as others see us!
It wad frae mony a blunder free us
and foolish notion.

Robert Burns

Sin divides

Whenever we indulge our selfish cravings (Morgan calls this instant gratification of desires), we avoid taking responsibility for something that we are meant to do, or say. We put up defences within ourselves, and they become a barrier between us and others. When we live behind barricades, how can we discern what is beyond them? Jesus had to shock people out of this way of living by saying, 'Forgive your enemies.' No two true duties conflict. But when we are trying to serve two masters, we fail to do right by either.

> If you are half hearted ... the devil will take a firm grip of one half of the heart, and use it to subjugate the other ... If you constantly try to compromise, finding some middle path between the way of Christ and the way of the world, you will become confused and lost. Jesus never compromised: neither should you.
>
> *Morgan: to a new Christian*

Finally, Morgan gives a warning which, if we heed it, may spare us from giving up the faith journey because we tried to follow God's guidance but things still went wrong. Morgan points out that, even if we avoid the snares of the evil one, a decision made in good faith may still have bad consequences. The reason is that the web of life is complex. So we are not immune from things going wrong, even when we have made decisions with a pure conscience. We are responsible to make decisions in a pure conscience; we are not responsible for the outcomes.

Ignatius's insights into discernment

These ground rules for discernment have been built upon over the centuries. A Basque who lived in the fifteenth century, Ignatius Loyola, became almost a cult name for discernment and spiritual direction in the closing years of the second millennium. 'His insights have a Celtic feel about them,' said someone during a group discussion. 'Of course,' piped up a Catholic former nun, 'because he was a Celt.'[3]

It has been widely observed that Ignatius was a sharp contrast to the typical Latin and continental spiritual leader. Whereas continental thinkers would typically 'live to think', Ignatius, like the pragmatic Anglo-Saxons, would 'think to live'.

My friend the former nun, however, was not as interested in ethnic origins as in style. 'He was a Celt in two ways,' she insisted. 'He was passionately red-blooded, and he went into the marketplace.' That is most certainly true. Inigo, as he was called by his parents, was passionate with women, and took an active part in jousting, socialising and battles until he was invalided out with a nearly fatal leg injury. After bearing agonising operations with heroic courage, he began a dalliance, through his bedside books, with saints. He discovered that dalliance with women and dalliance with saints affected his spirit in clearly different ways. Ignatius transposed his passion from women and the high life to Christ and the higher life. Soon, he had founded an army of Christians, and had worked out spiritual exercises which would help his old flames and friends 'in the marketplace,' as much as churchy people, to get discernment for the course of their lives. His *Spiritual Exercises* has proved to be a classic on spiritual direction.[4]

Ignatius's starting point was the same as that of Morgan, that each person has the ability to choose between good and evil. You don't question certain basic choices, he said, since they have already been made. If you are married, for example, you stick with your spouse through thick and thin, because God has already made clear in Scripture that that is his will. That still leaves you with many other choices. The next step is to be completely open to whatever the Lord desires for you. The third step is to say no to any choice that is evil, that is, which goes against the moral teachings of the Bible. The fourth step is to wait on God (ideally in a retreat) until God speaks with a voice so clear that you cannot mistake it, as when Christ called the apostles to follow him. There is a time for a revelation from God, and it is possible to sense when this is. When there is no such special time of revelation, we should use prayerful imagination.

Again echoing Morgan, Ignatius suggests that another approach is to use our reason to work out a right course. We should become tranquil, clarify the decision to be made, and look at it from the point of view of why we were created. Then we should weigh up the advantages and disadvantages of each option.

These steps in discernment are most helpful, but Ignatius, like Morgan, says there is a complication. There is an evil and therefore a deceiving spirit as well as a good spirit. Delusions and confusions can afflict us. How do we circumnavigate these, whether they come from the devil or from other psychic or spiritual forces? Ignatius deals with this problem in his *Rules for the Discernment of Spirits* which he appends to his *Spiritual Exercises*. After much testing born out of his own experience he came up with two indicators of the good or the bad way, which again echo Morgan. Instead of using Morgan's terms of 'guilt' and 'peace', Ignatius uses the terms 'desolation' and 'consolation'. If our intended choices produce desolation, we should reconsider our choice. If they produce consolation, we should proceed.

Fears about our own resources, depression, self-pity and ebbing strength are all forms of desolation which can lead us to stop journeying forward and settle into a false comfort zone. It is the purpose of devils to use these fears to afflict us with anxiety, confusion and distractions, and to probe and test us in such ways until they find our limits. Ignatius advises us never to make a change during a time of desolation; instead we should remain firm in the course we were on before the desolation beset us. He advises people to combat desolation by penance, but I think sometimes we would do better to combat it by rest, fun or by nourishing ourselves. Although desolation is from the devil, and can be brought on by our own slackness, sometimes, Ignatius suggests, God uses it to help us find a true understanding of ourselves, or to test and so build our character. Our response to it should be to open ourselves like a defenceless flower before God.

Consolation, which comes from God, gives us a deep sense of being at peace in the will of God. The good spirit gives courage, strength, tears, inspirations. Anything that shakes our commitment will be from the devil, anything that builds our commitment will be from God. The danger in consolation is to coast along in our own strength or to become conceited. So Ignatius advises us to humble ourselves when we feel especially blessed with consolation.

Ignatius concluded that a person who fundamentally wants God's way will feel desolation when they sin, or when the devil tempts them, and consolation when God's will is being done. The reverse, however, is true of a person who at heart does not want God's way. That person will feel apparent consolation or pleasure in wrongdoing, but desolation when influenced by the good spirit.

There is one other complication. Although true consolation comes from God, the devil can mimic it in order to lead us away from our true path. How can we discern the difference between a true, God-given consolation and a false one? Pseudo consolations never end up with us being closer to God, as true consolations do. Pseudo consolation can never give the deep peace and peaceableness towards others which is the fruit of God's Spirit. The devil can never fake unconditional love

A few soul friends have a particular gift of discerning spirits. One such is Martin Israel, who has a chapter on this subject in his book *The Spirit of Counsel*.[5] But every soul friend needs to become familiar with these ways of improving discernment in their own life, if they are to use them to facilitate discernment in a seeker. No two situations in life, nor the make-up of any two individuals, are identical. So, as a co-discerner, the soul friend will be very attentive to the course of action that seems to uniquely fit each particular seeker.

Summary

The basic work of a soul friend is to help a seeker to discern God's will. Morgan advises that we can learn to do this by eliminating choices which do not square with Christ's teachings, by figuring out the likely good and bad consequences of any intended action, and by observing which of these brings us peace or disquiet. Areas that are still resistant need to be prayerfully examined in the light of the power of evil, in its various modes, to blind and ensnare us.

Exercises
For soul friends and seekers

1. Think of a choice you have to make. Draw up two lists of likely consequences if you do and if you do not follow plan A. Repeat this for plan B. What do you think your choice will be?

2. Think about your fundamental choice. Are you clear you want God's will more than anything else?

3. Recall an experience when it was hard to know what you really felt. Can you put a name to your different feelings? What can you learn from this in the light of these guidelines?

4. Recall an experience of spiritual defeat. What dragged you down? What tactics did the evil spirit employ?

5. Recall an experience of victory that brought consolation. What choices or inspirations brought you closer to God?

6. Think of a choice you have to make. How would you advise another person who came to you for advice about the same choice?

7. Think of another choice you have to make. If you were on your death-bed which choice would you wish you had made?

Further reading

Van der Weyer, Robert, *The Letters of Pelagius, Celtic Soul Friend* (Arthur James, 1995).

Green, Thomas H., *Weeds Among the Wheat – Discernment: Where Prayer and Action Meet* (Ave Maria Press, Notre Dame, IN, 1994.) This gives a concise outline of Ignatius's advice on discernment, and each chapter ends with useful exercises.

CHAPTER 7

FOSTERING – IRISH INSIGHTS INTO SOUL FRIENDSHIP

The fifth to eighth centuries after Christ

Although the roles of foster-parent and soul friend are distinct in our society, the Irish experience can inspire all soul friends to grow in a love that fosters all that is of God in a seeker.

> Spiritual mentoring can be seen as a significant part of what historians have come to call the flowering of Ireland.
>
> *Edward Sellner*

There are two threads in the ancient Irish soul friendship tradition: the provision of foster-parents of children and young adults, and the provision of soul friends by monasteries. Both of these forms of soul friendship kindled warm bonds of human affection.

Soul friends for young people

It was the custom for better-placed families in sixth-century Ireland to employ a foster-parent to help bring up their child. The foster-parent was not, as in modern society, a married substitute for the physical parents, but a cherished supplement, who was often a widowed or unmarried celibate. The foster-parent would not live with the family, as would a British nanny; the child would live with the foster-parent for quite long periods.

As the child shared in the life of the foster-parent, they would learn to cook, fish, pray, repeat stories, make relationships, and grow confident in both practical living and in their inner life. As Christianity spread, committed Christians would sometimes sense that their child was being called to a spiritual vocation, and they would place them under the care of a holy hermit or nun who lived in their district. A good foster-parent would be both worldly wise and spiritually wise, and there are references in the written *Lives* of Celtic saints to these Christians continuing to visit their foster-parents for as long as they lived.

Monastic soul friends

Do nothing without counsel.

The Rule of Columbanus

In the early days of the Irish church, foster-parents of children would guide a young person into adulthood, but as large monasteries became widely established young people marked out for a vocation might be placed instead under a soul friend in a monastery.

The wider family of the tribe readily took to its heart the monastic family, with its spiritual father or mother. These were known as 'abbot' or 'abbess', but since those terms became over-formalised in later centuries, the term 'poppa' or 'mama' might, as with ammas and abbas of the deserts, more readily convey how the people regarded these dear folk.

Jesus and his apostles numbered thirteen, and the Irish often thought this to be the ideal 'family size' for a new monastery. Quite often, though, these grew into communities numbering hundreds. When they grew to such a size the abbot or abbess could not be a soul friend to every monk, let alone to visitors, so others were allocated this role. Some of these were ordained, and others were not.

In the early days of the monasteries there was such trust and desire to move along God's path that a trainee monk was expected to pour out his soul each day to the senior who was his soul friend; in this way things that clogged relationships with God or the brothers could be confessed and forgiven. These monks also became soul friends to many people outside the monasteries who were keen to follow God in their ordinary jobs.[1]

There are many references in medieval *Lives* to Celtic saints and their various soul friends.[2] The following stories, drawn from the *Lives* of Irish saints, furnish us with insights into this way of soul friendship. They reveal that soul friendships of various kinds were normal; also that the Irish enjoyed more relaxed relationships between men and women than existed in the Egyptian deserts. The stories are presented in chronological order so as to reflect the developing process.

Patrick 390 to 461:
'Learned every benefit to soul and spirit'

Patrick was a Briton, but we include him here as an adopted Irishman. His own two writings tell us little about his personal friends, but the medieval Irish *Life* gives us greater, albeit legendary, detail. At the age of thirty Patrick is thought to have set out for Rome, but on his way through Gaul he stayed at the monastery of Germanus, a God-inspired bishop. It seems likely that Patrick stayed with Germanus for many years and was mentored by him. The Irish *Life* states that with Germanus 'he learned, loved, and treasured wholeheartedly knowledge, wisdom, purity, and every benefit to soul and spirit'.

91

Ciaran *c.* 512 to 545:
'There was complete union between us'

The Life of Ciaran of Clonmacnois portrays him as 'a soul friend . . . blazing with light and instruction'. Ciaran himself nevertheless needed a soul friend, and *The Life* reveals that Ciaran placed himself under the guidance of Finnian, spiritual father of the outstanding monastery at Clonard. While Ciaran was there a local ruler brought his daughter, who had taken vows, to be discipled at the monastery, and Finnian entrusted her to Ciaran. We are told that they learned psalms together but that Ciaran guarded against sexual temptation by only looking at her feet! On a later occasion, however, we learn that a family whom Ciaran had helped gave their whole estate over to him, and he agreed to give spiritual guidance, even to their beautiful daughter, if she dedicated her body as well as her soul to Christ. Boundaries need to be established in every soul friendship.

This estate soon had a group of monks as its hub and, in common with many estates in Ireland at that time, became known as a monastery. When the time came for Ciaran to move on from Finnian's tutelage, he offered this monastery, whose site is unknown, to Finnian. The aging Finnian refused this, and instead offered his own monastery to Ciaran who wept at this act of trust. Finnian took this as a sign: 'From now on there will be complete union between us, and whoever tries to spoil our union shall possess nothing on earth or in heaven.' 'Yes, let it be as you say,' said Ciaran. Then, united in spirit, he left Finnian and went to Enda, the great teacher of the Irish church at the Aran monastery, 'to commune with him'. In this story we see how two soul friends may cease to meet, and yet retain deep spiritual bonds for ever in their hearts, which can be reactivated as needed.

Ciaran made friends throughout Ireland. They included, according to *The Life*, Columba of Iona, Enda, his guide at Aran Island, his colleague Senan of Scattery Island, and his close friend Kevin of Glendalough.

Ita d. about 570: Foster-mother of the saints

As we have seen, children were sometimes placed under a foster-parent who combined the roles of nanny and teacher. When Christianity took root, the element of prayer guide was added, and foster-parents were chosen for their ability to make saints out of promising children, and young adults too. An eighth-century poem of Alcuin describes Ita, who lived some fifty years after Brigid, as 'the foster-mother of the saints of Ireland'.

Before she could become a spiritual foster-mother, Ita, like the mothers of the desert, had to gain mastery of herself and of the spirits. She learned to fast and pray with great effect even as a child, but her baptism of fire came in her teens. One day Ita told her parents she wanted to become a nun. Her father, who was related to the rulers of Tara, vehemently opposed this. Ita calmly and confidently told everyone who was upset about this: 'Leave my father alone for a while. If nobody pressurises him he will come round, and in fact he will order me to take vows of his own conviction, for he will be compelled by my Lord Jesus Christ to let me go wherever I wish to serve God.'

Not long after this, Ita fasted for three days and three nights, during which time the devil waged war against her, and she resisted him. Eventually the devil left her with these words: 'Alas, Ita, you will free yourself from me, and many others too will be delivered.' That very night Ita's father dreamed that an angel spoke these words to him: 'Why do you forbid your daughter to be a virgin for Christ's sake? She will be a great and famous virgin before God and God's saints and will be the protector of many on the Day of Judgment. You will let her be a nun, and you will let her go wherever she wants to in order to serve Christ. She will serve God in another people, and she will be the mother of that people.' Ita's father immediately gave her his blessing, even if it meant her becoming a spiritual mother to a hostile clan.

God directed Ita to live among the neighbouring people of Uí Conaill, where with some companions she established a convent.

Young women flocked to her from all parts, as did the local people and their ruler, who offered her more land. Blessings flowed from Ita to the people, and they showered the convent with gifts. This did not deflect Ita from living simply, though she had to learn not to punish her body with too much fasting. Though she always refused to buy food, it was said an angel persuaded her to eat the food that was given to her.

The account of her life gives us glimpses of her ability to discern spirits. This prevented much time being wasted in her spiritual direction of others. For example, one of her nuns committed fornication, but kept it secret. The next day, Ita summoned her, told her exactly when and where she had transgressed, and urged her to guard her virginity. This prophetic word brought a change of heart; the nun willingly undertook exercises to build up her ability to master sexual temptations, and thereafter succeeded in living a pure life. Another of Ita's protégés, a nun who lived far away in Ita's native Connacht, secretly committed adultery. Ita knew even this, and requested that the nun be released to visit her. When Ita confronted the woman with what she had done it shocked her into repentance and she made restitution.

Ita combined a lovableness with an awesome authority. Many people came to her to confess their sins, even though they knew that she would not let them off lightly. They understood that they would be given disciplines to follow which would require them to make restitution to a wronged person, and which would strengthen their ability to overcome weaknesses.

Ita did not give these penances, as they were called, for their own sake; she liked to build people up. A man once confessed to her that he had killed his brother. She sensed that he was truly sorry before God; so, to encourage him, she told him, 'If you carry out my counsel you will have a happy death.' A later incident with this man shows that Ita did not bury her head in the sand when something went wrong; her policy was to overcome evil with good. At some later date it was reported that a group of men had been killed in battle, including this man. When Ita heard this she told a friend, 'I promised that man he would have a happy end. Go to the place of devastation and call upon him in God's name and in my name to rise up. I believe he will come and meet you.' The man did just that, and lived long.

We can learn from Ita to fast and pray until we win the battles in our own soul; the very battles that seekers who come to us may be facing for the first time.

Findbarr *c.* 560 to 610: Resurrection together

The person the Irish named the *anamchara* (soul friend) was sometimes very different from a desert ascetic, even though the Irish drew inspiration from the desert soul friends. Their soul friends often had a homely, earthy flavour, and they did not in every case have to be older then their disciple, as this delightful legend about Findbarr reveals.

When Findbarr was still a boy he was dedicated to God, and sent to live under the guidance of a soul friend named Lochan. One day a rich man named Fidach arrived and asked Lochan to be his soul friend. Instead of responding as Fidach expected, Lochan said to him, 'Kneel to that little lad there.' Fidach, insulted at the thought of kneeling to a boy as young as Findbarr, parried, 'If I take Findbarr to be my soul friend will you do the same?' To Fidach's surprise, Lochan said he would. Both men knelt before Findbarr and asked him to be their soul friend. The young Findbarr, with most delicate wisdom beyond his years, addressed his tutor: 'Will you please be responsible for soul-befriending Fidach and his offspring in return for teaching me the psalms?' These words also reveal delightful humour and a canny attitude; the issue of how to pay for fostering seems to have been a mixture of good will and negotiation in due time. In this case Findbarr seems to suggest that his act of giving back to Lochan the privilege of soul-befriending these well-able-to-pay people would be in lieu of his parents' fee to Lochan for teaching him!

Irish Christians who took vows often placed themselves under a tutor who trained them in a total life experience of head, heart and practical knowledge. How did they normally pay for such training? Another experience of Findbarr, also laced with humour, indicates that fees could be paid either in money or in spiritual kind.

Findbarr had moved on in order to study the Gospel of Matthew and the Acts of the Apostles with Bishop MacCuirb. In due course the bishop requested a stipend for his instruction. 'How much do you require?' Findbarr asked.

'That the resurrection of us both may be in the same place on the Day of Judgment,' the Bishop responded.

'You will have your wish', answered the prophetic Findbarr, 'for you will be buried in the same place as I am, and we will have our resurrection together.'

After another interval Findbarr went to live near Loch Iree. He started a school, whose tutor was Eolang, and Findbarr's sister and many male and female students came to live there. In due course Findbarr himself moved on yet again to make cells by the lake at Gougane Barra, where new people devoted themselves to the Lord under his guidance. While he was there Bishop MacCuirb died, and Findbarr himself no longer had a soul friend. He decided to make an unannounced return visit to Loch Iree and ask his old friend Eolang to be his soul friend. Eolang had a premonition that Findbarr was coming, and did a wise thing. When Findbarr asked the guest-master if he could go straight to his friend, Eolang asked the guest-master to arrange for Findbarr to bathe and rest overnight, and then go to his cells some miles away, with his travelling group, for a few days of quiet reflection. It was Eolang who then made the journey to Findbarr; kneeling, he placed himself and his community under Findbarr's oversight. Findbarr wept. 'This was not my thought; I intended to place everything, my soul and my community under your guidance,' he sighed.

'Let it be, for this is the will of God,' replied Eolang. 'You are dear to God and you are greater than myself. I ask only one thing, that our resurrection will be in the same place.'

'That wish will be fulfilled', Findbarr assured him, 'but I am still troubled about the soul friendship.'

'You will receive today a friend worthy of yourself,' Eolang assured him. Eolang then took Findbarr's hand, and offered it to God, placing it, as it were, in the hand of the Lord. 'Lord, take this man to yourself,' he prayed, and he began, in the beautiful words of *The Life*, 'leading him to heaven'. From that time, it was said, no one could look upon Findbarr's hand because of its radiance, so he always wore a glove.

This story is a lesson for us as it was for Findbarr. Whenever his demand for a human soul friend reasserted itself he knew he only had to look in the other direction, and he would be led hand in hand by the Lord. If ever we outlive our soul friend, or if circumstances prevent us from having one, we should remember this: Foster-parents foster us into maturity, and it is then fitting that they leave us. Soul friends are provisional helpers; they are companions on the way, but Jesus Christ himself is the way, the truth and the life.

Maedoc d. 626: Soul friendship is a gift

Maedoc trained at St David's Welsh school, returned to his native Ireland and founded communities at Ferns and elsewhere. Several centuries later these various communities produced *Lives* of their founder, which mostly comprise legends. One thing that shines out through all of these accounts is Maedoc's great capacity for friendship. He was thought to have retained a lifelong friendship with his tutor David, with Molaise, with his colleague Columba, and with Ita.

It was claimed that Maedoc's birth had been foretold by Ireland's chief sage, Finn Mac Cumaill. Shortly before Finn was buried at Ferns he was said to have uttered this prophetic poem:

> *Ferns of the green strand!*
> *Excellent will be the man who will own it.*
> *Soul friends will come from here,*
> *It will be a place dear to God.*
> *Maedoc with his company will come*
> *Like the sheen of the sun after showers.*

A company did indeed come to Ferns to see Maedoc for spiritual direction, and many went on from there to be soul friends to others. At the time when Maedoc had returned to Ireland after some years with David's Welsh community, he confided that he wished he had asked David who should be his soul friend on his return to Ireland. He continued to be so concerned about this that a group of brothers prepared a boat to take them back to Wales to consult with David about it. They were about to leave when the crew went on strike, and the elements erupted. As Maedoc strode through the pounding waves God taught him to live without human dependency. A divine messenger told him, 'You need no soul friend but the God of the elements, for he understands the thoughts and secrets of every person.'

Once Maedoc learned that lesson, God in fact gave him a most beautiful soul friendship with a holy monk named Molaise, but it came as a gift, not as a right to be clutched at, and they recognised when God was bringing it to an end. Though Maedoc and Molaise loved each other deeply, they knew from the start that, as God led each of them onwards, it might mean separation. One day they sat praying at the foot of two trees. They asked Jesus, 'Is it your will that we should part or that we should remain together until we die?' There must have been either a tree-cutting programme or a gale, for one of the trees fell to the south and the other to the north. They took this as a clear indication that one of them must go south to found a new community, and the other should go north. They kissed, embraced and said farewell. Maedoc went south to Ferns and Molaise went north to Devenish.

We can learn from Maedoc about letting go of friendships. If we are clutching at a special friendship, or if we are jealous lest others replace us in our friend's affections, we may be sure God is calling us to let go of that friendship. The willingness to receive friendship as a gift, and to let God show when and if we meet together, is vital to true soul friendship.

Once Maedoc was at Ferns many people sought his guidance, as Finn had once prophesied. An episode which throws light on this soul-friending process concerns some Christians who wanted to know where their 'place of resurrection' would be. One way in which spiritual direction came to Irish Christians in their journey through life was through the the discovery of their 'place of resurrection'. This was the place to which they were called, which would become their spiritual home, their place of burial, and the place where they would continue to pray for others after their death.

When these Christians prayed about this matter, God told them to visit Maedoc. Maedoc first of all tried to discern whether, since these folk had been drawn to him at Ferns, that was to be their place of resurrection. So he asked them, 'Did any of you hear a bell ring when you arrived?' They did not. Maedoc sensed that, though Ferns did not ring a bell, their place of resurrection would be somewhere within the region to which they had been drawn. So he walked with them to a rise from which they could see miles of countryside around. Speaking out what the Spirit put in his mind, he pointed in a certain direction and told them that would be their place of resurrection.

This principle still seems to apply today, and the first exercise at the end of this chapter helps us to explore this. For some people the geographical location is less important than being in the right context in other ways at death.

Samthann d. 739: Prayer guide

Samthann, Abbess of Clonbroney, was married before becoming a nun, and her foster-father was a king. She was powerful in prayer and ministry. We learn of a nobleman named Flann who spent much time studying with her, and of a monk who asked her advice about ways of praying. He wondered whether a person should pray lying down, sitting or standing. Samthann replied, 'A person may pray in every position.' A teacher whose enthusiasm outweighed his wisdom came to her and proposed to give up study in order to use the time to pray. The wise woman asked him a question: 'What, if it is not study, can prevent your mind from wandering all over the place as you pray?' The same man told her that he intended to go abroad on a pilgrimage. 'By all means travel overseas', she advised him, 'if God cannot be found on this side of the sea. But since God is near to all those who call upon him we have no need to cross the sea.'

Samthann was the soul friend of Mael-Ruain who, as we shall see in Chapter 12, was one of the leaders of an eighth-century reform movement known as Friends of God (*Celi De*). Their soul friendship came about in this way. A travelling peddler used to carry Samthann's greetings to the Friends of God in Munster. On one occasion she made him promise not to add or subtract one word from her message: 'Tell Mael-Ruain that he is my most favoured priest of the desert. Another thing, ask him whether he accepts women for confession, and will he accept my soul friendship?' Samthann knew how to bring on a shy young Christian with leadership potential!

When the young monk Mael-Ruain received the first message he stood up and praised God, stretching out his arms in the shape of the cross. When asked if he would accept a woman as a soul friend he blushed deeply, bowed three times to the Trinity, remained in silence, and then said, 'Yes'! When Samthann learned of his reply she is reported to have said, 'I think something will come of that youth.'

These Irish soul friends seem so human as well as holy, homespun yet wise, humorous and hospitable. They warm our hearts, they speak to us across the centuries, and they invite us to foster Christ in others. Increasing numbers of Christians are following the example of Irish soul friends, and choosing to live lives of prayer and reflection in quiet places. Many others seek such people out, either in a short- or a longer-term soul friend relationship.

Summary

The early Irish soul friends lived alongside a seeker and helped him or her to make the best of life in body, mind and spirit. Stories of Irish saints reveal different and endearing facets of soul friendship, which is seen as a gift which is specially precious at life's transitions.

Exercises

1. To find one's place of resurrection. Make a list of places which resonate with ('ring a bell for') you. Number these in order of priority; the place that rings deepest and longest should be numbered one, and so on. Now pray about this place, and see what natural links might develop. You may begin to sense that this place 'is near but not quite it'. Then keep on opening doors. Remember, *your* place of resurrection might be yours alone, so beware of jumping on to a bandwagon.

2. Make a list of your most prized friendships. Are you clutching, possessive or jealous about any of these? Release your friends into God's hands; also any persons they are helping or drawing closer to, pray for them to be built up in Christ.

Further reading

Sellner, Edward, *Wisdom of the Celtic Saints* (Ave Maria Press, 1993).

Stokes, Whitley (trans.), *Lives of Saints from the Book of Lismore* (Llanerch, 1995).

CHAPTER 8

FAITHFULNESS – BRITISH INSIGHTS INTO SOUL FRIENDSHIP

The fifth to seventh centuries after Christ

The various accounts of holy men and women who lived in Britain[1] seldom use the Irish term anamchara, *yet they breathe a spirit of transparent friendship and deep spiritual counsel.*

> Now Cuthbert had great numbers of people coming to him not just from Lindisfarne but even from the remote parts of Britain . . . They confessed their sins, confided in him about their temptations and laid open to him the common troubles of humanity they were labouring under – all in the hope of gaining consolation from so holy a man.
>
> *Bede, Life of Cuthbert 22*

Ninian, fifth century: 'Deservedly was that soul called friend'

Ninian apparently learned his Christian faith from his parents, who became Christians during the Roman occupation of Britain. We have no information about any particular soul friend relationship. We do, however, learn from *The Miracles of Bishop Ninian*, composed at Whithorn in the eighth century, that nobles and freemen entrusted the education of their sons to Ninian who instructed them in knowledge and moulded their characters, restraining vices with wholesome discipline and inculcating virtues. The anonymous author, no doubt a monk at the monastery Ninian founded at Whithorn, recounts that as Ninian was dying Christ's voice called to him, addressing him as 'my friend, my dove'. The author comments: 'Deservedly was that soul called "friend", since it consisted entirely of love with no fear in it.'

So although we have few details, we sense that deep friendship that expressed itself in the spiritual formation of others was integral to this foundational period in the Christianising of Britain.

David and Brother Aidan, sixth century: 'Of one mind and desire'

The eleventh-century biographer of David of Wales sometimes casts his praises of David in the mould of the gospel accounts of Jesus. Thus, like Jesus, who took his inner circle of three friends to the mountain or to the garden, David had an inner circle of three 'most faithful disciples, namely Aidan, Eliud, and Ismael'.[2] Of these three, Brother Aidan emerges as the one most akin to Jesus's 'beloved disciple' John. The biographer describes David and Aidan as being 'alike of one mind and desire', and the rapport between them transcended setback and separation, as the following episodes illustrate.

Once Aidan was outdoors studying one of the monastery's books, which had no doubt been painstakingly copied, when David asked him to go on an errand. This involved taking two oxen and a wagon to carry timber from some distance away. Aidan was, as always, so keen to carry out errands in a good spirit that he promptly left, leaving his precious book still open. On his return journey, the wagon and oxen careered over a cliff. Aidan made the sign of the cross over them, and retrieved them safely from the sea, but soon there was such a downpour that the ditches overflowed. Then Aidan thought of that precious book!

Having unloaded the timber he went to retrieve the book, doubtless fearing the damage the downpour had done to it. He found it, however, in exactly the same condition as it was when he left it. The brothers saw in this episode a link between an edifying soul friendship and the protecting hand of God. They felt that the humility and faith with which Aidan carried out the errand had provided a shield for the oxen in their fall, and that David's fatherly faith on behalf of his dear brother had provided a shield for the book.

Aidan's deep spiritual rapport with David continued even when he moved back to Ireland. He was praying in his monastery one Good Friday, when he had an intimation that someone would poison David's food at their Easter Day supper in Wales. Aidan sent one of his monks, who managed with divine guidance to cross the sea and reach David in time to warn him.

Rhigyfarch's *Life of St David* tells us that the monks generally would 'reveal their thoughts' to him. I have been to a number of Christian communities where brothers or sisters seem to flow together in mutual love. They have trust in their eyes, and esteem in their hearts for one another, and they help each other in practical ways. That spirit marked David of Wales and his brothers, as these stories reveal.

St Aidan's loving friendships with the English, seventh century

Oswald

Before King Oswald welcomed Bishop Aidan (who had no connection with Brother Aidan) to his Northumbrian kingdom, Aidan was at the Iona monastery, where he would have been assigned an Irish *anamchara*. But now Aidan himself had to be spiritual father to his eleven monks, to the Christians around King Oswald's court and to the new communities of Christians he hoped to establish in Northumbria. To whom could he bare his own soul? I have sometimes wondered whether, among the eleven monks who were sent with him to Northumbria, one was an older man who acted as his confessor and spiritual father. We know that many more monks subsequently arrived from Ireland, perhaps some of them reviving links of friendship with Aidan.

What is certain is that Aidan had a flare for developing new and deep spiritual friendships with both men and women, even though they were of a different race and language, and that these friendships bore great fruit. Aidan developed close friendships with succeeding Saxon kings. Can you imagine a king of a warrior race not only being willing to act as an interpreter among poor villagers as did Oswald (because no one else was at first available to interpret Aidan's Irish dialect), but also being willing to walk with Aidan rather than ride a royal horse? This could only have happened because there was a profound bond of trust and friendship between Aidan and Oswald.

Oswin

The famous story of how Oswald's successor, King Oswin, reacted after Aidan gave his gift of a royal horse to a passing beggar, indicates that these two men also had a soul friendship. Oswin, Bede informs us, was tall, handsome, courteous and beloved by all. The king, who had reprimanded Aidan for giving away such a horse, then accepted Aidan's rebuke: 'Is that son of a mare more precious to you than that son of God?' He received Aidan's words deep into his soul. After a time of reflection he knelt before Aidan in contrition, and promised never again to interfere with Aidan's ministry. Aidan was so moved that a king could be such a humble man after God's own heart that he had a premonition that brought tears to his eyes. He perceived that Oswin's lack of warlikeness would bring his imminent defeat and death in war. This indeed happened. Some scholars speculate that Aidan's own unexpected death only eleven days afterwards was brought on by a broken heart. Soul friendship indeed!

Hilda

No doubt Aidan was introduced to Hilda through Oswald, who was a relative. He heard that Hilda, who had gone to reside with relatives in the court of East Anglia, had decided to become a nun and join her sister for novice training at the French monastery of Chelles. Aidan pleaded with her to help develop the monastic life in her own kingdom instead. Hilda agreed, and Aidan seems to have offered her a personalised form of training. Bede informs us that Aidan, along with other devout men who had befriended Hilda, 'visited her frequently, instructed her assiduously, and loved her heartily for her innate wisdom and her devotion to the service of God'.[3] Hilda herself became a spiritual mother to many people, and Bede tells us that ordinary people and rulers sought her counsel.

Cuthbert and Boisil: 'He knew everything about him'

The anonymous monk of Lindisfarne, who wrote the earliest *Life* of Cuthbert, fitted the experiences of Cuthbert into the pattern established by the authors of two *Lives*: *The Life of St Antony*, ascribed to Athanasius and made available in Northumbria in the Latin translation of Evagrius, and *The Life of St Martin of Tours* by Sulpicius Severus. It is likely that Cuthbert himself, as well as his fellow monk and biographer, allowed the desert and ascetic tradition to shape his life, not least in the value it placed upon spiritual fathers and mothers.[4]

The *Anonymous Life of Cuthbert* seems to have been written within twenty years of Cuthbert's death in 687. The author was able to draw on the recollections of a number of people who had a particularly close friendship with Cuthbert. There was the priest Plegcils, the nun Kenswith, who had been Cuthbert's foster-mother, and Prior Aethilwald of Melrose. Either the Lindisfarne monk or Bede, who added to this account, also wrote down recollections of people who had known of other close friendships in Cuthbert's life, each with a distinctive hue, such as those with Boisil the prophetic prior, Herbert the Cumbrian hermit, and Herefrith, the spiritual father at Lindisfarne at the time of Cuthbert's dying.

Cuthbert, aged seventeen, saw a vision of Aidan being taken to heaven while he was guarding sheep on the Lammermuir hills one night in 651. The next day he rode with his servant to Melrose monastery, and offered himself for monastic service to the prior, Boisil. Why, in view of the fact that it was his vision of the death of Lindisfarne's Aidan that led him to so dedicate himself, did he choose Melrose rather than Lindisfarne? According to Bede it was because Cuthbert was attracted by Boisil's reputation as a wise teacher and guide.

As soon as Cuthbert and Boisil met there seems to have been a rapport between them; each recognised the high calling of the other. As Boisil saw the way Cuthbert dismounted from his horse, and bade farewell to his servant, to his horse, and to the sword he had handed to his servant, he said to his companion, 'You are looking at a true servant of God.' It brings to mind, Bede suggests, Jesus's assessment of Nathaniel: 'Here is a true Israelite, a person without guile' (John 1:47).

Boisil took Cuthbert as his pupil and taught him a deep love of the Gospels, especially St John. Bede, in his *Prose Life of St Cuthbert*, records these words of Cuthbert: 'In Boisil's old age, when I was but a youth, he brought me up in the monastery at Melrose and amid his instructions predicted with prophetic truth all the things which were to happen to me.'

For some years Cuthbert was away from Boisil at the Ripon monastery where he was guest-master. After his enforced return to Melrose, Cuthbert 'most diligently paid heed to both the words and deeds of Boisil as he had before'. Soon there was an outbreak of the plague. Cuthbert himself caught it but, unusually, he recovered; then Boisil succumbed. Boisil asked Cuthbert to be with him and spoke to him in a prophetic way, 'You will not get the plague a second time, but I will die of it.' Herefrith, a priest at Lindisfarne and later abbot there, who was in the monastery at the time, told Bede how, in the last week of his life, Boisil proposed to spend his time teaching his disciple:

Cuthbert asked, 'And what is best for me to read that I can finish in one week?' Boisil replied, 'The evangelist John. I have a book consisting of seven sections; with the Lord's help we can get through one every day, reading it and discussing it so far as is necessary.'

Bede sees significance in the way they read the Scriptures together: 'They dealt with the simple things of "the faith that works by love" (Galatians 5:6).' Love was the key to John's soul friendship with Jesus; and it was the key to Boisil's soul friendship with Cuthbert.

Boisil shared the accumulated wisdom of his heart and his head with his disciple. During those last seven days of reading and sharing, Boisil also 'declared all Cuthbert's future to him'. Boisil's prophetic prayers for Cuthbert did not come in a functional way; they came out of their reflections upon the Scriptures and out of their love for one another. It is not too often that a soul friendship combines such a rapport with such a prophetic edge; when it does, it is something we should prize, as Cuthbert prized his friendship with Boisil.

Bede's summary of Cuthbert's life is that he received from Boisil 'a knowledge of the Scriptures and the example of a life of good works'. A knowledge of holy Scriptures and an example of a good life form foundations of soul friendship that lasts.

Cuthbert as a soul friend

Cuthbert, who drew so deeply from his own spiritual guides, became a spiritual guide to others; at first as a busy pastor and later as a hermit. When he became Prior of Melrose he sometimes went away for up to a month offering pastoral care to people even in the most inaccessible villages. From Melrose he was transferred to be Prior of Lindisfarne. Bede says that there he continued the practical 'works of mercy' that he had displayed at Melrose, and his reputation as a holy man who ministered to people's bodily and spiritual ailments in the power of God continued to grow. No wonder, then, that when he withdrew to the solitary Farne Isle for nine years, great numbers of penitents and pilgrims, even from the remoter parts of Britain, sought the guidance of this holy man.

> They were not disappointed. No one left uncomforted, no one had to carry back the burdens they brought with them. With a word from God he would rekindle spirits that were chilled by sorrow. He brought back to the joys of heaven those weighed down with worry... To people beset with temptation he would skilfully disclose the ploys of the devil, explaining that a person who lacks love for God or others is easily caught in the devil's traps, while a person strong in faith can, with God's help, brush them aside like so many spiders' webs.
>
> *Bede, Life of Cuthbert*

A house was built where those who made the crossing could wait to meet Cuthbert; in due course Cuthbert would come over and give each visitor counsel and prayer. Cuthbert was continuing the tradition of the fathers of the desert who, like him, were sought out as spiritual guides.

Although the accounts of Cuthbert's life give sparse details, we can glean that, in addition to the villagers to whom Cuthbert gave pastoral care and the visitors to Farne Isle who sought guidance, certain people used Cuthbert as a spiritual guide over a long period. There were his relations with various women. Kenswith, the first nun in Northumbria whose name we know, was asked to be his foster-mother when he was a boy. It seems that the Saxons who embraced Christianity also embraced the custom of the Irish Christians who evangelised them in providing holy foster-mothers for children. Kenswith outlived Cuthbert, and it is likely that Cuthbert outgrew her in discernment as well as in learning. We learn from Bede's account of a fire that broke out in her village while Cuthbert was there, that he maintained visits to his foster-mother as an adult, and that she immediately turned to him for help.

Hermit bonds between Cuthbert and Herbert

Herbert was a hermit priest on an island in Derwentwater, who, Bede tells us, 'had long been bound to Cuthbert . . . by the bonds of spiritual friendship'. During Cuthbert's years at Lindisfarne and Farne, Herbert walked across the land each year to spend time with him. After Cuthbert become chief pastor of the Northumbrians he made plans for a pastoral visit to Carlisle and Herbert decided to make Carlisle the venue for his annual visit. Bede pictures Herbert hoping to be inspired to heavenly desires by Cuthbert, and the two of them 'refreshing each other with draughts of living waters'.

Herbert no doubt stayed overnight with Cuthbert as a fellow guest. During their time together Cuthbert said, 'Remember to ask me now whatever you need to know and to discuss with me, for I am sure this is the last time we shall meet in this life, and that I shall soon move into the next life.'

Herbert wept. On his knees he pleaded with Cuthbert, 'Remember your most faithful companion, and ask the Lord in his mercy that as we have served him together on earth, so we may journey together with him to heaven. For you know that I have always tried to live my life in accordance with your guidance, and when I have gone the wrong way through ignorance or frailty I have always tried to put things right according to your advice.'

Cuthbert went aside to pray this through, and God gave him the assurance that he would grant this request. Events confirmed this. They never saw each other again. Herbert underwent a long illness, and they both went to heaven on 20 March the same year.

The soul friendships explored in this chapter have two things in common: community and faithfulness. The wisdom of these soul friends grew in relationship to a community of which they remained part even when, like Cuthbert and Herbert, they were called away to the solitary life. Those who divorce themselves from the community of Christ's Church, as do many secular counsellors, lack that wholeness of understanding and feeling that is the heart of true soul

110

friendship. It was the stability of community that enabled these soul friends to remain faithful through the vicissitudes of the years.

Hermit soul friendships continue today. For example, Brother Harald, hermit of Shepherd's Dene, Northumberland, travels each winter to southern France to spend time with his hermit soul friend there.

Christians in ordinary life, when they seek a soul friend, continue to turn to members of religious orders. Sometimes they seek out someone who has dedicated themselves in greater or lesser degree to a hermit life. In order to find the necessary solitude some of these soul friends, by the nature of things, live in places hard of access. Then it is that, like Herbert and Cuthbert, the visits become fewer but longer.

Summary

The thread which runs through most of the accounts of these saints is the faithfulness they showed in their friendships and counsel. Without this faithfulness we may question whether Hilda would have made Britain her missionfield, whether the Irish–British fellowship would have survived, and whether hermits would have died with such peace.

Exercises

For soul friends and seekers to do together or separately

1. At Eastertide Brother Aidan's thoughts turned to his old soul friend David. Use a time of vigil to recall and bless those who have helped you in times past.

2. Hilda might have been lost to the Christian Mission in Britain were it not for Aidan's friendship and belief in her. Pray for your friends, imagining how God sees and wants to use their potential.

3. Cuthbert gained from Boisil a knowledge of the Scriptures and the example of a life of good works. Review your life. How can you

gain a more complete knowledge of the Scriptures? Are there good works which you have yet to do?

Further Reading
Rollason, D.W. (ed.), *Cuthbert: Saint and Patron* (Dean and Chapter of Durham Cathedral, 1987).

CHAPTER 9

WILDNESS – HERMITS' INSIGHTS INTO SOUL FRIENDSHIP

The fifth to seventh centuries after Christ

Celtic Christians who journeyed to wild places were sought out as soul friends. They also became ikons for the majority of soul friends and seekers who stayed at home, but who recognised that one's life journey needs to go beyond comfort zones.

> A friend is a loved one who awakens your life in order to free the wild possibilities within you.
>
> *John O'Donohue*

eltic Christians who ventured across land or sea to seek God in wild places were admired as 'white martyrs' because their long, dangerous pilgrimages required a letting-go and a self-giving second only to physical martyrdom. The stories of Brendan's hair-raising adventures on the ocean, of Samson's victories against serpent or wild wolf, of hermits confronting elements and demons on rocky outposts – these spurred those who heard them to seek God's next steps for their own lives. These 'pilgrims for the love of

113

God' became models for the majority who did not travel, but who did not want to get stuck in a rut.

In the Bible the Hebrew and Greek words sometimes translated as 'desert' are also translated as 'wilderness', and this word is often used in classic Christian descriptions of the spiritual journey. This reminds us that we are called to get to grips with the wild things in our lives and harness these to God. To know God means that no part of life is kept in a separate compartment. It was surely not for nothing that the Bible translators came to use the word 'wilderness'. None of us is for long without some wilderness that we need to traverse.

In Orthodox Christian theology the Holy Spirit arises within the Trinity through *spiratio* (from the Latin word for breath, *spirare*), the breathing of the Father and the Son. The Celtic theologian John Scotus Eriguena perceived the movement of God's Spirit in creation (Genesis 1:1, 2) as a turbulent swirl of the four elements, a wildness of energy that gives rise to creativity. The breathing of a human being reflects something of the breath or Spirit of God in the soul. The Spirit can move through the turbulent waters of our lives. The focus of spiritual direction in the Celtic tradition lies less in helping a seeker to conform to norms of convention than in helping a seeker to be true to the movements of the Spirit that transcend convention.

I once asked a respected Christian, 'What draws you to follow the Way of Life of the Community of Aidan and Hilda?'

'There is a wild man somewhere inside me waiting to get out,' he replied. 'The Celtic Christians knew how to move out of their safety zones. They had no no-go areas for God.'

A soul friend in the Celtic tradition never encourages a seeker to hide from their wild inner spirit, but to acknowledge it and harness it to the Great Spirit. In this chapter we shall allow some outstanding wild and holy wanderers to teach us.

Ireland's John the Baptist

Ciaran of Saigir, who was known as 'the first born of the saints of Ireland', became an early type of the holy, wild wanderer. He was born on Clear Island off the coast of Cork, the southernmost point of Ireland. Clad in skins and living in caves with wild animals, biographers cast him in the role of Ireland's John the Baptist, preparing the way for St Patrick's mission. A wild boar and a wolf became his first 'monks' at Saigir. The sources refer to a manuscript, now lost, entitled *Ciaran's Journey*. According to *The Litany of Pilgrim Saints*, fifteen people went with Ciaran to Scotland. The ruins of a medieval chapel on the Rhinns of Islay is probably the site of Ciaran's cell there. His voyage to Scotland became the first to capture the popular imagination.[1]

Celtic hermits deliberately chose to live lives exposed to the elements. They called God 'the Lord of the Elements'. They sensed that the elements of nature mirror raw elements in our own natures, and that by exposing themselves to the one, they got in touch with the other.

E.G. Bowen[2] charts the journeys of many of these wandering pilgrims, known as *peregrini*. Some went along the western seaways from Sutherland to Finisterre. Others went to the warmer lands of the south, but most ventured into the dark and stormy waters of the north, reaching the Orkneys, Shetlands, the Faroes and even Iceland. The heroic voyages of the few became archetypes of the inner journey of the many.

These Celtic Christians were following, in their own way, the example of Old Testament believers, of Jesus himself, and of the spiritual fathers and mothers of Egypt, who all journeyed into deserts. Columba's biographer, Adamnan, tells the story of Cormac's dangerous voyage north to find a 'desert in the sea'. Columba revealed that Cormac, in his desire to reach this 'desert', had to voyage three times through stormy waters.

In the Hebrides the leading angelic being, Michael, rides a white, unharnessed horse with a sword of elemental flame to combat the dragon. He does not rise to subdue the wind, nor does he domesticate the wild horse. The dragon represents the destructive potential; the wind and the wild horse represent the creative potential in elemental forces. So in spiritual direction we learn to embrace and harness the good in the wildness in order to master the destructive in it.

Carl Gustav Jung helped twentieth-century folk to understand that there is a wilderness in the psyche of Western people. He wrote that the undercurrents of the psychic life of the West are uninviting; we have slaved away to build a monumental world around us, but it is only imposing because we have lavished all that is imposing in our natures on the outside, and we have left what is shabby to the inside. It is necessary, he says, even though it is hard, to look into the psychic depths, because it is only there that we shall find the creative currents for something new.

> At first we cannot see beyond the path that leads downward to dark and hateful things – but no light or beauty will ever come from the person who cannot bear this sight. Light is always born of darkness, and the sun never yet stood still in heaven to satisfy a person's longings or to still their fears.
>
> C.G. Jung[3]

Each of us has to journey on beyond our comfort zones, into those dark, wild or untrodden places within ourselves, if not in physically distant places, that beckon to us. This requires us to let go of the control patterns that we impose upon our lives, and to become open to what lies beyond. To do this we need guides along the way.

Kevin and our hidden monsters

In their book *Glendalough: A Celtic Pilgrimage*, two guides, Michael Rodgers and Marcus Losack, portray the experience of Kevin, Glendalough's 'hermit of the wild', as an image of our own inner journey.[4] For them, the stories of Kevin suggest his life was driven not only by a desire for solitude but also to reach for the edges of life.

Kevin was a wild man clothed in animal skins. He is said to have prayed for one hour every night in the cold waters of the lake where a monster used to distract and annoy him by curling itself around his body, biting and stinging him. In another story he banished a monster from the lower lake to the upper lake. As Kevin lived alone at the upper lake, in effect he took the monster to himself. It was said that the fervour of his prayer, his patience, and God's love in him rendered the monster harmless.

Rodgers and Losack write:

> The story of the monster in the lake is revealing in the light of modern psychology's understanding of the unconscious mind which can have such an impact on our behaviour and responses. It has been said that the history of monsters is the history of humanity's struggle to see its own inner face. Certainly there lurks in all of us 'a little monster' that tends to push down deep inside us in one way or another. What happens when we consign our dark thoughts into the deep waters of our mind? Do they not tend to re-emerge in 'monstrous' form, perhaps even as the 'monsters' we see in others? What did Kevin do? It appears that he moved the monster to the Upper Lake where he himself lived. It might be said that he acknowledged its presence and tried to befriend it. Perhaps there is a key in that story for each of us.

Kevin lived in a small cave, now known as St Kevin's Bed, fifty feet above the lake. He chose to live on the side of the lake that is in shade for a full six months every year. His decision to go to this dark and inhospitable place seems to lie at the heart of the Glendalough experience, out of which, after Kevin's death, grew a most significant monastic city.

Why did Kevin do this? Perhaps he needed to go the very edge, to stretch himself to the limit, in order to get to the place of total, childlike dependence upon God, to experience the innocence of the first human beings, who like Kevin were clothed in skins, and who walked naked and alone with God in the shade of a primitive garden.

Kevin's Bed challenges us to enter our place of vulnerability and fear. 'Go to the place of your greatest fear and there you will find your greatest strength.'

Enquirers who ask the Community of Aidan and Hilda if they can test out its way with a soul friend for a trial period are known as explorers. The next step, the making of first promises, is known as 'making the first voyage of the coracle'.[5] A member of the community welcomes them with these words:

> Brothers and sisters, God is calling you to leave behind everything that stops you setting sail in the ocean of God's love. You have heard the call of the Wild Goose, the untamable Spirit of God; be ready for him to lead you into wild, windy or well-worn places in the knowledge that he will make them places of wonder and welcome.

Richard Rohr, the co-author of the book *The Wild Man's Journey*,[6] had to go to India to find a culture where the concept of the wild person is generally understood. He discovered that Indians traditionally divide a person's life into four stages. These are the student, the householder, the seeker and the wise person. The third stage, regarded in the West as a time of householding and business which is the main focus of life, is viewed by Indians as merely a transition stage. They sometimes refer to the seeker as a forest dweller; he does not necessarily go off to the woods, but he does go off alone to explore the meaning of life. 'After years of having experienced life', Rohr writes, 'they are now in a position to begin to understand it, to look for the big picture.' Compared with this, Rohr claims, the Western view of life is short-sighted and pleasure-centred; and Westerners do not expect old people to journey into wisdom in the fourth stage of old age.

Accompanying a seeker through wild places

How do we apply this aspect of life to our soul befriending of a person who spends their life amid the dull routines of an office-bound city? The role of a soul friend is to discern if and when the time is right to point the seeker towards this kind of journey. The seeker themselves will know when they are ready. The soul friend must respect their choice. On the one hand, never try to push; on the other hand, never try to pull back the seeker. For example, if the seeker is in a dark place, journey with them into this, rather than try to find an escape route or give pat answers to agonised questions. Or perhaps the seeker is coming near to a place of anger. Listen most certainly; sympathise and look at temporary ways of coping if this is appropriate, but do not let attention to symptoms deflect the seeker from going deeper into the things that feed the anger. Likewise a soul friend will try to find out what is the fear behind a fear.

What if the soul friend feels out of their depth? They can respond in one of three ways: give up; realise that, though they have not travelled where the seeker is now travelling, they need not be intimidated by this, since they have travelled to other places; or, third, learn to travel humbly alongside the seeker.

The soul friend can pray for the seeker. Pray forth release from entanglement in false inner networks of negativity; pray forth fluency of feeling; pray forth movement towards the as yet untrodden areas that beckon. A soul friend may repeat this prayer for a seeker:

> *Wild Spirit of the Almighty*
> *Be your eye in the dark places*
> *Be your flight in the trapped places*
> *Be your host in the wild places*
> *Be your brood in the barren places*
> *Be your formation in the lost places.*

Exercises
For soul friends and seekers

1. What apron-strings are there still in your life? To what or to whom are you clinging?

2. How far have you journeyed into your creativity? What might it mean to do this?

3. How far have you journeyed (if you are female) into the masculine side of your nature, or (if you are male) into the feminine side?

4. What areas of emotional pain do you try to avoid?

5. 'Go to the place of your greatest fear and there you will find your greatest strength.' What is the place of your greatest fear? If you are not sure, jot down fears you become aware of during the days and during the nights. What do these tell you? What are some fear-busting actions that you have taken? What fear-busting actions might you recommend to a disciple?

6. What about a journey into responsibility? What areas of life have you abdicated from?

7. What are the monsters in your life, the 'destroyers of life' which you need to confront and conquer?

8. What is your equivalent of Brendan's Paradise Island (i.e. your unrealised God-given hopes)?

Further reading
Parker, Russ, *The Wild Spirit* (SPCK, 1996).

CHAPTER 10

PROPHECY – COLUMBA'S
INSIGHTS INTO SOUL
FRIENDSHIP

The sixth century after Christ

The Irish have a tradition they call 'soul-making' – reviewing the direction of one's life, having the courage to change, and seeking to relate harmoniously to the physical and the spiritual environment. The link between prophecy and soul friendship, which is necessary to this process, is seen most clearly in Columba, as Adamnan's Life *illustrates.*[1]

Purity, wisdom and prophecy,
These are the gifts I would ask of Thee;
O High King of Heaven, grant them to me.
COLUMBA'S PRAYER FROM THE PLAY WITH MUSIC, *COLUMBA*

Columba (521–97) had the benefit of an upbringing in one of Ireland's ruling families, and as a young Christian he chose Ireland's best mentors in different aspects of the Christian way. First, he travelled far from his home in Donegal, to study at Moville under Finnian, who had acquired knowledge in the magnificent library at Ninian's Whithorn. Next he travelled south to

Leinster to draw from the bard Gemman the wisdom of poetry, folk memory, and the creative flow that facilitates Christ-centred nationhood. Then, to fulfil a need for mentoring of a different sort, Columba moved to the renowned monastery at Clonard, where, under another Finnian, he became immersed in the spirituality of the early fathers of the church and, through the writings of Cassian, in the fathers and mothers of the Eastern deserts. No doubt, too, he would have learned to network with the church in Wales, where Finnian had been trained.

Innumerable people soon sought out Columba himself as a soul friend. Most of them travelled a long way to seek his advice, then moved on in their life journey, keeping just occasional contact through the years. A few remained natural soul friends for life. The reason for this pattern was partly Columba's stature as overseer of his large family of churches, but partly his clear perception of an individual's future path. The story of Libran illustrates the link between prophecy and individual care.

Columba and Libran

A farm worker in Connaught, Ireland, committed a crime of passion; he killed a man. He was later to be named Libran. While he was in prison under sentence of death, a wealthy relative paid a large ransom fee, in return for Libran's promise to work as his slave for the rest of his life. After but a few days as a slave Libran escaped, and went on a long journey to make penance for his crime. Arriving at Columba's island monastery at Iona, Libran asked Columba to accept him as a novice monk. Columba put him through a rigorous appraisal, explaining that to someone who was not truly called to the monastic life, the duties would be too much to bear. Kneeling before Columba, Libran made full confession of his sins, and dedicated himself to do anything, or go anywhere under Columba's direction. The obedience he had refused to his relative, he now willingly gave to Columba.

God flashed into Columba's mind what he wanted for Libran. He was to serve in Columba's Mag Luinge monastery at Tiree for seven years, refraining from certain meals and from Holy Communion as a penance. Following this probationary period he was to return to Iona for Lent. This he did. Following the penances of Lent, he was welcomed back into the full fellowship of the church and received the sacrament with joy at the Easter celebration.

Inwardly, however, Libran was still agonising over the oath he had failed to keep with his relative more than seven years before, so he asked to talk this through with Columba. Once again God flashed into Columba's mind what lay ahead for Libran.

'Your former master and your father, your mother and your brothers are still alive,' Columba told him. 'You must prepare yourself for a long voyage.' Columba then gave Libran a ceremonial sword, which was a mark of the bond between a ruler and his subject. 'Take this as a gift you can offer your master in return for your freedom. He has a wife with many virtues; he will take her advice, and release you there and then without demanding any fee.'

A serious sin can lead to one tangle after another. Life is not as simple as we would like; nor was it for Libran. By going to prison, and then escaping, Libran had neglected the service due from a son to his father. This had caused resentment in his brothers. Columba intuitively understood all this and was given prophetic guidance to deal with this second tangle. Columba informed Libran that although he would be released from the first obligation about which he was so anxious, he would not be released from his family obligations. His brothers, he told him, would force him to make good the service he owed to his father.

This was Columba's advice, combined with an assuring prophecy:

> Obey your brothers without hesitation, and take your old father
> into your care. Although this will seem a heavy burden, it will not
> be for long, for one week after you begin the care of your father he
> will die. Your brothers will press you to take on the care of your

mother, but your younger brother will volunteer to take your place.

All this came true. The wife of Libran's former 'employer' told her husband, 'Holy Columba's blessing will do us more good than this gift, so release this man to Columba without payment.' And when Libran's brothers demanded that he stay to look after their mother, the younger brother spoke up: 'Our brother has spent the last seven years working for the salvation of his soul with Columba in Britain; it is not right that we should hold him back.'

So Libran made his farewells and tried to board a boat that was leaving Derry to take him to Scotland. The help of his soul friend was needed even at this distance, for the sailors refused to let him on board. Libran started to talk to Columba as if he were physically present. 'I bet you are not pleased that these men have full sails and a fair wind but they won't take me,' he said loudly to Columba. At that the wind changed, the boat slowed, and Libran ran beside it. The men, who probably heard Libran's words, started to discuss whether the wind might change again in their favour if they took him with them. 'The prayers of Columba, with whom I have spent seven years, will be able to get you a fair wind,' Libran told them; they took him on board. Libran, conscious of Columba's unseen support, prayed in the name of Almighty God, and God's winds took them to their destination.

When Libran reached Iona it was not he, but Columba, who related everything that had happened. That was the occasion when Columba gave him the name by which we know him, Libran, because he had been so truly liberated and permitted to take full monastic vows.

Columba sent Libran back to the Tiree monastery with this prophetic blessing: 'You will enjoy life long into old age. Nevertheless your place of resurrection will be in Ireland, not Britain.' This made Libran weep, so Columba comforted him with these careful words:

You need have no distress. You will die in one of my monasteries
and you will have your share in the kingdom among my specially
chosen monks. You will wake from death into the resurrection of
eternal life with them.

Libran was comforted, indeed enriched, by this blessing and went
away at peace. After working many years in the reed beds of the
monastery at Tiree, and after Columba himself had passed to heaven,
the aged Libran was sent to the Columban monastery of Durrow, in
Ireland, on some community business. He became ill, died and was
buried there in peace.

Without Columba's prophetic support, Libran would never have
had the assurance he needed to go and do right by his former boss
and by his family. If this unfinished business had not been dealt
with, he would have lacked the inner healing which enabled him to
live such a long and fruitful life.

Columba was not alone among soul friends in his use of prophetic
gifts. Though few are given foreknowledge in such detail as was he,
more people are given mental pictures which carry a vision for
another. Such were the prophetic visions that guided Ciaran and
Samthann.

Ciaran (512–45) and the prophecy of the spreading tree

Young people with a sense of vocation went to the island of Aran to
study under Enda, the most famous teacher in Ireland. Some sought
the advice of this monastic leader, and others sought after a soul
friend. Ciaran, an outstanding young leader who was searching for
God's next steps for him, was one such. During Ciaran's period of
study there both men had a similar vision.

A large and fruitful tree grew beside a river in the middle of
Ireland. The tree protected the entire island, its fruit crossed the sea
and the birds carried off some of its fruit to the world. Enda then
interpreted the vision to Ciaran:

The tree is you. All Ireland will be sheltered by your grace and many people will be fed by your fasting and prayers. In the name of God, go to the centre of Ireland and found your church on the banks of a river.

As a result of this guidance Ciaran founded the monastery of Clonmacnoise, which was a major influence for a thousand years, and whose ruins still evoke awe today.

Samthann (d. 739) and the prophecy of the great flame

Samthann was given leadership of a monastery through a prophetic vision given to Funecha, the foundress of Clonbroney monastery. Funecha saw Samthann as a spark of fire which grew to a great flame and blazed over the monastery. She understood this to mean that Samthann was burning with the Holy Spirit and that through her the monastery would come alight with the power and wonders of God. So Samthann was made its leader.

The purpose of prophecy is to build up people and release them into their destiny. Yet how many people never fulfil their destiny because Christian friends fail to pray over them and pass on what God flashes into their minds for them? It is true that few of us are given Columba's frequency and clarity of prophecy, but many of us are given what is needed for a particular person or situation.

A soul friend should not be shy to ask a seeker if they would like to have a time of silent prayer, during which the soul friend (or, indeed, the seeker) shares any pictures or Scriptures that come into their minds and which they feel may be from God. Many of us fear to do this, not out of embarrassment, but in case we get it wrong. We have a healthy horror of brainwashing, and do not wish a seeker to do something that is not right for them but that we have put into their minds in the name of God. There is no need to let this fear discourage prophetic prayer. We simply need to offer what we feel God has put into our minds, and make clear that the seeker should weigh this, as St Paul says we should with any prophecy (1 Corinthians 14:29). If both the soul friend and the seeker have a sense of peace and rightness about something that is shared, it is best to move ahead in the light of it, though still keeping open the possibility that God may have to correct distortions.

We do need to beware of giving people what pleases their ego. In his book *Soul Friend*,[2] Kenneth Leech recalls a critique that R.A. Lambourne made of the pastoral counselling movement in the 1960s: 'There was an excessive preoccupation with self-development at the expense of justice and matter.' In contrast he cites Thomas Merton, who sees the monk as a spiritual guide who questions the fundamental values of society, and who sees monasticism not as an escape from the incarnation and from a sharing of ordinary life, but as a way of sharing it that is free from illusions and idolatries.

Sometimes a conviction will come to a soul friend which feels as if it is not their own insight, it is 'pure gift'. Perhaps they are quaking with this conviction, or a picture or a word flashes through their mind out of the blue; and it seems as if God has directly given them something for the seeker. As with all prophetic messages, this needs to be weighed, so it should be offered humbly, in a provisional way. It is wise for the soul friend to say to the seeker that they may have got it wrong – but it is worth offering it none the less. The seeker can then be included in the process of discussing and interpreting it, and this can be creative. Such an input can sometimes give the seeker a motivation that was previously lacking; sometimes it can break through a mental log-jam, or it can open up a new process or direction.

Summary
The purpose of using prophecy in soul friendships is to free a seeker from acquiescence in a comfortable or defensive status quo, so that they may travel the road God has for them. The majority of soul friends who lack the precision of Columba's seeings may still offer what they do see, drawing out the seeker until they see it for themselves, or sharing it for a seeker to weigh.

Exercises

1. Columba recognised that Libran could not go forward until he had dealt with the unfinished business in his past life. Take time to write down any unfinished business in your life; then ask God to show you how you should deal with it.

2. If you are a soul friend, invite God to give you a picture for the seeker(s) for whom you pray.

Further reading

Adamnan, *Life of St Columba*, edited and translated with extensive footnotes by Richard Sharpe (Penguin, 1991). A third of this *Life* is a record of Columba's prophecies to friends.

CHAPTER 11

FITNESS TRAINING –
COLUMBANUS'S INSIGHTS
INTO SOUL FRIENDSHIP

The sixth and seventh centuries after Christ

Celtic 'penitentials' and modern fitness programmes have some things in common. Soul friends today will not copy the details, but can use the principles in their work with those seekers who invite them to do this.

Faithful are the wounds of a friend.

Proverbs 27:6

enance is not what you think it is. It is often thought of in a negative light as confessing sins to a priest and making an act of self-punishment. In the Celtic tradition penance is thought of in a positive light, as making an act of dedication for love of God, in order to overcome and leave behind the things that have hindered that love. The person making an act of penance is like a lover saying to their spouse, 'I give you the gift beyond price – all of myself, always. To help me to do this, and to show it, I will visibly leave behind all counter attractions to you, and accompany only you. In this way you will know at all times that you alone are the love of my life.' In this light penance becomes something beautiful.

The beauty of the fish in his bright lake
Beautiful too its surface shimmering.
The beauty of the word with which the Trinity speaks
Beautiful too doing penance for sin.
THE LOVES OF TALIESIN

Penance, which seems bizarre to some liberal minds today, was really fitness training. It was the means of becoming fit for a destiny with an eternal king. That is why those who led the way in this were known as athletes of the Spirit, and why the leaders of many Celtic Christian communities wrote out fitness-training programmes not only for their members, but also for those in the general public who looked to the communities for guidance.

These were known as penitentials. On the continent, penitentials were less effective than those drawn up in Celtic lands. A person might confess their sins, to a priest they hardly knew who would declare that they were forgiven, without them having to make restitution to anyone they had wronged; and the priest might suggest a perfunctory act of self-discipline which rarely increased real self-mastery. Penitentials produced by Celtic leaders were more far-reaching. Columbanus, along with David of Britain, was a front-runner, and he exported these most rigorous fitness-training programmes to the continent of Europe. These influenced many people, including local bishops who sought Columbanus out as a spiritual guide.[1] There are large collections of penitentials in places as far from Ireland as Warsaw and the Ambrosian Museum, Milan.

In one penitential, Columbanus explains that just as doctors use different medicines to treat bodily ailments, so spiritual doctors should use different cures for the various wounds of the soul. He acknowledges that few of us have the gift of being a spiritual doctor, so he sets out 'a few prescriptions according to the traditions of our elders, and according to our own partial understanding'.[2] These prescriptions focussed on eight principal vices that destroy our ability to be effective human beings: gluttony, avarice, rage, self-pity, lust, slackness, vanity and pride. They had to be healed by 'taking', as medicine, their opposite virtues. The principle was cure by contraries. These vices can also be viewed as hurdles that runners in a race have to overcome.

The fitness-training programme

This consisted of the following elements:

1. To acquire mastery over personal drives by doing without good, as well as bad things.
2. To develop positive strengths by doing good works. The purpose of these was to learn to channel energy creatively that had previously been used in a negative way.
3. To instil a habit of appreciation, particularly of God's Presence in all things and at all times. The chanting of psalms was the main method.
4. To start a healing process by making restitution to any wronged person.

A programme was voluntary, though in the case of monks and nuns it was part of the contract they made at the outset. The soul friend would find out from the seeker themselves what their weak points were. These would be shared in complete trust, in an outpouring of the soul known as 'confession'. Occasionally, of course, some foul play by a monk or a priest caused public outrage and a complaint against them was brought to their soul friend as part of the contract.

We shall now look at how the early Celtic training programmes, particularly those of Columbanus, dealt with the eight hurdles.

1. Gluttony
This includes excessive eating, drinking or talking. Doing without is the principal remedy, but in a way that helps to overcome the vice. Columbanus inducted oversleepers to prayer vigils during night hours; excessive talkers to extra periods of silence. Girl Guides who

agree to sponsored silences in order to raise money for poor children of the Third World retain something of this idea. Seekers today may fall prey to excessive TV watching, Internet surfing, or car driving. A soul friend should have creative alternatives to suggest for each.

2. Avarice

This is love of money, which can lead to stealing, cheating, lying, manipulative business practices or workaholism that robs family and friends of one's presence. Columbanus's antidote was to foster generosity in the seeker, which develops their trust in God's providence, and others' trust in them. One exercise was for a seeker to give money to the poor. A seeker who had stolen from somebody was to repay them, not from savings, but from the earnings of their own work, in weekly instalments. That kind of exercise has the added benefit of helping us to put ourselves in the shoes of the other person; it inculcates service as the model of supreme achievement.

3. Rage

This includes verbal abuse, violence to a person or their property, abortion and murder. The inclusion of these acts under the heading of rage is perceptive. It shows that Columbanus's training programme addressed the roots as well as the symptoms. The remedies were varied, but they all aimed to bring about a deep change of heart. Quarrelsomeness had to be replaced with understanding; damage to property with replacement items; injury with medical attention; angry words with acts of forgiveness; and murder with an offer of time and effort in lieu of that which the dead person might have given. In the case of abortion and some kinds of murder, the restitution could not consist of like for like. Instead, the miscreant publicly entered a long period of penalty which included fasting and exclusion from Holy Communion. The seeker who had no money had to work for the wronged person instead.

In our society the element of personal restitution has been lost. Young people who vandalise do not have to make personal restoration because they do not earn and it is not administratively cost-effective (in the short term) to oversee this. Insurance companies cover car drivers who cause damage through road rage. A popular movement towards voluntary restitution could have a leavening effect.

But what can be achieved in the context of soul friendship far outweighs that which can be achieved by any public programme. Columbanus sought to replace rage with its opposite, love. Tears that flowed as the seeker poured out his heart to his soul friend led to a deep receiving of forgiveness, and a love for the person who had been wronged.

4. Self-pity

This includes small-mindedness, resentment, miserableness, indifference and self-induced despair. This despair is to be distinguished from what later was termed 'the dark night of the soul', which might not be caused by a sinful attitude. The primary cure was joy. Columbanus urged all young people to expect trials and disappointments from the outset, but to look upon these as opportunities for growing more selfless, and therefore more receptive to the unending joy that is God's gift and their destiny. The chanting of psalms, which are so full of praise, was a chief means of moving into joy.

When a little book entitled *From Prison to Praise*[3] hit the headlines in the early 1970s it transformed many miserable Christians. They got the idea, for the first time, that they could praise God in all things, at all times. All over the world Christians started to practise this, praising God in prayers, songs, Scriptures and tongues. Soul friends should be alert both to the self-pity syndrome and to the praise antidote.

5. Lust

This includes all genital sexual acts outside marriage, and enforced sexual acts within marriage. The penitentials provide remedial programmes of varying intensity for adultery, fornication, homosexual acts, child abuse, sex with animals, and self-abuse. In order to gain mastery over craving, fasting from food as well as from sex (even within marriage) was prescribed. The seeker undertook not to live again in the same house with a person who had been a sexual partner unless, of course, they got married. If a man had violated a virgin, he would pay compensation to her parents. A person who had abused a child would undertake one year's fast (i.e. reduced intake of foods) and so on.

But how can restitution be made, for example, by a married man who has a baby by another man's wife? This common failing devastates both his innocent wife and the innocent husband: their deepest bonds of trust have been violated. Respect, trust, innocence, love – all have been severely damaged. How can a healing process get under way that is not just a plastering over of the wound? How can the guilty man prove to both victims and, indeed, to his collaborating sex partner who shares his shame and guilt, that a professed change of heart is real? Columbanus's drastic remedy was for him to be celibate, even with his wife, for three years. The desire, that threatened to destroy him, had to be mastered and be seen to be mastered.

Columbanus was wise to admit his 'partial knowledge'. In the light of modern research into sexual therapeutic processes, it may be sensible to bring the wronged wife into the decision-making. She might indeed welcome a period of abstinence to help her overcome her own revulsion at the unfaithful act, but sooner or later she may again desire and need sexual intercourse with her husband. Columbanus's principle can be retained if sexual intercourse is not resumed until the circumstances have been explored with the soul friend, and prepared for with prayer.

In the case of a homosexual act, simple diet for a long period was prescribed, and the penitent was also asked to abstain from receiving Holy Communion. At Columbanus's monastery at Bobbio, they wrote special prayers for use when a such a penitent was restored to Communion. The principle, which is to establish clear boundaries, is essential to effective spiritual guidance. Andrew Comiskey, who has helped many people who have committed regular homosexual acts to move out of this habit, hammers home the importance of boundaries. If we have a propensity to fall over cliffs, we need to decide not to walk along cliff-top paths.[4]

In our confused society sexual experimentation is often thought to be a good thing. The Celtic guides knew that multiple sexual relationships tend to become depersonalised or, if depth of encounter is sought, tend to be lacking in integrity, since real depth cries out for faithfulness, shared sacrifice, and single-mindedness before and after the event. They understood that this applied to homosexual experimentation as much as to heterosexual. Much modern insight confirms the wisdom of this. In Jungian understanding the degree of individuation ultimately attainable is likely to be more limited when the interior masculine and feminine components are drawn into lively response only by another of the same sex.[5]

The 'cure by contraries' approach, and not just abstinence on its own, is now understood to be vital for homosexuals. Soul friends should encourage them to develop close non-sexual friendships with heterosexuals of the same sex. This may help them to discover the intimacy and the gender identity that they were seeking and not fully finding in homosexual activity.[6]

The sex drive is one of the most powerful forces in life, for good or ill, and the purpose of the Celtic penitential programmes is to bring order to these drives. In Celtic spirituality sex is a good servant, but a bad master. So the sex drive must never be split off from the Spirit. Detached sexuality, which is not part of a deepening relationship with a spouse and with God, is wrong.

> It is biologically evident that to gain control of passion and so make it serve Spirit must be a condition of progress.
>
> *Teilhard de Chardin*

The natural energies that the love drive represents should not be pushed down, but they should be harnessed and transformed. Celtic soul friends encouraged the practice of sexual abstinence on Fridays and Saturdays, not only as a means of developing discipline, but also to create the opportunity to become immersed in the presence of God.

What if the seeker frequently fails in sexual morality? Discernment is necessary, to know whether the seeker fundamentally wants to choose God, or not. If the seeker does desire God but has an abnormal weakness, the seeker needs affirmation of that which is of God within them. Rather than propose unrealistic goals – which lead to guilt, fear of the soul friend and a downward spiral – it may be better to aim gradually to reduce the number of lapses. The soul friend should never condone any act of sexual immorality, and should help the seeker to establish boundaries that keep them away from the traps of temptation; nevertheless, a seeker who struggles but sometimes continues to fail should be steered rather than condemned.

6. Slackness

This includes neglect of duties, oversleeping, unreliability, wandering off without notice, lack of attentiveness to others, carelessness and slipshod work. Training exercises include doing extra work on behalf of someone else, keeping prayer vigils during normal hours of sleep, and chanting psalms when sleepy. Sleep was thought of as an image of death, and wakeful activity as a Christian's imitation of the Creator. So the aim was to motivate the seeker to a life of zeal, stability, perseverance and excellence, and in this way to become an ikon of God.

'What is your secret?' I asked my friend Derek, who had been a major in the British army, a shop steward in a laundry, and a tireless church worker into his eighties. 'The battle for the day is won or lost at the moment of waking,' he told me. 'If you let the downward pull of the flesh dominate you at the start of the day, and fail to get up the moment you wake up, everything else in your life will be lethargic.'

7. Vanity

This includes boasting, self-advertisement, or causing discord through promotion of ideas that are not God-centred (heresy). The fitness programme required a seeker to be accountable to another person, and to embrace self-imposed silences during meetings. A seeker who had fostered discord through sectarian or heretical ideas had to publicly condemn these, and also to work to win back to unity in the faith those whom the seeker's influence had led astray. Columbanus geared his programmes to the concept of life as a pilgrimage. The aim was to produce Christians with trusting, childlike attitudes who never took their L-plates down, and who never thought that they 'knew it all'. The present-day Taizé Community in France fosters such an attitude. A soul friend whose seeker has 'everything buttoned up' should encourage the seeker to attend to how others perceive them, and should point them to desert-style experiences where they get in touch with their vulnerabilities.

8. Pride
This includes disregard of those in authority, envy, complaining, criticism and contempt of others. Acts of humility are prescribed for the disobedient. The training exercise to overcome envy is to practise kindness towards those the seeker most envies. Defamation of another is seen as a sin against justice and love, so the culprit has to openly admit and apologise for this. The role of the soul friend is to affirm what is good in the accused person; to confront, correct and elicit compassion in the seeker. Columbanus's aim was always to excite a passion to be like Christ. So his training programme includes taking to heart St Paul's great hymn about Christ humbling himself: 'Christ Jesus was in the form of God yet he did not cling to equality with God. Instead he emptied himself taking the form of a servant and became obedient even to death on a cross' (Philippians 2:6–8).

Behind all these penitential practices lay the concept of accountability. This was a saying of one of the desert fathers: 'Therefore we ought to live as having to give account to God of our way of life every day.' Soul friendships were sustained in that perspective; and what fruit they bore. Mrs Concannon, reflecting upon mutual influences in the lives of Columbanus and Francis of Assisi (who made devotion to Columbanus at his foundation at Bobbio) writes of the former: 'His mission of penance[7] was accomplished in that ministry of "Soul Friendship" which did so much to build the laity into the solid masonry of the Church.'[8]

The relevance of penance today

Sports people often say that confidence comes as a result of training to their utmost. So it does with character training. Those who enrolled in the first flush of the fitness-training programmes described in this chapter were motivated by the love to God to give their utmost, and many of these ordinary people grew confident in God. In later generations guilt and traditional expectation played a part in maintaining these training programmes, and their innocence and integrity became tarnished. Just as sports training has updated its tools and facilities, so training of athletes of the spirit needs to do the same.

In the days of the Celtic monasteries, penitentials were used with monks who had already made a commitment of obedience. It seems they were also used selectively with lay people. We must remember that the lives of most Christians revolved around a monastery, and a soul friend and a seeker would share common expectations about their obligations. Those conditions do not exist in our multi-choice society. A soul friend today might wish to introduce the idea of fitness training, and ascertain whether the seeker wishes to include this as part of the contract between them. No one today would wish to copy the precise regimen used by Columbanus. The principles, however, have never been bettered, and are, I believe, due for a come-back.

An article on New Year resolutions and healthy eating habits in the London *Times* began:

> Our more heinous unhealthy habits show a disregard for one or more of the seven deadly sins, each of which can lead to medical disaster. But it requires more than a good resolution to convert,

and thereby spare the heart of a type A personality – competitive, striving and ruthlessly ambitious – to a type B, no less clever and sometimes as successful but laid back and contemplative. Unless the type A's respond to beta-blockers or are very determined, they will continue to journey through life burdened with a heavy load of avarice, pride and envy.[9]

How may a soul friend apply penance today?

If a seeker is in a mess and asks a soul friend's help, the soul friend should focus on two things: the best way the seeker can make restitution, and the best meditation exercise for building up self-mastery. In order to give the potential soul friend a feel for this kind of encounter, there follows an imaginary but true-to-life example.

Brian was a zealous US Christian in his twenties. After being repeatedly betrayed by his fiancée his anger erupted, he turned his back on God, who he felt had let him down, and decided to live for himself. He took a holiday flight to the UK and made a girl pregnant. She decided to keep the baby, but she and Brian had nothing in common. Back home, riddled with guilt, Brian eventually sought out a soul friend whom he had known from his past. How did the soul friend respond?

First, the soul friend asked Brian to tell the whole story. It is important that the seeker 'gets everything out', and that the soul friend gets the full picture. Second, they decided what they needed to do during these three days together. There were three phases, each interspersed with plenty of space for Brian to be alone.

1. Talking through the anger and getting to its roots. Brian confessing it in prayer, the soul friend praying for release and healing.

2. Talking through the guilt, identifying steps of restitution (payments to the mother of 15 per cent of Brian's salary until the child was eighteen years old; monthly contact by phone; the offer

of a month together with the child each year; the offer to bring up the child if ever the mother relinquished her); identifying the unmet emotional needs (lack of parental love) which led Brian to try and meet these needs inappropriately; adopting a repetitive spiritual exercise which would develop mastery of these spiritual needs (an exercise meditating on the mother love of God was chosen which Brian agreed to repeat often); confession by Brian of sin and guilt, and prayer by the soul friend assuring him of God's forgiveness, encircling and releasing the baby and mother to God.

3. Preparing for the future, identifying the temperament and aptitudes of Brian and envisioning a spiritual pattern he could follow which would reflect these; affirming it is OK to ditch previous spiritual patterns which were driven by false church conditioning and were alien to Brian's nature; exploring contacts, books, and praying meditatively together.

Confession and sorrow

Many evangelical Christians who do not believe it is necessary to confess their sins to a priest or to receive formal absolution nevertheless confess sins to a non-ordained soul friend, believing that it is God who forgives. Some of these Christians do, however, need human assurance that their sins are forgiven. A non-ordained soul friend can give a penitent some preparation before confession, and if assurance of forgiveness is needed, may read a Scripture such as this: 'If we confess our sins, God is faithful and just and will forgive our sins and cleanse us from all unrighteousness' (1 John 1:9). The preparation may include silence, readings from Scripture, or prophetic prayer. It might be followed by anointing with oil if this helps a seeker go forth healed and calmed.

Sometimes a person is so conscious of guilt that they never think to name anything as being wrong. A soul friend might prompt them by asking: 'For which of these events that you have recounted do you wish to say sorry?'

Although, in general, we should adhere to the link between confession and restitution, we should not be legalistic about this. Some people do need to separate the exploration with a soul friend of how to deal with a situation from the sacramental confession of their sins to a priest.

Summary

Soul friends in Celtic monasteries used penitentials produced by their monastic leaders as a tool to build up seekers. These penitentials were based on two principles: the need to make restitution for sins against other people, and the need to develop self-mastery. A contemporary soul friend should have tools with which to develop restitution and self-mastery.

Exercises
For soul friends or potential soul friends

1. Carefully go through each of the eight vices listed in this chapter. Think of an example of each vice that has blighted the experience of someone you know. Now prayerfully think through a training exercise and suggest a remedy that would help to master each of these sins.

2. Now make a list of other vices that you think should be added to this list, and write out a training exercise for each.

3. Brian was a Christian who, after being repeatedly let down, blamed and turned his back on God, and decided to live for his own pleasure. Imaginatively reconstruct another example, and decide how you, as the soul friend, would use the time together, and what restitution and self-mastery exercise you would recommend.[10]

Further reading
Connolly, Hugh, *The Irish Penitentials* (Four Courts Press, 1995).

CHAPTER 12

ORDER – LATER IRISH
MONASTIC INSIGHTS INTO
SOUL FRIENDSHIP

The eighth to tenth centuries after Christ

When most of the population became Christian, the many Irish monasteries became responsible for providing soul friends for the population through (male only) clergy, who developed this role in a ritualistic way. Lessons from these widespread practices were translated into regulations which most monasteries drew up. Although this was in many ways a retrograde development, the regulations contain warnings and advice from which we can learn.

> The monastery should have a priest who is devout and faithful to the monastic life, steadfast in his ministry, and a sure and compassionate guide in the art of good living.
>
> *The Rule of Ailbe (eighth century)*

A shift had taken place since the time of Brigid and Columba, several centuries earlier. Hermits and other wise individuals still acted as soul friends here and there, but in general soul friendship became more ritualised and clericalised, and therefore, incidentally, more male. People from the surrounding area flocked to their local monastery to confess and receive penances, and the monastery appointed one or more priests to make this their full-time ministry.

According to some students of the history of religious movements it is an unwritten law that communities need reform at least every two centuries. The first generation or two remain fired up by the vision of their founder. Then, as success increases the size, bureaucracy replaces spontaneity; as disagreements arise, code replaces relationship; and what began as a movement becomes a monument.

It is our loss that we have few written guidelines from Irish communities in the time of the sixth-century founders. This is either because they did not write things down, or because their writings were lost, along with the libraries, at the time of the Norse invasions. As with other religious communities over the centuries, we sense that the fires lit by founders tended to burn low after a few generations. To counter this, more detailed rules were laid down to maintain discipline and to prevent abuses.

In the eighth century a reform movement began in Ireland known as *Celi De*, meaning the Servants or Friends of God. The reform sought to wean members of communities from formalism and kindle in them prayer, sensitivity and unity of heart with like-minded Christians, while acknowledging that they needed to organise in order to provide ministry on a large scale.

Rules of monasteries which embraced these reforms in the eighth and ninth centuries have come down to us, some in fragmentary form.[1] They reveal the pivotal role of the soul friend, both for monks and for lay people who looked to the monastery for nurture. A monastic soul friend was grounded in the Scriptures and in the Rules of the saints. Among the monks and nuns, daily confession was as normal and useful as sweeping the floor. Correction 'without harshness, and without blame, and with laughter' was the aim, rather than reproof. In spiritual direction two things were all important: counsel and mortification.

In this chapter we shall record extracts from the various Rules

143

drawn up by monasteries who accepted reforms in the eighth century. The Rules are often named after the founder of the community, although they were written some centuries after the founder's death. It may be that during the twenty-first century the church will face a larger-scale demand for the provision of soul friends. If so, we shall find useful advice from these Celtic monasteries.

The Rule of Ciaran (seventh or eighth century) – Wander only to consult wise people

A partial copy exists of a Rule attributed to St Ciaran. If this refers to the Ciaran who founded Clonmacnoise monastery, this is no doubt because his monastery was later influenced by the *Celi De* reform. This fairly early Rule contains the following interesting advice: 'It is dangerous to form the habit of leaving one's monastery unless it be to visit a church, to consult the wise, or to make the round of the cemeteries.'

We learn from this, not only that Christianity was becoming more institutionalised (monks who suddenly wandered off at the prompting of their heart made life difficult for the rest who had to keep the organisation going, so they were warned against doing this), but also that it was a custom for monks to travel around in order to consult mentors, or 'the wise'.

The Rule of Comghall (late eighth century) – Place yourself under another

This Rule, attributed to Comghall, the founder of the famous monastery at Bangor, includes these strong words: 'The advice of a devout sage is a great asset if one wishes to avoid penalty. However self-confident you are, place yourself under the direction of another.'

The Rule of Tallaght (eighth century)

The village of Tallaght, near Dublin, was built on the site of the monastery founded by Mael-Ruain, who died in 792, and who was a leader of the reform movement. *The Annals of Ulster* mention a hermit, Mael Dithruib, who was a great friend and disciple of Mael-Ruain, and who kept a record of his sayings. These give us insights into their approach to soul friendship. The numbered extracts that follow are from this record.

Preparation for a soul friend session

63. Those of the laity who came for spiritual direction were ordered to remain apart from their wives on the nights of Wednesday, Thursday and Saturday. When they did likewise on Sundays and during their wives' monthly periods, it was in line with the teaching of Peter as outlined in the *Liber Clementinis*.

The basis of soul friendship

71. A person enters God's service when (s)he promises what (s)he has set out to do, and takes this upon themself under the direction of someone else.

The perils of a soul friend

74. Mael Dithruib used to say that the office of soul friend was perilous because, should the soul friend impose on a penitent a penance commensurate with the gravity of the sin, it was more likely to be breached than observed. But if the soul friend did not impose a penance, the debts of the sinner would fall upon himself. It is safer for the soul friend to send them advice, but not to receive their confession.

When to stop being a soul friend

75. Elair rejected all those whom he had accepted previously for soul friendship because they would not give their best effort, and because they concealed some of their sins in confession. He would allow no one to approach him for the purpose of soul friendship. He did, however, allow and

encourage penitents for their peace of soul, to go and question devout men, that is monks of perfect life who would have some proficiency in teaching what would be beneficial for their souls. He himself, however, did not receive any one for soul friendship, anyone, that is, whom he suspected had a soul friend of his own and from whom he might receive counsel.

Changing a soul friend

76. Mael-Ruain was of like mind. He was unwilling to accept even Mael Dithruib until he learned whether or not he had already a spiritual father to direct him. When Mael Dithruib first came to Mael-Ruain for soul friendship, Mael-Ruain said that, 'artisans such as smiths and carpenters do not like to see those whom they are training go to another craftsman for instruction. Why then should your spiritual father be happy to see you come to me for direction?' 'It is for that very reason', replied Mael Dithruib, 'that I obtained from my spiritual father permission to come to you.' Mael-Ruain then agreed to become his soul friend, and Mael Dithruib submitted himself to his authority.

What kind of soul friend to place yourself under

77. Mael-Ruain then said to Mael Dithruib: 'We regard the first year spent under our spiritual direction as a year of purifying, and so you will have to spend three periods of forty days on bread and water, except for a mouthful of milk and water.' And he added: 'When you place yourself under the guidance and control of someone else you should seek out the fire which will most fiercely burn, that is, which will spare you the least.'

This throws light upon the seriousness with which spiritual guidance was taken. It is not clear how frequently people came for spiritual direction, but the principle is one we can adopt to our benefit.

From the ninth-century Rule of St Carthage – Integrity

A Rule has come down to us from the ninth century, which has sometimes been attributed to St Carthage, who was abbot of a large monastery near Offaly in the eighth century. There are copies of this in the British Museum and in Trinity College, Dublin. The Rule includes an entire section on the duties of the clerical soul friend. Reading between the lines, we can see that a large section of the population must have come to one or more priests set aside by their monastery for the full-time work of spiritual direction. Soul friendship had almost become an industry, and with it came abuse. We can see also how easy it must have been for a priest who was in great demand, and who lived off donations, to give more time to some than to others.

Here is a paraphrase of some pieces of advice from the Rule:

> If you are a soul friend to someone, do not neglect them just because they have no money to offer you; and refuse to accept a donation from any one who refuses to take seriously your advice.
>
> Take care not to let those who give you large donations have a hold on your affections, instead, let them be like fire on your body.
>
> Do not begrudge giving time and attention to those who can give you nothing, for the integrity of your soul is worth more than money.
>
> Indeed, you must share the spiritual treasures God has given you with everyone: strangers, even though they have no high connections, the poor, the elderly, the widowed, though not with people who are intent only on sin.

This raises the issue of charging for spiritual direction. Generally, in Britain and Ireland in recent centuries no charges were made because most soul friends were already provided for by the church if they were a priest, pastor or a member of a religious community, or because they were on a pension. Increasingly, today, this is not so, and it is important that seekers should be responsible in giving donations to soul friends who are not otherwise supported. There is a warning here, however, to such soul friends. Never refuse spiritual direction to someone just because they cannot afford to pay. This marks out a difference between Christian ministry and commercial secular agencies.

> The soul friend should look for candour and integrity in the confessions of penitents. Fast and pray on behalf of these; if you don't, you will pay for it because the results of their sins will become a burden upon you.

> Instruct the unlearned, both by what you teach and by the life that you model, so that they follow your example rather than sin.

> Each person should be treated the same; in simplicity and complete confidentiality.

Institutionalism, even superstition, crept into the church over the following centuries. The *Celi De*, which began as a reform, acquiesced in abuses. A 'Rule of the *Celi De*' from the twelfth (or perhaps eleventh) century reveals a bureaucrat's approach to soul friendship. The Rule states that there should be a bishop for every territory – in the early years of Christianisation people-groups, not territories, had bishops. The bishop's duties included that of being a soul friend to rulers (presumably holy hermits or foster-mothers were not considered fitting now). Each area had a parish priest with students he prepared for ordination. Any priest who took upon himself the care of a church, also took upon himself the duty of giving spiritual direction to all the 'subjects' [*sic*] of that church, men, boys, women and girls. Anyone who refused the guidance of this spiritual father was to be denied Communion or inclusion in the intercessions. Was the power game, which the Irish church had for centuries been so gloriously free of, now entrenched at its heart?

The role of the soul friend soon became fully institutionalised throughout the pre-Reformation Western church. In 1215 the Fourth Lateran Council made confession to a priest obligatory. Although nuns no doubt continued to give spiritual direction within certain circles, soul friendship as a creative bond between two free spirits was a thing of the past.

After the Reformation the Roman Catholic Church at the Council of Trent (1546) defined confession as one of the seven sacraments of the church. More recently that church has renamed this the sacrament of reconciliation, in an attempt to recover something of the human process involved in it.

The churches that broke away from Roman church control during the fifteenth- and sixteenth-century Reformation rejected clericalism and compulsory confession; they believed in 'the priesthood of all believers'. This did not, however, see a revival of the role of the soul friend. It seemed that almost all the practices of the old church were now suspect, and spiritual direction had been too closely identified with the priesthood to be allowed back in a lay form. In theory members of Reformed churches were encouraged to 'confess their sins to one another' as the New Testament letter of James urged (James 5:16), but this was not practical in village communities where gossip abounded.

The Church of England, which claimed to embrace the best of the old and of the Reformed churches, did, in time, restore spiritual direction as a valued part of its tradition. Although its formularies do not mention this, it has taught this about the making of confessions: 'All may, none must, some should.' It has taken a similar approach to spiritual direction in general. The spiritual director need not be, but often has been, a priest. Although that church proclaims belief in the priesthood of all believers, spiritual direction tended in practice to be restricted to its more catholic wing, and to bookish people who could afford to stay at retreat houses.

The wheel has now come full circle. The freedoms of travel and information have made possible, and indeed necessary, a new flowering of soul friendship which transcends, though it does not devalue, the church's formal arrangements of the past. If there is a large-scale revival of soul friendship some of the lessons of this chapter will need to be learned.

Summary

As enormous numbers of adults in Ireland joined the church and expected to have a soul friend the provision of a soul friend was organised from the top down, and the spontaneity of early days was lost. This was the price of success. Eventually the confession of sins to an allocated (male) priest replaced soul friendship as the norm in spiritual direction. This practice went into steep decline at the close of the second millennium. Today's multi-choice society makes possible a revival of the original type of soul friendship.

Exercises
For a soul friend

1. Consider how the Rule of Tallaght advised people to prepare for soul friendship sessions. How do you recommend yourself or others to prepare?

For a soul friend or seeker
2. According to the Rule of Tallaght a person enters God's service when they promise to adhere to what they have set out to do under the direction of someone else. Are you and your soul friend clear what you have set out to do? If not, work on this now, and write it down to discuss with your soul friend when you next meet.

For a seeker
3. Elair refused to be a soul friend to people who only told him half the truth. Do you have a soul friend (or, if not, a priest or pastor) to whom you can entrust your deepest faults and longings? If so, have you confided all? If not, what should you do about it?

CHAPTER 13

AN ART – AELRED'S
INSIGHTS INTO SOUL
FRIENDSHIP

Twelfth century after Christ

Aelred had a great gift of friendship; he studied it, fostered it, and wrote about it. Although much of what he wrote is about friendship in a general sense, we, with him, can view that general friendship as the base of a pyramid. Near the top of the pyramid certain friendships meet the criteria which mark out a soul friend.

> Friendship is the best medicine in life. It is . . . a bridge between us and the perfect love of God.
>
> *Aelred*

Aelred's great-grandfather looked after St Cuthbert's shrine at Durham, which was one of the few parts of Northumbria's Celtic heritage to survive the ravages of the Vikings. This devotion to Cuthbert was handed down through the married priests in his family, and was continued by Aelred's father, Eilaf. Eilaf had to leave his post at St Cuthbert's shrine and retire to Hexham when William the Conqueror, at the pope's urging, began to enforce clerical celibacy. Here Aelred, who was named Ethelred in his early years, was born. Soon monks replaced married clergy there, too, so in 1118 Eilaf entered Durham's new cathedral monastery of St Cuthbert, in the presence of Ethelred and his two brothers. There a call to the monastery began to stir in the young Ethelred.

It was a custom of that first feudal age that sons of members of the upper class were sent away to be fostered by a person of high influence and education. Ethelred was sent over the border to the court of David, King of the Scots. There he proved most popular, and made close friends with David's two stepsons, Simon and Waldef, who became models for him. It was probably there, too, that his Anglo-Saxon name was softened to the Norman form by which he is now known.

During his childhood education Aelred became familiar with the dialogue of the Roman philosopher Cicero *On Friendship*,[1] which influenced him ever after. At the court he had opportunity to develop a variety of good friendships for which he had great aptitude. Yet he recorded that even friends whose company he most enjoyed did not enter into the things that went on deep inside him, and this sometimes brought him near to despair. His were highly successful social friendships but they lacked the spiritual element.

In 1134, while returning from a visit to York on church business, Aelred called in at the new Cistercian monastery at Rievaulx. The impact on him was so powerful that he offered himself as a humble novice there, and was accepted. He got on as well with everyone there as he had at the royal court, and before long was sent to Rome to represent his abbot. On his return to Rievaulx Aelred was appointed Master of Novices, then he was sent to found a new monastery at Revesby, and in 1147 was recalled to become Abbot of Rievaulx. His duties included regular visits to a daughter monastery at Wardon.

Aelred brought a fresh approach to monastic life. The old attitude had been that monks should have no special friendships, and should therefore not express affection. Aelred had no place for friendships that shut anyone else out, or that were not accountable, but he did not believe in suppressing thoughtful friendships that grew out of the flow of personalities given to God. So the Celtic way of seeing the presence of God in human lives that were fully lived triumphed over the formal, standardised approach that had by then become the norm in the church.

Aelred's work *Spiritual Friendship*[2] reflects this new attitude which was in fact restoring the spirit of friendship that marked Celtic Christians such as St Cuthbert. The work consists of three books. The first was probably begun at Wardon. The third was completed some twenty years later. The framework owes much to Cicero's treatise *On Friendship*, with its questions and answers, but Cicero did not know Christ. Much of the content of Aelred's work explores the transforming power of Christ as the source and sustainer of friendship that embraces the soul and is eternal.

We know that Aelred drew inspiration from the Celtic saints. It was he who wrote *The Life of St Ninian*.[3] In this book he laments that in his own time 'mouths consecrated for the praise of God are daily polluted by backbiting' and contrasts this with Ninian 'the radiant one', 'whose miracles do not cease to shine forth even to our own times'. Aelred compares Ninian to a bee 'who formed for himself the honeycombs of wisdom'. There seems little doubt that Aelred sought to do likewise, and that this was reflected in his soul friendships.

The rest of this chapter is a paraphrase of extracts from Aelred's work:

Book 1: Questions about general friendship

When I was a boy I loved to give affection to my friends, but because I did not know the laws of friendship I was pulled in all directions. Once I had read Cicero's treatise on friendship I had something against which to check my changing affections. Then, when I committed my life to serve Christ in a monastery, Christ and his words in the Scriptures became the centre of my affections. But I never forgot Cicero's thoughts about friendship, so I wrote my own treatise on spiritual friendship, drawing on the Scriptures and the friendships of Christian saints.

Ivo: I should like to learn how the friendship which ought to exist among us begins and is sustained in Christ, of whom Cicero was ignorant.

Aelred: You can get an imperfect idea of the nature of friendship in this definition of Cicero's: It is mutual harmony in human and divine affairs coupled with love and care.

Ivo: But I am convinced that true friendship cannot exist among those who live without Christ.

Aelred: The word friend (in Latin *amicus*) comes from the word love (*amor*). I have explained the affections and movements of love in my book *Mirror of Charity*. A friend is guardian of mutual love. He guards my spirit so as to preserve its secrets in faithful silence; he should endure the defects he finds in my spirit, rejoice and sorrow with me, and feel as his own all that his friend experiences. Friendship therefore consists of ties of love and sweetness. A true friend offers unconditional love at all times, whatever the other may do wrong. That is why true friendship was so rare before Christ.

Although friendship is so difficult to achieve, it is possible. Remember that Jesus said, 'Ask, and you shall receive.' The early Christians received this grace. We read in the Acts of the Apostles that they 'were of one heart and mind' (Acts 4:32). How many martyrs gave their lives for their brothers and sisters? 'No one has greater love than the one who lays down their life for their friends' as Jesus said.

Ivo: Is there no difference between love and friendship?

Aelred: Yes, for God requires us to love our enemies as well as our friends. We only call those people friends to whom we can entrust our heart and all its secrets.

Ivo: Don't godless people have such bonds, too?

Aelred: They may have a harmony of vices, but this cannot be called spiritual friendship. For the person who loves sin hates himself, and will not be able to love another. The fact that even friendships polluted by lust, greed or comfort are so valued only goes to show how much more precious is pure friendship.

Selfish friendship lusts after people as objects for gratification. Friendships that are inflamed by lust or greed are not open to reason, or to the judgment of others. That kind of friendship manipulates, and becomes consumed by deceit. It carries within it the seeds of its own destruction.

In contrast true, spiritual friendship springs from the feelings of the heart, which have their own dignity, and no ulterior motive. This kind of friendship is born of those who share a similar calling in God. Prudence directs, justice rules, fortitude guards, and self-control moderates this kind of friendship.

Ivo: What is the source of friendship in the Divine plan?

Aelred: God built companionship into all creation; not one created thing exists alone. It is the same in the spiritual world, among the angels. Pleasant companionship and delightful love among the angels enabled them, though they have free will, never to have envy or discord. Finally, when God created human beings God said it was not good for man to be alone, that is why there are men and women. From the beginning nature implanted the desire for friendship and love in the heart of each person.

155

However, after the fall into sin human beings became divided by envy. Friendship was violated by the many and only lived by the few. Law was brought in to regulate friendship, and to put bounds upon the power of sin to destroy it. Although many so-called friendships have mixed motives, it is possible for people who do not serve God to get a taste of natural friendship through these, so that they then want to find true friendship and wisdom.

Ivo: What is the link between wisdom and friendship?

Aelred: Friendship is inextricably linked to wisdom. This may surprise you, but if true friendship is eternal, we see that wisdom consists in following what is true and everlasting. As the Scripture says: 'The person who lives in God lives in friendship.' In this sense we can say that God is friendship.

Book 2: The blessings of friendship

Walter: What are the practical advantages of friendship?

Aelred: Nothing more sacred is striven for, nothing more useful is sought after, nothing more difficult is discovered, nothing more sweet experienced, and nothing more profitable is possessed. For friendship bears fruit in this life and the next.

It combats vices by its own virtue, it tempers adversity, moderates prosperity, and assuages loneliness. What happiness, security and joy to have someone to whom you dare to speak on equal terms as to oneself; one to whom you need not fear to confess your failings; one to whom you can without embarrassment share your progress in the life of the Spirit, one to whom you can entrust the secrets of your heart and before whom you can place all your plans. Friendship heightens the joys of prosperity and lessens the sorrows of adversity by sharing them. It is the best medicine in life. More than all these, friendship is a bridge between us and the perfect love of God.

In friendship there is no pretence, it is holy, voluntary and true. Its adjuncts are honour and charm, truth and joy, sweetness and goodwill, affection and action. The ever-flowing inspiration of the love by which we love our friend is Christ.

A good goal of friendship is that we behave towards our friend as we would like our friend to behave towards ourselves. True friendship is therefore only possible among good people. For as long as one delights in something that is not good more than in the good of another, one cannot be truly their friend.

Objections

Gratian: But surely I am not good, so how can I have such friendship?

Aelred: I mean by a good person someone who by God's grace, as St Paul writes, lives a self-controlled, godly and upright life (Titus 2:12).

Walter: I wonder whether friendship is so difficult that it is best avoided. Are not my own burdens enough to bear, without having to bear those of a friend? Since it is so difficult to keep loving someone even to death, isn't it better not to start than to let them down later?

Aelred: What is the wisdom of avoiding friendship in order to avoid care, burdens or fears? Can you achieve moral growth in your own life without struggle? Then why expect to achieve mutual growth without struggle? Cicero reminds

157

us that to take friendship out of life is like taking away the sun. Or take the example of St Paul, who was weak alongside the weak, and strong alongside the strong. Do you think he should have given up those ways? Those who urge you to take no care for others are more like wild beasts than human beings.

Walter: What sort of friendships should be avoided?

Aelred: As well as the so-called friendship that is based on interest in a common vice, the aimless friendship that pursues anyone who passes by without thought should be avoided. We should never follow physical attraction which lacks integrity, reason and openness to others. We should guard against unfaithful, unstable, impure loves. This kind of relationship is better called friendship's poison than friendship. The beginnings of a spiritual friendship should possess purity of intention, the direction of thought, and the restraint of a balanced spirit.

A friendship entered into for no other reason than to gain benefits is also unsound. Certainly, some benefits such as advice and understanding are lovely fruits of friendship, but they should not be the roots of it. The blessings proceed from the friendship, the friendship does not proceed from the blessings. As with biblical friendships such as that between David and Jonathan it is not so much the benefits obtained through a friend that delights as the friend's love in itself.

Book 3: The conditions, limits and fruits of friendship

Aelred: The source of friendship is love. Love can proceed from nature – as a mother loves her child; it can proceed from duty, such as the act of forgiving an enemy; or it can proceed from affection alone, as when a person's beauty, strength, personality, or character steals into the soul. Friendship should only proceed from the love that is both pure according to reason as well as affectionate according to the heart. An impulse to affection that is not willing to be tested and weighed should be guarded against. We should never be ruled by only the head or by only the heart, but by both together.

The foundation of all true friendship is the love of God; all other attractions must be submitted to this. We cannot love another if we do not love ourselves, since we learn how to love our neighbour by doing to them what we wish for ourselves.

Not all whom we love should be embraced as friends. Since your friend is the companion of your soul, to whom you wish to entrust yourself completely, you should choose someone who is fitted for this. Then you should test this friendship, and only then embrace it. For friendship should be stable and manifest a certain likeness to eternity. We should not, like children, change friends by whim. There is nothing more detestable than the person who injures, deserts or insults a friend. A friend should be chosen with extreme care and tested with the utmost caution, for after that, the two should become as one.

The four stages of soul friendship

The four stages by which one attains such friendship are selection, probation, admission and harmony.

1. Selection

We should draw our friends from that reservoir of people who seek to supplant anger with patience, and suspicion with the contemplation of love. These qualities undergird friendship: love – a delight in doing good to another; affection – an inward pleasure that is naturally expressed; security – the ability to keep intimacies so that there is no fear or suspicion; happiness – a friendly sharing of everything in one's life.

Avoid selecting as a soul friend someone with faults such as backbiting, impugning one's integrity, arrogance, breaking of a confidence, or secret undermining, which make this unattainable (Sirach 22:27, Vulgate version). However, there are some persons who have a fault but who do not give way to the vices which break friendship; these faults can be confronted and healed, and the person can then be considered. Fickle, suspicious, talkative or irritable persons *can* develop into soul friends, but it is vital that the healing process is under way before you go further.

2. Probation

These qualities must be tested in a friend: loyalty, right intention, discretion, and patience. Loyalty is friendship's nurse and guardian. With it a friend remains a true companion through fortune and misfortune alike. A truly loyal friend sees nothing in his friend but his heart. By right intention, we mean that a friend should expect nothing from the friendship except God and the natural good that flows from this. By discretion we mean an understanding of what to seek, do and suffer for a friend, what to confront and what to affirm, and the manner, time and place for these. Patience means that we do not hit back when our friend confronts something unacceptable in us, and that we faithfully bear adversity caused by something our friend does.

A friend of mine who lost his temper nevertheless did not break a confidence or impugn my integrity. Though he transgressed the law of friendship, that was no reason for me to cease to treat him with the utmost confidence and solicitude, since I have made that commitment.

Most of us fall into a fault at some time or another. When this happens to a friend, we should take great care to help him make amends, and to put right what has gone wrong between us.

If your friend refuses to do this, if he breaks the foundations of friendship, or if he injures another person who is also your friend, then you are right to end the friendship. In this situation we should make a gradual withdrawal of the friendship, little by little, so that it dies away without causing more harm. Even if a former friend hurls public abuse at us we should never wage war on someone who was once our friend. Even if friendship has to be withdrawn, love should still be shown, which will include traces of the former friendship.

3. Admission

How can we cultivate friendship? By giving whenever our friend is in need, if possible, before he needs to ask us. Do this in a way that preserves mutual cheerfulness and self-confidence. One should not, however, give promotion or honours on a basis of favouritism, and a true friend should never expect those sort of rewards from the friendship. If we are in a position to appoint people to posts, we should not do this because they are friends, but because they are suited to the post. Think of Jesus, who appointed Peter to a chief post, but had such a profound rapport with John.

4. Harmony

We can cultivate friendship by praying for and being solicitous for one another, and by taking pleasure in one another's progress. It can happen that as a person prays to Christ for a friend, the sweetness they find in Christ passes over to their friend.

Give each other such respect that if your friend sins you yourself blush and feel the pain of it. In this way your very demeanour can help your friend to regain a right demeanour himself. Praise your friend often, but never be subservient. Offer advice and counsel from the heart, but not in a paternalistic way. If you perceive a fault developing in your friend, bring it to his attention in private, thus maintaining sympathy and respect. However, if he continues to resist, do it openly, even if it wounds him, but always without bitterness. The friend needs to feel that your correction is born of love, not rancour, so do not hide your feelings. It is good if your tears flow.

Study, too, your friend's type of personality, and adapt your responses to this. If he is under pressure, wait for an appropriate moment to sort out something that is wrong. To bide your time, not giving the impression that anything is wrong, is not the same as dissimulation, which is always wrong.

In true friendship there is equality of regard, regardless of the different social standing two friends may have. There is a preferring of the other before self, as Jonathan, a king's son, preferred David before himself (1 Samuel 23:17). The best companion of friendship is reverence. True and eternal affection is where there is no deceit. It begins in this life and is completed in the next.

A personal example of soul friendship

I will give you an example of friendship from my personal experience. I recall choosing one friend, when I was young, because we had similar interests. I demanded nothing and bestowed nothing but affection. He had no share in the burdens of my duties and died while still young. Another person was a co-worker who shared in many burdensome duties with me; I only admitted him into the intimacy of friendship in later years. I was drawn to the first person through affection but was never able to test this. I was drawn to the second person through duty; he was tested over many years, and only then, as my admiration for his qualities grew, was affection born, and we became the closest confidants. There was no pretence, evasion, half-truths, but everything was open and above board. We corrected each other without getting indignant. He exposed himself to dangers and forestalled scandals on my account. He was the refuge of my spirit, the solace of my griefs, whose heart of love received me when I was worn out, whose counsel refreshed me when I was despondent. He calmed me when I was distressed and soothed me when I was angry. When anything unpleasant occurred I shared it with him so that we carried it together shoulder to shoulder. Was not this a foretaste of the blessedness of heaven? If you see anything in this example which is worth imitating, please make sure you profit by it.

There is more. Once as I walked amidst my brothers in the monastery the affection of all passed into my soul and I was transfused by joy. As we ascend from the holy love with which we embrace a friend to the love with which we embrace Christ, fear, even of death, departs and we partake of the spiritual fruit of friendship, waiting the fullness of heaven, when the friendship we have known on earth with a few, shall be outpoured by God upon all, and all shall outpour upon God, and God shall be all in all.

Summary

Aelred restored the freshness, integrity and spontaneity of friendship which had been overlaid since the first flowering of the Celtic church. If we apply the principles of friendship that he expounds we create the seedbed in which soul friendships can come to flower. Only one or two of the friendships Aelred describes can be described as true soul friendships. He, however, was limited to those who were members of his monastery; we are not.

Exercises
For all readers

1. Draw up a list of people you are acquainted with to whom you are

naturally drawn. Cross out those with whom you could not sustain thoughtful, rounded conversations about things of the mind. Now cross out those with whom you could not sustain a sharing of the deep things of the spirit, because intimacies would either not be understood or not be respected. If anyone remains on this list, what prevents you taking further steps to develop the friendship?

2. Review in your life, in the light of what Aelred writes, these four qualities of a friend that need to be tested: loyalty through good and bad times; absence of 'demand'; understanding of the developmental process in a relationship; willingness to be corrected.

3. Review your friendships in the light of these suggested ways of cultivating a friendship: mutual meeting of needs; prayer; high regard; encouragement; counsel; loving correction; transparency.

4. Contemplate heaven as the place of accelerated and maximum friendship.

Further reading
Aelred of Rievaulx, *Spiritual Friendship*, translated by Mary Eugenia Laker SSND (Cistercian Publications, Kalamazoo, MI, 1977).

CHAPTER 14

DYING – SOUL FRIENDS AT HEAVEN'S DOOR

The sixth, seventh and nineteenth centuries after Christ

A soul friendship that deepens into old age can be a deep solace when one is dying. Stories from early Ireland and from nineteenth-century Scotland give us a feel for what a soul friend can offer at death. But there are limits to this. That is why we do well to learn how Celtic Christians made soul friends of those who were already in heaven.

> To accompany other people, along with their loved ones, up to the gate of death is to enter Holy Ground. To stand in an awesome place where the wind of the Spirit blows; to encounter peace and grief, insight, intimacy and pain on a level not found in ordinary living. By the side of the dying we learn stillness, waiting, simply being; the arts of quietness and keeping watch, prayer beyond words.
>
> *Penelope Wilcock*[1]

When death draws near, we have no energy with which to keep up appearances. We need to be with those in whose presence we do not have to strive. We need someone who will hold our hand, and be a bridge for us between earth and heaven. Soul friends are there for each other at life or death moments.

The Celtic tradition places much value upon soul friends being present to one another at death. When Columba intuited that the monk Cailton would not live long, he sent a message inviting him to come to Iona to rest, 'for, loving you as a friend, I want you to end your days with me here'.

When Ciaran of Clonmacnoise was dying he waited alone in his little chapel for his soul friend Kevin of Glendalough to arrive. Unfortunately Ciaran died before Kevin arrived. However:

> Ciaran's spirit returned from heaven and re-entered his body so that he could commune with Kevin and welcome him. The two friends stayed together from the one watch to another, engaged in mutual conversation, and strengthened their friendship. Then Ciaran blessed Kevin, and Kevin blessed water and administered the Eucharist to Ciaran. Ciaran gave his bell to Kevin as a sign of their lasting unity.
>
> *The Life of Ciaran*

As we read in Chapter 7, the grief of the aging Findbarr was again renewed when Eolang, his last soul friend became terminally ill. Just before he died Eolang said to Findbarr, 'I place you under the charge and guidance of Jesus Christ himself.' When Findbarr himself became ill, he visited his friend Colman at Cloyne; he became worse and prepared for his end while on this visit. Colman sat beside his bed to the end. On 25 September 623 Findbarr yielded his soul to his Creator. His body was taken to Cork where there was a twelve-day wake. One of those at the wake, Bishop Fursey of Ferns, saw a golden ladder reaching from the tomb to heaven.

Learn to embrace death as a friend

To be fully present when we come to that time of final parting we need to have embraced death as a friend. It is said that Columba took back to Iona a clod of earth from the grave of his friend, Ciaran of Clonmacnoise, and that he took this with him wherever he went. People today, however, go to great lengths to deny the presence of death.

The Rule of Columba urged each member to prepare for their death. Columba, Cuthbert, Brendan and others were given prophecies about the time and manner of their death; they died triumphantly. A soul friend should prepare a seeker for death. That means learning to transfigure the faces of death that leer at us on our journey through life. One face is fear. Fear is rooted in the fear of death, of loss, of the unknown. Death, for a seeker who has been enabled to overcome fear, will be a meeting with a friend.

Fear flees as we become familiar with the company of heaven, and with the borderlands that form a bridge between earth and heaven. In the Celtic tradition the world of heaven was seen to be so close to the world of earth that death was thought of as an opportunity more than a threat.

A soul friend's prayers at the deathbed

In the folk memory of the nineteenth-century Hebrideans, 'the Death-croon was chanted over the dying by the anam-chara, the soul friend, assisted by three chanters'.[2] Later on the rite passed into the hands of the town elders and the mourning women who eventually sold their services as a profession.

Alexander Carmichael tells us in the *Carmina Gadelica*[3] that prayers said by a soul friend over a dying person are known as death blessing, soul leading or soul peace. The soul friend makes the sign of the cross on the person's forehead, and asks the Three Persons of the Trinity and the saints in heaven to receive the departing soul.

I pray Peter and I pray Paul
I pray Virgin and I pray Son
I pray the twelve kindly apostles to seek you and find you.

When the soul separates from the body
And goes in bursts of light
Up from out its human frame
O holy God of eternity
Come to seek and find you.

May God and Jesus aid you
May God and Jesus protect you
May God and Jesus and the gentle Spirit
Eternally seek and find you.

Sleep. sleep and away with your sorrow
The great sleep of Jesus
The restoring sleep of Jesus
The sleep of the kiss of Jesus of peace and glory.
On the arm of the Jesus of blessings
The Jesus of grace has his hand round you
In nearness to the Trinity farewell to your pains
Christ stands before you and peace is in his mind
Sleep, O sleep in the calm of all calm
Sleep, O sleep in the love of all loves
Sleep, beloved in the Lord of life
Sleep, beloved in the God of life.

May Kindly Michael, Chief of the holy angels,
Take charge of your beloved soul,
And tenderly bring it home
To the Three of limitless love,

Creator, Saviour, Eternal Life-giver.
CARMINA GADELICA (EDITED)

A soul friend may place a crucifix before the eyes of the frail or dying person. A well-known Bible passage, psalm or hymn may be read, and further prayers such as this may be repeated from time to time.

In the Name of the all-powerful Father,
In the Name of the all-loving Son,
In the Name of the enfolding Spirit
I command all spirit of fear to leave you,
I break the power of unforgiven sin in you
I set you free from dependence upon human ties
That you may be
As free as the wind,
As soft as sheep's wool,
As straight as an arrow;
And that you may journey into the heart of God.

A soul friend's presence at the deathbed

A member of staff at St Christopher's Hospice for the Dying, London, told me that three things stand out as most important to a dying person: relationship, rhythm and creation. A soul friend (even if it is a staff member who 'stands in' as a soul friend in a patient's last weeks) can encourage the dying person to talk about their nearest and dearest, what they want to say to them, when and how. Letters and messages might be conveyed through the soul friend to dear ones who cannot be present. The soul friend may draw out whether there are relatives or friends who have need to be forgiven. Perhaps the dying person can voice their hurt or their forgiveness to the soul friend.

Rhythm means much: waking and sleeping, light and dark of the day and of the seasons. The ongoingness of this life's rhythms reflects something of the other side, and provides reassurance and hope. Creation means much. A simple thing such as a ray of sun falling on a cheek becomes a cherished experience.

It is good for a soul friend to unfold memories for the one who is dying, to recall important events, to give assurance that there is nothing to fear. A dying person returns to the specialness of the moment, so it matters that we become present to the one who is dying, and become present to one's own grief only when away from the bedside.

By the side of a dying, loved friend we feel helpless. But that very helplessness can be our best gift to the helpless friend. We can stay with them in peace, saying, 'I am here,' or stroke them in wordless prayer. From time to time, out of this silence, beautiful words of prayer may be spoken.

When a soul friend can't be present at a seeker's death

In the Celtic tradition death, like life, is itself a journey. The soul takes its time to leave the body, so it is important not to let the body of the dead person be unattended. There is no arbitrary cut-off point when we must cease to pray for someone who is on our heart. Even if they die, we can continue to pray, because timing is not ours to command, it is God's.

Whenever Flann was about to engage in a battle he would go to Samthann, his local abbess and friend, for prayer. One day he went to battle without first obtaining her prayers, and he was killed. On hearing of this, Samthann called her sisters to prayer, telling them, 'Our friend Flann is being led by demons to painful places.' She fell into an ecstasy. When she awoke she said to the sisters, 'Let's give thanks to God because the soul for whom you prayed has been taken from torment to peace through our prayers and God's immense compassion.'

A child was with Maedoc (the sixth-century Bishop of Ferns, Ireland) by a large standing cross. The child saw Maedoc mount a large golden ladder which reached from earth to heaven. When Maedoc came down again the child could not look in his face for its brilliance. 'Where did you go?' the child asked him. This was his reply: 'I went with the gladness of the company of heaven to meet the soul of Columcille as it went to join them for he was my own soul friend in this world.'

The role of soul friends who are now in heaven

Make friends of the dead.

Columba

When a person is close to death, the curtain between this world and the next is sometimes drawn aside for a moment. They may become aware of presences coming near to them, friends or loved ones who have gone before them, or holy people who lived and died in the place where they are. An awesome energy can surround the moment of death.

> The life and passion of a person leaves an imprint on the ether of a place. Love does not remain within the heart, it flows out to build secret tabernacles in a landscape.
>
> *John O'Donohue*

Jesus asked us to remember, when we think about our forebears in the faith, that God is God of the living, not of the dead (Matthew 22:32). The Bible teaches us that through the birth, death and resurrection of Jesus Christ death has been vanquished; that is, it no longer becomes a barrier between us and eternity. The belief of the church in Celtic days, in relation to Christians who have died, was that they had joined an innumerable company of living witnesses to Christ (Hebrews 12:22, 23).

We find many indications in Scripture that those who have died are alert and aware of what is taking place both in heaven and on earth. This passage surely would not say that in the church's worship

171

we are in the presence of angels, God the Father, Jesus and 'the spirit of just people made complete' if these spirits were somehow inactive or unaware? They would not have been called 'witnesses' if they were unconscious of their surroundings.

There is a strand in church teaching – based on 1 Thessalonians 4:13–18, where Paul refers to those who 'sleep in Jesus' – that the soul is unconscious after death until it is awakened at Christ's second coming. This teaching did not appear until the fifteenth century, and was alien to Celtic Christians. They understood this 'sleep' to be a deep peace, a cessation of earthly activity but not of spiritual presence.

All Christians believe that there is only one mediator between God and humans – Jesus Christ. We can, and do, pray directly to God through Christ. But that does not mean that we do not need human friends who pray for us. The Scriptures frequently command us to pray for one another (e.g. 1 Timothy 2:1; Colossians 4:2–4). The saints in heaven can answer our prayers no more and no less than can our friends on earth. They have no power to answer them of their own accord; they can only plead with Christ on our behalf. Since the departed remain alive in Christ, why should they cease to express their love and concern for us in prayer? Which most reflects the nature of God, that they do or that they don't? Freed from the concerns of day-to-day survival on earth, more intimately knit to Christ than we are, they are able to intercede for us more frequently and powerfully than many an earthbound friend.

Biblical examples

The Old Testament contains rich examples of God sending messengers from heaven to believers on earth, as in the account of Abraham (Genesis 18). Jesus needed friends to strengthen him before his great trial. He was given three earthly friends (John, Peter and James) and two heavenly friends (Moses and Elijah) (Matthew 17:1–13). Through the centuries close friends of Christ in heaven have appeared to people living on earth, to strengthen them in time of need. There are, of course, the well-known apparitions of Jesus's mother. Apostles, saints or Christians who were once acquaintances on earth appear in the dreams of many people. As our culture grows more sensitive to the otherworld, it is almost commonplace for sensitive people to become aware of presences which leave impressions on the soul. I shared a meal in Glastonbury with a group most of whom had encountered presences that day. Christians will apply the test 'By their fruit you shall know them' (Matthew 7:16) to such encounters.

Later examples

The flock of Ignatius, the third Bishop of Antioch, who was thrown to the lions in about 110 AD, wept and slept together through the following night, when suddenly Ignatius appeared, embraced some and prayed for others. The company was greatly strengthened by these appearances and sang many praises to God.[4]

The night before the young Northumbrian King Oswald had to confront a barbarian army three times the size of his, Columba appeared to him, and promised that he would be protected and given victory. That he was.

The example of Monenna

When the local people of Killeevy, in sixth-century Ireland, learned that their much loved founding abbess Monenna was on her deathbed, they asked her, as those who were linked to her by blood and by the Spirit, to give them one more year of her presence with them, for they knew that God would give her whatever she asked. She replied:

> If you had asked before yesterday I would have granted your request, but from today I cannot do so. You see, the apostles Peter and Paul have been sent to guide my soul to heaven and they are here with me now. I see them holding a kind of cloth with

marvellous gold and artwork. I must go with them to my Lord who sent them. God hears your prayers. He will give a life to one of you. I pray God's blessing on your wives, children, and homes; I leave you my badger skin coat and my garden tools. I have no doubt that if you carry these with you when enemies attack God will deliver you. Do not be sad at my leaving you. For I truly believe that Christ, with whom I now go to stay, will give you whatever I ask of Him in heaven no less than when I prayed to Him on earth.[5]

Angels as soul friends

I am told that in Gaelic the 'you' in the blessing 'God be with you' is in the plural; the meaning is 'God be with you and with your guardian angel.' Many of the *Lives* of Celtic saints refer to them developing a soul friendship with an angel. Adamnan's *Life of St Columba* contains breathtaking accounts of his encounters with angels. David of Wales received significant guidance from his angel companion.

Before them was Patrick. He may have had no senior soul friends to turn to in some of the areas he laboured in. One thing he had – his guardian angel. Some years after Patrick (a slave) escaped from Ireland, he had a dream in which a figure named Victor brought letters from the Irish, urging him to 'come back and walk with us once more'. Patrick himself records this. Writers some centuries later wrote about a guardian angel who guided Patrick throughout his life, and this guardian angel became identified with the dream figure Victor.

According to the later writings, an angel used to visit Patrick every seventh day, and talked to Patrick as one person talks to another. Even during his six years as a slave it was believed that the angel talked with him some thirty times. When Patrick knew he was shortly to die he made his way to his headquarters at Armagh. But an angel came to him during his journey there and said, 'Why do you go on a journey without Victor's guidance?

Victor calls you. Change your route and go to him.' This Patrick did.

Summary
Accounts of early Irish soul friends give us insight into tender sharing and giving at the time of death. The *Carmina Gadelica* recalls a way of being fully present through gestures and words. A good soul friend, however, will do themselves out of a job, and help a seeker to become familiar with the angels and saints of Jesus in heaven.

Exercises
For soul friends and seekers

1. Ask yourself of what are you really afraid? When you can name it, your fear begins to shrink. Now place this fear on an imaginary altar, which is surrounded by a heavenly company. What happens?

2. Edward Sellner describes how a 'Cuthbert figure' recurred in his dreams, so he began, in waking life, to hold dialogues with him about the concerns of his heart.[6] Think of a saint with whom you strongly identify, and begin an imaginary dialogue.

For seekers

3. Find an unhurried time when you and your soul friend (or another person) can talk through what you would like from your soul friend on your deathbed or vice versa.

Further reading
Wilcock, Penelope, *Spiritual Care of Dying and Bereaved People* (SPCK, 1996).

Callanan, Maggie and Kelley, Patricia *Final Gifts* (Hodder & Stoughton, 1992).

Part 3

A beginner's guide to finding and becoming a soul friend

A beginner's guide to
finding and becoming a
soul friend

CHAPTER 15

CHOOSING AND CHANGING A SOUL FRIEND

Some readers may not yet have found a soul friend. If you have, or are, a soul friend, imagine you are a shy person who desires a soul friend, but that you have no idea how to go about finding one. This chapter looks at the mechanics (or is it the art?) of finding one.

Seek, and you will find.

Jesus (Matthew 7:7)

The phone rings. A voice tells me, 'I want to follow a Celtic spirituality with the help of a soul friend; please will you put me in touch with one.'

'I suggest you talk to your pastor or priest about whom you might approach,' I reply.

'Oh, he wouldn't be interested. Nobody in my church understands what this is about,' the caller replies.

'Is there a religious community within travelling distance to which you could go', I ask, 'where you could talk to a sister or brother about what soul-friending they might be able to offer?'

'I don't know any religious communities. Anyhow, a sister told a friend of mine who did visit one that she did not think the sisters were up to providing the kind of soul friendship he was looking for.'

'My problem is', I respond, 'that I know of only a handful of soul friends in your part of the country, and they are already overloaded. In any case, even if we had a long list of soul friends who are available in your area, it is highly unlikely that the right match could be made just like that. I think you need to approach this in a different way. I *can* suggest someone with whom you could talk through what your needs are, what sort of soul friend is appropriate for you, and how you might begin the process of finding the right one.'

That is a typical phone conversation, and it highlights a challenge in my work as Guardian of the Community of Aidan and Hilda. So let us explore, step by step, a more organic way of going about finding a soul friend. Before we begin, let us be still, for these steps may not be necessary. Many people already have a soul friend-in-waiting of whom they are unaware. This lack of awareness causes the potential soul friend to seem distant or unavailable. Perhaps this lack of awareness stems from fear that *such* a person could not possibly have time for you. Or may be it is the fruit of your low self-image: Such a person would not have an interest in *me*. It could be caused by overbusyness; you have never been still long enough to become aware of that mysterious chemistry that draws one soul to another.

Regard this search for a soul friend as part of your spiritual journey. Discard conditioning which makes you falsely prejudge where you are likely to find one: Only among priests? Only from my particular church stream? Only among older or learned persons?

Look at it from God's angle. There are people all around you of varying personalities and aptitudes. Some of these have an aptitude for listening. Some distil wisdom beyond their years; they may not even know they do this. Some of these will have wisdom, but they have not yet discovered the Trinity. But some have. Observe the people you are with now. Which of them do you sense has such aptitudes in greatest measure? Talk to them. Ask them about the people who guide or inspire them. Is there a lead to follow? Maybe not this time. Keep observing, talking and looking for leads. Go on a retreat and meet a new group of people. Sooner or later you will be led to a person with whom you can explore soul friendship.

If we go out to a wild place alone, and we wait in stillness, how often do we find that a bird or animal becomes aware of us, and we of them? It can be like that in finding a soul friend. Try going away to a place apart, where your spirit relaxes in a prayerful rhythm. Let the kaleidoscope of people who have ever entered the horizons of your life flow through your mind and heart. Is there a person, however well or little you know them, who resonates in the deep places? Think through whether there is any good reason why you should not approach them. There may be, in which case desist. Or is it that you fear rejection? Ask their help in a way that does not put pressure on them. For example, you could write to them as follows, enclosing a checklist (see the Exercise at the end of this chapter): 'I need help in finding an appropriate soul friend and wonder if you would consider being my soul friend, or else discuss with me other people I might approach?'

If you have done this, and it has not so far yielded fruit, then it is time to take the steps that follow.

Step 1: Get clear what sort of soul friend you need

Choosing a soul friend is a very personal decision. We may each want a soul friend for different reasons according to particular circumstances.

Soul friends come in many shapes and sizes, and we should be open to someone becoming our soul friend who does not fit our preconceptions. This person is not your type physically? You may have to make a mental adjustment, but once you have made it, do you think you can live with it? The same principle applies if the potential soul friend is of a different temperament to you; perhaps you are an extrovert and the potential soul friend is an introvert, or vice versa. We may look for someone with similar experience to ourselves, whereas it may prove to be more rewarding to open up our lives to someone with contrasting experience.

Most new seekers need a soul friend of the same gender, since it prevents physical attractions distorting the spiritual process; but some older people, or seekers who are not attracted to the opposite sex, may welcome a soul friend of either gender. No two people want exactly the same thing from a soul friend. One person may be quite content to have as their soul friend a mature Christian friend who is a good listener, and who will meet with them a few times each year; another person feels the need for a well-trained soul friend, who has learned about different forms of Christian prayer and spirituality. One person seeks a soul friend who will always be there for them; another person needs to make formal confession of sins to a priest, and wants that priest also to be their soul friend.

There is a wide spectrum of needs and of soul friends who meet those needs. If you already know someone who fits the bill for you, there is no need to delay in explaining to them clearly what you hope for, and asking them if they will respond. If your need for a problem to be solved dominates your life, fix up with a counsellor first. To find one, contact a Citizens Advice Bureau (CAB), a priest or pastor, or look in the *Yellow Pages* telephone directory. Once that problem is being addressed, continue your search for a soul friend.

It is usually best to have a soul friend who is not involved in your own sphere of work or church ministry. If you wish to talk about a difficulty in this work, they may have views about this that prevent them focussing objectively on your own spiritual journey.

Beware of choosing someone who will only ever be nice to you and who will never confront you. Remember the advice given by Mael Ruain in Chapter 12. You should 'seek out the fire which will most fiercely burn,' that is, which will spare you the least. The most successful soul friends may well be those who initially know you least and who can ask questions without becoming involved in the situation.

As we have seen, most people who seek a soul friend require someone who is mature, warm, understanding, close to God, a good listener, and who can keep confidences. Other desired characteristics will vary according to the needs of the seeker. Write down the three qualities that you put at the top of your list. Now add any other qualities which for you are important in a soul friend.

Step 2: Talk to someone who can advise you about your choice

Is there a priest or pastor in your area with whom you could talk about your need for a soul friend? If this is 'not their scene', why not go to a religious community for suggestions? If you belong to a wider church stream, try them. An increasing number of Anglican and Roman Catholic dioceses now have in a place a spiritual direction network; an enquiry at the diocesan office or to the bishop's chaplain may yield results. A friend of mine just turned up at a cathedral and asked for a spiritual director; he was not disappointed. In Britain the National Retreat Association[1] can give you a contact person in your region with whom you can discuss your need for a soul friend.

Step 3: Have a trial period

It makes sense to have a year's trial period at the end of which both seeker and soul friend review whether they are right for each other. It may be that temperaments are not compatible, circumstances change, the seeker finds this is not actually what they want to pursue, or the soul friend does not resonate with the seeker. There is no shame in acknowledging this. That is the value of a trial run for both persons, either of whom may feel somebody else is more appropriate for the next stage.

When Donan, the leader of a community on the island of Eigg, asked Columba if he would be his soul friend, the saint declined, saying it was not fitting that he should be *anamchara* of one destined to be a red martyr. This revealed unusual discernment of spirit, since some twenty years after Columba's own death, Donan and about fifty monks were massacred by Viking invaders on Easter Day.

Columba may have felt that he had nothing to offer a person whose 'martyrdom' was more total than his own 'green martyrdom'. Or he may have felt that he should not take on further responsibilities and, whereas with another person he would have made an exception, out of concern for their eternal destiny, in Donan's case he was assured that his eternal destiny was secure.

In order to test out the suitability of a soul friend it can be useful to become aware of different types of personality and of their compatibility. The Enneagram is one way to do this. Those who come out as types 2, 3 or 4 in an Enneagram test tend at all costs to want to create a good impression. If a soul friend is not to collude with a seeker of this type, the soul friend should either have got free of a compulsion to impress, or be of a different temperament.

Enneagram 2s may feel so hollow inside that they question who they really are. So they put up defences, perhaps of jokey or cynical banter, or of psychosomatic complaints, in order to prevent anyone, including a soul friend getting near to the hollowness that they hide from. A soul friend needs to stay with the seeker through all this. Some types of soul friend will feel instinctively that this is wasting time. If you are impatient with this type of person, you are probably not the best person to be a soul friend to them.

Here is a checklist to use when you review your trial period:

- Have you got anywhere?
- Are you at ease with one another?
- Do you feel affirmed?
- Can you say the things you most want to say?
- Are you challenged, informed, stimulated or stretched?

If the answer is mostly 'no', it may well be wise to change your soul friend. Otherwise, why not continue?

Step 4: Be mutually committed

In the Egyptian desert, as we saw in Chapter 4, the loyalty a disciple owed an abba or amma was nearly absolute. It is as important for a seeker as for a soul friend to prove trustworthy. Mutual self-giving and respect provide the right seedbed for growth. Once the trial period has been completed, and a mutual commitment has been made, it is important to remain true to that for the foreseeable future, other things being equal.

Step 5: Consider bad and good reasons for changing a soul friend

Other things may not in all circumstances be equal. Bad reasons for changing a soul friend are that they cross our will, or put their finger on things that we do not want to face, or refuse to collude with the mental 'games' we play, or have an off day, or are not well connected, or are not as interesting as some new soul friend who becomes available. Each of us needs a soul friend who will hold us to the highest and help us not to collude with the renegade within us. So if a seeker announces a wish to sever the relationship, the soul friend should suggest a review before a parting takes place. The soul friend should search out if the seeker is running away from something, and make sure the new soul friend is contacted.

It can be appropriate to consult different advisors, of course, as do many people in government, education and business. At certain times a seeker may need to have recourse to a therapist, a counsellor, a vocational advisor, a pastor, or a confessor as well as to a soul friend. But it is unwise, and unfair to the soul friend, to do work together upon the deepest intimacies of the soul with more than one person at the same time. This causes confusion and fails to show the respect due to a soul friend.

There *are* good reasons for changing a soul friend, for example if the soul friend becomes inaccessible, perhaps through illness or preoccupation with other things, through disobedience to God, or through moving elsewhere.

There are rare but beautiful soul friendships, often between two people with equality of experience and insight, which flower into lifetime friendships; but, because one of them moves far away, each needs also a locally accessible 'working' soul friend. If that is the case, this should be explained to the local soul friend.

There is a more subtle reason for making a change. We should expect to grow. We may begin to journey to places which our soul friend neither knows about nor has a feel for. In the body of Christ there are ears, eyes, hands, noses and feet. We may need to find another member of that body who can travel with us for a season. Antony, once he had laid the groundwork of purity, sought out different soul friends over his long life. He did this, his biographer Athanasius tells us, because he wanted to learn different virtues from each; he 'observed the graciousness of one, the eagerness for prayers in another, freedom from anger and the human concern of another – getting attributes of each in himself, and striving to manifest in himself what was lost from all'.[2]

Few of us are likely to work through all the things we can learn from one soul friend, let alone several, so assiduously as Antony because, unlike him, we live in a frenetic society. We would be wise to take this to be a principle that we apply most sparingly. So we should not change a soul friend lightly or quickly, or we could be out of the frying pan and into the fire. In the process we could be causing havoc with the psychic energy of those we ask to help us. It may be better to honestly explain our felt needs to our soul friend, and explore together how best to proceed, perhaps taking a sabbatical leave from our soul friend, which might or might not become permanent.

Ultimately, as the following story shows, each seeker must take responsibility for their own decisions:

A brother questioned Abba Poemen, saying, 'I am losing my soul through living near my abba; should I go on living with him?' The old man knew that he was finding this harmful and he was surprised that he even asked if he should stay there. He came back again and said, 'I am losing my soul.' But the old man did not tell him to leave. He came a third time and said, 'I really cannot stay there any longer.' Then Abba Poeman said, 'Now you are saving yourself; go away and do not stay with him any longer,' and he added, 'When someone sees that they are in danger of losing their soul, they do not need to ask advice.'[3]

Step 6: Make the change decently

A new soul friend does well to check out that the former soul friend has given their blessing. We can learn from our friend Mael-Ruain of Tallaght (Chapter 12) who pointed out that master craftspeople do not like those they are training to go to another craftsperson for instruction, so why should we expect soul friends to be any more happy with this practice? It was only when his applicant, Mael Dithruib, assured him that he had first obtained his soul friend's permission to transfer that Mael Ruain accepted him, after which Mael Dithruib submitted to his authority.[4]

Exercise
A checklist for a seeker to fill in or for a soul friend to give to an enquirer who wants help in finding a soul friend

Do you want* your soul friend to be

male □ female □ ordained □ in a religious order □ older than yourself □
someone you don't otherwise have contact with □
grounded in a particular tradition (e.g. Catholic, evangelical, charismatic) □

*Only tick those things you are definite about. Write details where appropriate.

trained in a particular field of prayer or personality indicator ☐
available outside scheduled meetings, e.g. through phone or mail ☐
within an area that is accessible to you ☐ without charge ☐
someone who listens ☐ prays with you ☐ remains formal ☐

Do you want

help in organising your time and working out your priorities ☐
help to work out what your are really thinking/feeling ☐
help to develop spiritual life and understanding ☐
help to make decisions, e.g. on changing work ☐
help in obtaining skills or knowledge ☐

CHAPTER 16

QUALITIES AND DISCIPLINES
OF A SOUL FRIEND

This chapter explores qualities a seeker might expect to find in a soul friend. Clarity about these will help would-be soul friends to nurture these qualities in themselves. To do this, they need to develop disciplines and knowledge, and these too are explored.

> A person is competent to be a soul friend when they can answer for their own soul first and can correct themselves.
>
> *Columbanus*

What qualities should a seeker look for in a soul friend? I often invite groups studying soul friendship to write down the qualities they think are most important. One group drew up the following list:
Soul friends should be

- vulnerable (loving is painful)
- free to risk the relationship
- aware of short- and long-term goals
- aware of their own limitations
- able to create a space for the other

- prepared to challenge
- open to and able to listen well to the other person
- someone with whom we can freely share our deepest thoughts.

The list that follows consists of the ten most important qualities that I have gleaned from the experience and reflection of a cross-section of people.

1. Acceptance

A seeker needs to feel that they can open themselves up to their soul friend, warts and all, without causing the soul friend to bristle or throw a wobbly. The seeker needs to know that there is nothing about themselves that they dare not talk about with their soul friend; they need to feel at ease about sharing their deepest thoughts. In order for a soul friend to be at ease with the seeker, the soul friend must be at ease with themselves. A soul friend who does not know themselves, including their own shadow side, will be no help to the seeker, because the seeker may trigger things within them that they have not come to know or accept. If that happens, the soul friend may become defensive, and try to keep the seeker at a distance, to project things on to the seeker, or to condemn.

To accept a person does not mean that you accept as good everything that they do or believe. The soul friend is there in order that the seeker may off-load their burden. The very fact that the seeker is off-loading suggests that they already know that what they do is not right; so they do not need to know the soul friend's moral views at that point. At that moment they need, above all else, to know that they are accepted.

This quality of acceptance models God's attitude to each of us: 'While we were yet sinners, Christ gave himself for us (Romans 5:8)'. Acceptance springs from humility, which is the basis of all spirituality, for it acknowledges human limitations.

The soul friend needs to be able to accept the temperament of the seeker. For example, seekers of type 2 in the Enneagram, tend to shy away from any feeling that they are being pigeonholed or analysed. So in this case a soul friend should not come to a session with a predetermined agenda, and should not recap and clarify as would be appropriate with other people. The soul friend should create a free and unstructured climate rather than focus on the seeker too much.

The soul friend needs to be unshockable. In my time outwardly conventional people have confessed to killing, adultery, secret suicide attempts; I once even had someone arrive at night dressed up as a transvestite. Treat all such confessions in a matter-of-fact way. They have happened, so you can do nothing to prevent what has happened. The point now is to address in a workmanlike way the needs these confessions reveal. Nothing is worse than to communicate a sense of disappointment in the seeker, who is actually risking much at that moment in order not to be a continuing disappointment to themselves. Emotional reactions by a soul friend merely add to the baggage that has to be discarded before headway can be made.

2. Accessibility

A person who surrounds themself with too much fuss, busyness or protocol spoils their chances of being a good soul friend. A shy seeker can be inhibited from intruding upon their time, even though, in reality, any time they would have spent together might have been more worthwhile than what took its place.

Although accessibility is often included in a list of qualities seekers desire in a soul friend, the seeker must beware of trying to eat the goose that lays the golden egg. A good soul friend will certainly be 'fully present' to you when you meet, and will change their schedule to meet some really genuine need, but the function of a soul friend is not that of, say, a good neighbour, or a pastoral carer.

There is a limit to the number of people we can make ourselves available to. Jesus made himself available, sometimes night and day, to twelve people for a period of three years. Jesus had other dear friends, but he did not make himself available to them on the basis of their requests. A classic example of this is Jesus's decision not to respond to the plea of Mary and Martha to visit their brother Lazarus when he was terminally ill (John 11:5, 6). Henri Nouwen, who wrote about Jesus's 'creative absences', pointed out that absences can be used as much as presences when they are in the will of God.

Some soul friends work on the basis of scheduled meetings only, while others are happy for the soul friendship to include spontaneous meetings; whichever is the basis, the soul friend needs to be accessible in spirit.

3. Confidentiality

Many more people would use a friend close at hand as their confidant if it were not for the fact that confidentiality is so necessary. For, with the best will in the world, it is hard to expect something to be kept confidential if the person in whom you have just confided one thing will soon be chattering with your mutual friends, or with their spouse, about all sorts of other things. Our lives are like jigsaw puzzles, and people deduce one thing from another. That is a reason for choosing as your soul friend, not just a friend, but someone who lives outside your immediate circle, or one who is professionally trained to keep confidences.

Sometimes a seeker shares things with their soul friend which are public knowledge, but mixed up with this is something which in their mind is not. Even a seasoned soul friend can sometimes unwittingly pass on information imparted in this way, not suspecting that it was shared in confidence. So, if a seeker is sharing with a soul friend in a general way, the seeker has a responsibility to make clear when something is to be kept confidential. A soul friend who is in any doubt might, at the close of a session, itemise the things that are thought to be confidential.

4. Attentiveness

This is a quality that portrait and landscape painters develop. They cultivate careful observation of both the overall feel and the details of their subject. A soul friend is attentive to the mood of the seeker on arrival, to the situation from which the seeker has emerged, to the strength or weakness indicated by their voice. Is there something difficult that the seeker wants to 'get out'? Or does the seeker actually want a bit of relaxing conversation? This quality is explored further in Chapter 19.

5. Respect

A good soul friendship provides time for trust, love and recollection to grow. There should be no possessiveness or clutching in the relationship, but a respect for the word that God may speak through the other. The seeker should not be dismissive of the soul friend because of any weakness, blind spots or ignorance. The soul friend should not be put on a pedestal or bound to a system imposed by the mind of the seeker. A soul friend should intercede for the seeker, and neither seek to pre-empt the way the Holy Spirit is working in a seeker nor expect the seeker to adopt the soul friend's ways, and vice versa. There is no place for repression, or shame before others.

6. Maturity

Most people lack the maturity needed to be a soul friend until they pass into the second half of life. Soul friends should have followed the journey with Christ for some years. There are exceptions to this rule; occasionally a person young in years has an innate wisdom, or is given a particular grace by God. Conversely, some people have existed longer than others, but they have not 'lived' longer, and despite their age would not make a suitable soul friend.

7. Reliability

A soul friend can appear unreliable to a seeker in a number of ways. First, if their body language or lack of attentiveness betray the fact that their own moods or agendas intrude upon their work of soul befriending. Second, if they too often change their appointments for reasons that are not sound, such as bad organisation, confusion about their priorities, or for reasons that are not made clear. Third, if they lose their cool, or talk too loosely about others, so that either their behaviour or their judgment seems unreliable. Fourth, if they become impatient. Fifth, if they cannot respond to an emergency without passing on panic or frustration to the seeker. For example, if in a genuine crisis a seeker rings for advice or asks for a meeting at short notice, and the soul friend is also under pressure, it is important that the soul friend explains in a clear, calm way what they can or cannot offer; and that they can suggest some step that the seeker can take even if they themselves are not available.

8. Discernment

The soul friend seeks to discern the patterns of the Spirit in the heart of the seeker. Although the Spirit's patterns in different people have some common resemblances from which we can learn, these patterns are unique to each individual, for God calls each one to walk their own special path. So the soul friend should not let their own preconceived ideas – for example, about behaviour or belief patterns – cloud their perception of what the Spirit is doing in the seeker. I have had to learn the lesson over and over again that God can work in people whose ways I do not approve of. Remember, Jesus told us that he did not come to serve respectable people, but those who were not (Mark 2:17). God starts where people are, and sometimes they are in a slimy pit, in a dysfunctional syndrome, or have a distorted understanding of God.

You may feel that you don't have great skills of discernment. For example, I do not know whether a person in a mid-life crisis needs medicine, a change from a pressured job, or to dig deep into hidden insecurities. But as I share in the seeker's own process of asking questions and trying different approaches, I can be the listening presence alongside, which helps the seeker to discover the way forward for themselves.

You may feel that you do not have a gift of 'seeing' such as that which enabled people like Columba to know exactly what sins someone was coming to confess! Perhaps, if there were enough such saints to go round, the rest of us could leave soul befriending to them, but there are not enough such people. (And if there were, I wonder whether all of us would wish to have them as our soul friend?)

The experience of Seraphim of Sarov, the nineteenth-century Russian hermit, encourages me. A seeker asked him how it was that he knew exactly what was in a person's thoughts, and exactly what he should say to that person. Seraphim replied that he had no idea! He simply spoke whatever the Holy Spirit put in his mind, and trusted that it would be right for the person. He spoke what he was given, but did not know what targets his words were hitting!

Of course, the Holy Spirit worked through Seraphim in that way because the things from his own psyche had been purified by constant vigil and contemplation. His ego was pure and was one with God's. That is why nobody should be a soul friend who is not prepared to spend prime time alone with God.

The discernment of spirits comes through the constant practice of purifying one's own spirit, there is nothing extraordinary about it. Wisdom can come from books; for certain seekers, a soul friend who is well read seems appropriate, but the essence of wisdom is to be found, not in books, but in observation.

9. Honesty

The seeker should not expect the soul friend to unburden themselves in detail in the way the seeker has, because that is not the purpose of the time together. In any case, the soul friend will have done this with their own soul friend. On the other hand, the soul friend should not just dispense advice and share nothing of themselves. The seeker needs to know that the soul friend can be vulnerable. The soul friend may share some current concern during small talk at the start of the session; or the soul friend may share some experience of their own journey which helps the seeker to realise that they are not alone in their struggle, or which throws light on the ways of God.

The soul friend should be willing to tell the seeker any necessary home truths, but should never rush into this. It is essential first to establish a relationship of trust and respect. A soul friend should never 'crush a bruised reed'.

As they get to know one another, a prevailing habit may become apparent to the soul friend which the seeker, having known nothing different, has not questioned. Perhaps, for example, the seeker exhibits a critical spirit, or belittles themselves, or talks big but never puts these thoughts into action. It can be helpful if, in a matter-of-fact way, and at a time when the seeker is not preoccupied with other things, the soul friend points this out.

The ability to listen in a non-directive way is vital, but it is not everything. A soul friend should certainly not say everything they feel in their heart, because some of this belongs to them or to others, but is not appropriate for the seeker at that time. But sometimes the soul friend will become aware of a conviction which is meant to be shared with the seeker, but which the seeker does not seem to have picked up themselves. This might be a commonsense conviction, or a practical suggestion, or a piece of wisdom, or a verse from the Bible.

10. Humanity

Warmth, compassion, understanding and responsiveness all appear on lists of qualities people desire in soul friends. To the extent that these are inborn we cannot command them. But often people who seem to lack these qualities are in fact merely failing to express them. Shyness, conditioning and lack of practice inhibit the growth of these qualities. A soul friend should be a person who can be gentle, who is no longer at war with themselves, who is growing.

If you are a would-be soul friend, but feel you lack these qualities, do not give up. It is possible to cultivate them. Pay attention to your prayers: Visualise Christ the Sun warming your friends. Pay attention to your meditation: Contemplate Christ's compassionate heart becoming one with yours, and offer this to everyone you meet. Pay attention to your conversations: Practise echoing back what you think you have understood. Pay attention to your body language: When you are sitting with someone, lean towards them, maintain eye contact, and make sure you *show* that you are responding.

Disciplines

Not every would-be soul friend needs to acquire learning from books, but every soul friend needs to practise spiritual disciplines. These enable a potential soul friend to develop the desirable qualities. True soul friends are not found 'in ivory palaces', however lofty or erudite their words or writings may be; they are found among those who live the life of prayer. Those who merely talk or write about spiritual disciplines fall into the category of those Jesus referred to as 'the blind leading the blind' (Matthew 15:14).

The experience of the desert fathers and mothers throws light upon this. Some of them were well versed in theology, but people who wanted primarily to acquire knowledge were more likely to go to a teacher in a city. Others had no books, but had acquired the wisdom of nature and of everyday experience. As we have noted, Abba Arsenius, who was learned in Latin and Greek, went to an Egyptian peasant for counsel. 'I do not even have the basics of the knowledge this peasant has,' he observed.

Nevertheless, we live in a society of mass education. Every soul friend should be an active learner. The Latin word for 'discipline' is the same as that for 'discipling' or 'learning' (*disciplina*), which reminds us that we cannot separate discipline from learning. Some will develop their learning through reading or courses of study; others will grow in wisdom through meditation on Scripture, life and nature. What follows is a kind of syllabus. Not every soul friend need be schooled in each subject, but some should be, and all should be aware of it. Many a seeker will use a soul friend without expecting to be introduced to a syllabus like this. So in some cases the syllabus will bear fruit mainly in the growth in the soul friend's mental and spiritual stature. In other cases, where a long-term and wholistic relationship has taken root, a seeker will want to link the exploration of their personal way with the exploration of this wider, ancient and communal way.

A syllabus

The Bible

The Bible is many wonderful things to many people. To a soul friend it can be cherished as the Book of Journeys. From it we learn about the journey of the human race, the journey of a people, the journey of humankind's ultimate representative Jesus Christ; and we learn about the God-shaping of men, women and children of every type and circumstance.

The book of Exodus yields many lessons about detachment. The psalms, as Calvin observed, are 'a mirror of the soul'. The book of Acts and the epistles tell us about the way of Christians. In short, the Bible is an ever-living source of wisdom for spiritual direction. We should ponder it every day. Sometimes words from the Bible will come to a soul friend's mind which are to be shared with the seeker, perhaps to console, challenge, affirm or envision.

Celtic Christians memorised the psalms and the Gospels, and meditated on them as they did so. Today schemes abound for daily Bible reading and for Bible study; soul friends should be aware of these and use and commend them as appropriate. They also do well to learn and reflect upon the creeds of the Church.

Ways of praying

During the course of the first two millennia of Christianity, schools of prayer have developed under the inspiration of certain great saints. Some of these have grown into religious orders, movements, or classic spiritualities which are accessible to anyone.

The classic way of praying and of meditating upon Scripture which began in the first millennium is known as the *Lectio Divina* (meaning the sacred reading). We read the chosen passage through thoughtfully several times, chew over those bits which ring bells for us, allow prayers of sorrow, praise and request to arise out of the reading, and then relax in the presence of God.

The Celtic stream which seemed to go underground in the eleventh century seems to surface again in the twelfth and thirteenth centuries with St Francis of Assisi (eleventh and twelfth century) who prayed by meditating on God in creation, and in a renewed mystical tradition. Exemplars of this are Rhineland mystics such as Hildegaard of Bingen (twelfth century) and Meister Eckhart (thirteenth and fourteenth century), and fourteenth-century English mystics such as Julian of Norwich and Richard Rolle.

St Teresa of Avila (sixteenth century) and the Carmelite movement has stressed contemplative prayer. St Ignatius Loyola (sixteenth century) developed imaginative meditation exercises on Scripture. St Francis de Sales (sixteenth and seventeenth century) taught people to pray by meditating upon God in the ordinary workplace. William Law's *A Serious Call to the Devout and Holy Life* (eighteenth century) fostered a movement of moral disciplines, ordered prayer and meditation among British Protestants. Appendix 2 contains a list of relevant books.

In recent years we have learned more about which approaches to prayer best suit different personality types.[1] Imaginative contemplation suits certain temperaments (e.g. the SJ Myers-Briggs type). In this form of prayer we step into an episode in Scripture and, using all our five senses, imagine we were there and how we are changed. A person of another temperament will project the experience they read about in Scripture on to their present situation (NF type).

The SP type may find that communing with God through creation is most helpful; while the NT type will use the mind more, asking questions such as what? why? when? how? who? about a Scripture passage.

Knowledge of good and evil

This involves knowledge of the seven deadly sins and the seven contrasting virtues and ways of discerning and combating these, much of which was covered in Chapters 4 and 6. A soul friend should practise and commend confession, repentance, restitution and the processes of inner healing. A soul friend should aim to become familiar with the gifts of the Spirit, the discernment of spirits, and the methods used in spiritual warfare. These things should not be forced, they can be learned as the soul friend goes along.

Readers who are 'post-modern children' may have questions about this area of the syllabus. A post-modern Christian might believe that

- to live together as an unmarried couple is more honest and responsible than to marry before knowing whether the relationship will work;
- to choose to be a lone mother is good, because it saves baby and mother from infringements a husband might impose;
- a practising homosexual partnership is good because it has more love in it than a partnership involving a person of the opposite sex;
- Christians should not impose values, propose rules or suggest that others are wrong;
- everyone should be free to follow their own way so long as it does not harm others.

A soul friendship is attractive to this post-modern approach in one respect: it is concerned with the individual path of the seeker rather than with public morality. But a soul friend in the Celtic tradition cannot pretend that a seeker can develop wholeness without facing up to issues of good and evil. True, the old way of presenting these issues, as standardised rules and punishments, does not speak to post-modern seekers. They reject value judgments made by representatives of fallible, out-of-touch institutions as hypocritical and valueless. A soul friend therefore has to reinterpret this tradition.

A way to do this is to frequently ask a seeker how their individual choices will affect the web of life. Natural (quite apart from Christian) wisdom teaches that a baby, born out of the sexual union of a man and a woman, is meant by nature to be offered the wholeness made possible by a father and a mother's dependable care. Thus we need to ask of every act: Does it violate nature's or God's purpose for this sexual organ, for the human community, for the human species, for the creatures, for the plants, for the soil?

Down-to-earth wisdom

Down-to-earth wisdom has been missing from the resource bank of church spiritual directors in recent centuries; it is vital to recover it. For the Jews, and therefore for Jesus, wisdom was the third partner in their threefold tradition of the law, the prophets and wisdom. Desert and Celtic Christians did not lose this, but Western Christianity in the second millennium did lose it.

Columbanus taught seekers that 'the person who tramples the world tramples themselves'. It follows that in order not to trample, that is, not to violate the natural and human world, we have to become familiar with it. Earth and the heavens have their own wisdom. This does not mean that soul friends should teach science to their seekers! It does mean that they should encourage the habit of observation of the creation that is around them by day and by night. It seems that certain rhythms and patterns with which God has endowed creation are archetypes of rhythms and patterns in human beings which God intends us to co-operate with. Primal peoples know that they are connected to the earth and to the web of life, and this brings humility. Without this knowing it is not possible to find wholeness. This we can learn from them.

A member of a new church runs a Christian bookshop. He discovered that biblical Jews devote themselves to three things – wisdom, knowledge and understanding. He also understood that these were three manifestations of the Trinity, so he dedicated his life to the pursuit of them. He befriended customers who followed New Age practices and told them of this. One of them, a druid, said: 'I have never met a Christian before who is dedicated to wisdom. Will you please spend time with me; I need to talk with a person who has wisdom.' Not all modern druids are nutcases or occultists; some of them have a deep love of the earth and are steeped in the wisdom of the earth and of nature. We can learn from them. It is important that they find soul friends who are Christians, just as did the early druids.

Knowledge of human ways is another aspect of wisdom. A soul friend in the Celtic tradition seeks to learn both from the rhythms of the earth and from the rhythms of human life. Wisdom is at home with the body, it develops a canny sense, and a practical know-how in human relations. Maybe you have no mind for academic pursuits, but you want to improve your awareness of down-to-earth problems? You could do worse than to read the advice of some of the more sensible agony aunts.[2]

Personal disciplines

Many a seeker will use a soul friend who is not expert in all these fields. Whether or not you are called to study any of these matters in a formal way, there can be no doubt that every soul friend needs to develop their own spiritual disciplines.

What exactly is a spiritual discipline? It is something you do regularly, as a priority, which trains your spirit, mind and body. Spiritual disciplines include prayer; meditation; abstinence from excess food, sleep, TV, etc.; self-examination and confession of sins; solitude; study; acts of service; worship.

These disciplines are means to an end. The end is knowledge and mastery of self, union with God and the conquest of all that distracts from or destroys this. A soul friend, first and foremost, is someone who daily dedicates themself to their own inner journey. The spiritual journey has to be lived. It has to be worked at daily. It has to be an experience that is shared, not just an idea that is broadcast.

How people live this fundamental spiritual discipline will be as varied as is the immense tapestry of human beings with which God has peopled the earth. There needs to be a dedication to some discipline in things such as prayer and Bible reading. But undergirding all particular disciplines will be one discipline that is common to all: reflection. A spiritual guide has to be someone who contemplates the Giver of life rather than attempts to control life. Some will contemplate in a cloistered way, others will contemplate 'on the job', but without the contemplation, all is lost; the inner person becomes vacuous.

All sound education is exposure to greatness.

Robert Hutchens

We are in the presence of greatness whenever we are in the presence of a person who contemplates. Be they somebodies or nobodies in this world's eyes, if they are contemplating they are royal souls, and something of the greatness of God's majesty shines through every humble soul. *That* is the essence of soul friendship.

Don't let lack of discipline deter you

Many people dismiss the idea of being a soul friend because they feel they lack the qualities and disciplines we have touched upon in this chapter. That is a mistake.

Think of people you know who have just become Christians, or who are immature. They need a person who is on hand to give them a helping hand, but they often cannot find such a person. Soul friends should certainly be willing to learn, but they can do this as they hold out the helping hand. They can learn about different ways of praying, and how to become more aware, as they journey. They can allow incipient gifts within them to unfold within the soul-friend relationship. It is good that they start where they are, sharing up to their experience, not beyond it. They have no need to pretend to be what they are not. That is the joy of the Celtic tradition; you don't have to be clever, or to have 'arrived' to be a soul friend. There must be many people who have these qualities to whom it has never occurred that they might become soul friends.

Summary

To become a soul friend we need to develop warmth, insight and trustworthy qualities. It helps to become familiar with the resource bank of Christian spirituality through the centuries. We also need to bring reflective prayer to bear on our motives, actions and relation-ships. We need to put in place sound, everyday routines which help us to do this. We should not be daunted, for we can start where we are.

Exercises
For actual or potential soul friends

1. If you have not already done so, make your own list of the qualities you think a soul friend should have. Number these in order of priority. How many of these qualities do you think you possess? Now ask a close friend to answer the same question about you.

2. Think about yourself (or, if this seems apt, about someone else who is a soul friend) and give yourself a mental score, allocating ten points to each of the above ten qualities. Do not expect soul friends to get 100 per cent. On the other hand, a score of less than 50 per cent may indicate that a person should work on developing these qualities before taking on the formal role of a soul friend.

3. Work on your weakest area – the quality which received the lowest score. Meditate on a New Testament story in which Christ

embodies this quality. Decide on an exercise which can make this weak area stronger. For example, practise the presence of Christ by making your emotional responses one with his.

4. Think about the syllabus above. Talk through with your own soul friend ways of developing your knowledge in one or more of these areas.

Further reading
Foster, Richard, *Celebration of Discipline* (Hodder & Stoughton, 1980).

CHAPTER 17

PRINCIPLES AND GROUND RULES FOR ACCOMPANYING OTHERS

We cannot escape the play of opposites, and the art of being human is the ability to honour both sides, thus not taking either to extremes. Like the ebb and flow of the tides, we need to weave the polarities of life into a creative pattern and rhythm.

Geraint ap Iorwerth[1]

If we are to make ultimate sense of our lives, all the disparate elements in us have to be integrated around call.

Elizabeth O'Connor[2]

Principles

1. Divine love

Part 2 of this book illustrated twelve facets of the Celtic soul-friendship tradition. Undergirding them all is a passion that human beings are true to the image of God that is within them, and thus reflect the unconditional love of the Three Persons of the Trinity. The Celtic tradition does not divorce spirituality from humanness; it understands that we <u>become more fully human by coming closer to God</u>. It has no place for self-improvement for

become more fully human by coming closer to God

purely utilitarian reasons; nor has it a place for piety which makes a person less than human. The dedication of the seeker's will to God is the *sine qua non* of their spiritual journey which a soul friend facilitates. For the Celtic soul friend recognises that our deepest reality is as a spiritual being with a mind and a body. To live apart from God ultimately affects our mental and physical wellbeing, and this has a chain effect upon our environment. Spiritual direction without God is a lost cause.

2. Flow

Just as the Celtic way of mission is to go with the flow of culture, so the Celtic way of mentoring is to go with the flow of character. A Celtic soul friend starts where people are, not where they think they ought to be. The Celtic way encourages the seeker's journey to unfold according to the unique nature of the seeker's personality and circumstances. The Celts recognised that the shape of each soul is different, and they had a profound respect for the difference and mystery of each person. A soul friend in the Celtic tradition accepts the fact that each person looks at life in a way which is different to others. Popular courses, such as those concerning Myers-Briggs and the Enneagram, which discover the different types of personality and how their dynamics can best be expressed fit well with this Celtic approach. It does not force a person into a blueprint.

For example, if the seeker works fifty hours a week in an office and spends two hours each day commuting to work, it might be better to explore how to use the lunch-hour or the commuting time more creatively, rather than to talk about a rhythm of rest in some mirage of the countryside.

Individuality is the only true gateway to blessing and potential. Flow refers not only to the personality of the seeker, but also to the personality of God.

3. Realism

In the Celtic tradition people speak from their heart and call a spade a spade. They don't button up bits that are 'not nice', they can talk about earthy and spiritual things in the same breath. Søren

Kierkegaard likened people in the West to a skater who always skirted round the edge of the ice because he feared that if he skated to the middle the ice might crack and he would drown. Skating round the edge is alien to the Celtic way; though, because we are conditioned by Western habits, a soul friend whose seeker is skating round the edges will be patient, and gradually draw out what it is they fear. The soul friend may encourage silences in which there is attentiveness to the deepest convictions of the heart, until the seeker is able to distinguish between conditioning and true convictions. The best way a soul friend can encourage a seeker to become real is to share real things about themselves.

4. Holism

Spiritual direction in the Celtic tradition is holistic. Through sin we separate ourselves from God, others and the created world. Having violated the laws of God we are fractured and dis-eased within our mind, body and spirit, and in relation to the world outside us. Spiritual direction seeks to bring the seeker into a right relationship with the physical, mental and spiritual laws of God.

A soul friend desires that the fragmented elements within the seeker are integrated; that the seeker is at home with their body and sexuality, with their emotions and creativity, with their intellect and intuition, with their surface life and their 'shadow', with their masculine and feminine (yin and yang). The soul friend and seeker together address the inner life and try to bring these polarities into balance. The aim should be that each of the seeker's senses and faculties is fully alive under the sway of God's Spirit.

Holism also means that in order to realise our full humanity we need to build a picture of our life as a whole, past and present. Once the significant jigsaw pieces of our life are present and known, the kaleidoscope shapes resolve into a pattern, and our relationship with self, God and others can be whole.

Holism also means that a person relates to the world as a whole, rather than to fragments of it as ends in themselves. So a soul friend and a seeker will explore how to prayerfully relate to money, home, work, neighbourhood and the earth. This will affect values, lifestyle and choices.

5. Accountability

It is generally assumed that a seeker gives account to the soul friend. If this is not what is expected it should be made clear at the first session. The soul friend needs to give time for trust to be established, so the early sessions may omit this element.

For what should a seeker give account? This will vary according to the nature and circumstances of the seeker, and may be mutually discussed. A seeker may give account for their use of time, talent, money, opportunity, power and sex; for their handling of weaknesses, and for their relationships in home, work, church and society. A soul friend might, at the appropriate time, ask a seeker to justify their life choices. The benefit of this is that the seeker is truly known, warts and all, by at least one person, and begins to know and be known before God.

6. Mutuality

Should the soul friend be accountable to the seeker? A soul friend should be vulnerable, and willing to share with their seeker anything that is appropriate. If a person is soul friend to a number of seekers it is not practical or helpful to spend as much time as a seeker in giving an account of their own lives. This would be repetitious, draining, and would rob the seeker of needed attention. Yet if there is space, and the seeker has the desire to receive this, the soul friend should, in addition to being accountable to their own soul friend, give some account of their use of these things to a seeker. There are, of course, all sorts of other ways in which mutuality can be expressed.

7. Openness

Human beings tend to make assumptions about everyone they meet, and soul friends are not immune from this. Styles of dress, speech or culture in the seeker trigger stereotypes in the soul friend's mind. A good soul friend rids themself of assumptions about the seeker's personality, motivation, calling and potential. The soul friend seeks to see beyond the externals of a person to the God-given treasure which is the core of their being. Spiritual directors can easily fall into another bad habit: they assume they know the prescription God wants them to give the seeker before they have truly listened to the seeker or to the Spirit. The Holy Spirit never works with any two people the same way; the Holy Spirit is always original and timely. So a soul friend needs to be attentive and open to the whispers of the Holy Spirit.

Some ground rules

These are not cast in iron; they can be adapted if there is good reason, but they have been tried and tested.

1. Have a contract

Seekers may put in writing what they expect from their soul friend. For example, one seeker may want to unload, another to clarify choices, and another may desire advice on prayer. Soul friends may state what they expect to offer. Put the two together, and there is an agreed basis. This avoids disappointed expectations caused by unexpressed assumptions.

It is best to agree at the outset how often you intend to meet, though this can be altered if needs or circumstances change. Some meet quarterly; others find short, frequent encounters serve them better. Fewer, longer meetings that enable seekers to gradually get into their feelings may be preferred. A seeker who has to make a long journey may come but once a year, and stay overnight.

2. Obtain appropriate information

The dynamics between the seeker and their parents, spouse, children, employer, social worker or doctor are frequently relevant to their journey. It might be useful for a seeker to provide a curriculum vitae, an assessment from an employer or college course leader, results of a psychological, personality type or gift detection workshop, or a letter of reference.

3. Have an agenda

It can be a good idea to establish an agenda at the beginning of each session. The soul friend may have asked the seeker to come with some reflections or jottings that follow up something in the previous session. Or on the seeker's arrival the soul friend might ask, 'Is there something you wish us to focus on?' If there is not, the soul friend might pick up something from the previous session that seemed significant and worthy of further exploration.

For a seeker who comes rarely but for an overnight stay a different kind of agenda is needed. The soul friend should mentally map out a provisional way of using the time, but ask the seeker how they envisage using the time and adapt this accordingly. Here is an example of a twenty-four-hour schedule, which will be interspersed by meals:

1. The seeker reviews their journey since the last meeting, and identifies issues to be addressed.
2. Walk, prayer.
3. Session on specific issues, prayer.
4. Space for reflection, reading, journalling, silence or sleep.
5. If the seeker is stressed, addressing of weaknesses, problems, tasks ahead. If the seeker is relaxed, a think-tank session to stimulate vision and creativity.
6. Recapitulation of spiritual issues that have been identified, things to work at, tasks to undertake, things to confess, people to release etc. Prayer, including any affirming or prophetic words.

4. Review

If an objective has been suggested, it can be reviewed and both partners can move on, avoiding red herrings. If the soul friend senses that an issue has been dealt with in the course of a session, it is good to recap and evaluate by posing a question such as: 'What have you learned?' 'What will you now do differently?' 'What is of God in this situation?'

Every year or so it is good to review whether it is felt the soul friend should continue for another year, or whether the soul friend has completed their work, or a soul friend of a different personality type, experience or gender might be more appropriate. If that is the case, explore who might be approached to be a soul friend who is suited to the next stage of the seeker's journey.

5. Centre down

On occasions, if both seeker and soul friend are instinctively aware of this need, it can help to start a session in this way. There are various ways to centre. It can be to focus on one's body, and become aware of what it is saying. The soul friend might simply suggest a time of silence in which to focus on what are the priorities from God's point of view. Some seekers may need to offload some immediate concern, or to set it aside, naming it and handing it over.

6. Check out

The soul friend needs to check out whether they are getting things right. If, as the soul friend, you are not sure whether the seeker has finished their agenda (remember the most important things are often kept till last) or has more things to discuss, ask them. Don't be afraid to admit you are not sure what should be done or said next. You might ask questions such as: 'Is this the main thing you want to talk about? If not, can we clarify how we leave this point?' 'Are you clear what you will do about it?' 'Shall we pray about this and then move on?'

7. Know when to refer to another helping agency

In the holistic Celtic tradition, other helping agencies are seen as allies, not threats. Physical, psychological and spiritual approaches all have their place in the journey towards wholeness. However, we are complex psychosomatic entities, and it is not always easy to know when a seeker's most pressing need is for another form of treatment.

How does one distinguish between the need for deliverance, inner spiritual healing, and mental treatment? Professor Andrew Sims of St James's University Hospital in Leeds, who is himself a

Christian, gave the National Schizophrenia Fellowship some clues to distinguishing between religious and psychotic experience. One test to apply to a client who claims to be hearing the voice of God about many things is: Can they hold a 'normal' conversation on another topic.[3] Another test is whether their conversation has coherence.

As regards bodily symptoms, there are now readily obtainable checklists of symptoms that can be checked out with a doctor. If the soul friend knows little about another discipline – be it medicine, psychiatry or homeopathy – the best thing is to encourage the seeker to explore possible treatments with the appropriate agent. If, for example, there is recurring depression, let both medical and emotional approaches be tried.

8. Recap and suggest a task

It is good to end a session with a recap of the key points that need to be taken hold of. The soul friend and the seeker might then decide:

- ❋ Is there something to try out, or do, which we will review when we next meet?
- ❋ Is there a Scripture for meditation which addresses the issue that has come up?
- ❋ Is there a virtue to develop in place of a vice which has been addressed?
- ❋ Is there a compulsive habit to refrain from or a relationship to restore?
- ❋ Is there something to pray for or to bless?

9. Share something of yourself

The soul friend should not seem to be a mere dispenser of spiritual pills. It should be possible, at the end of a session or over a cup of tea, to share something of what is on their own heart: a need for prayer or encouragement, or maybe a flavour of something that lies ahead.

10. Make a note after each session
Note (either mentally or in writing) what, if anything, you need to remember from that session which may form part of the next meeting's agenda.

11. Seek supervision
It is highly unlikely that a soul friend will have the temperament, experience or knowledge to meet every need of every type of personality at every stage of their journey. Sometimes the soul friend will feel stuck. When this happens, it is best to take it in one's stride, to reflect upon this, perhaps to seek out a book that relates to this.

Something more is also needed. A soul friend needs another person with whom they can check things out from time to time. Most counsellors in Britain, and many spiritual directors in the USA are now required to have regular supervision. This has not been the tradition with spiritual directors in Britain, perhaps because so many directors have been priests who are under the seal of the confessional. This absence of supervision is not tenable in a soul-friendship relationship. A priest, and any soul friend, can maintain confidentiality by giving the supervisor examples without naming the individuals concerned.

A checklist

This is a sample of a checklist we give to soul friends in the Community of Aidan and Hilda. The soul friend and seeker each have a copy and tick the items they have mutually agreed to address.

☐   Sharing of weaknesses, failings, concerns
☐   Information about the member's history, schedules, needs
☐   Frequency and length of meetings
☐   Venue (what is most conducive?)
☐   Inner journey – identify and help the member own the direction, blockages, next steps

☐ Money – how income is spent and given
☐ Sex
☐ Accountability – in work, family, church, society
☐ Study – what, how, when
☐ Retreats/pilgrimage/quiet days – what, how, when
☐ Prayer, work, rest – schedules, frustrations, options, patterns
☐ Guidance on ways of praying and spiritual disciplines
☐ Relationships – quality of, time for, dangers, boundaries, priorities
☐ Steps to greater wholeness, forgiveness, release (including non-verbal rituals)
☐ Detection and use of personality and/or gifts
☐ Challenge or prophetic input
☐ Shared silence and/or prayer
☐ Formal confession/absolution from an ordained person
☐ Suggest tasks/spiritual exercises/penances
☐ Take notes to review next session
☐ Recap points and action at end of session
☐ Tissues available
☐ Permission to take notes
☐ Other

Exercises
For a soul friend to give to a seeker

1. Make up your own checklist which you might use with a seeker.

2. Suppose a seeker wants to develop a rhythm of prayer, work and rest, but commutes to work and is away from home twelve hours each weekday. What possibilities would you explore with the seeker for developing this rhythm both at work and at home?

3. Write down several ways a soul friend can help a seeker feel that there is a mutual relationship.

4. Suppose a seeker has told you they have one of the following problems, and you are concluding the session. What questions would you ask in order to find out the cause of each problem, and what exercise would you suggest which will help the seeker develop self-mastery?

a) Too much social drinking
b) Getting overweight
c) Making nasty remarks about someone in authority
d) Working too late at night

Further reading
Miller, William, *Why do Christians Break Down?* (Augsberg, 1981).

Conroy, Maureen, RSM, *Looking into the Well: Supervision of Spiritual Directors* (Loyola Press, Chicago, 1995).

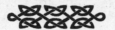

CHAPTER 18

SOME TOOLS FOR THE SOUL FRIEND

Part 2 explored the Celtic tradition of soul friendship. In Part 3 we have looked at the qualities, principles, resources and ground rules that a soul friend should espouse. But what are the means to achieve the end? In this chapter we take a look at some of the tools a soul friend can use.

Give us the tools, and we will finish the job.

Winston Churchill

The soul friend's own experience

Next to God, *you* are the greatest resource in your calling as a soul friend, a resource far, far more wonderful than anything that can be written down. Take time to get to know yourself and your journey, its turning points, blind alleys and its pools of inspiration. Pray that God will anoint the immense treasure of experience that is yours. Offer yourself in humility, in childlike attentiveness, in calm confidence. The only soul friendship that has lasting worth is that which comes out of a life of prayer.

Listening and questioning

Listening is such an important skill that we devote the whole of the following chapter to it. Questioning is a tool a soul friend should use with restraint. Do not normally interrupt a seeker, but if the seeker moves on to a new subject before you have understood the previous subject it is wise to ask a question for clarification. In order to offer true understanding to the seeker the soul friend needs to have understood correctly. Sometimes a seeker is inhibited or confused, and then it can be helpful to ask a question that gently draws out the deepest issues of the heart. Such questions can be blessings that help the seeker to see more clearly for themselves.

Confession

'Confession is good for the soul', whether it be formal confession to a priest or informal confession to any soul friend. A soul friend who is a minister outside the Catholic tradition may, on occasion, be asked by a seeker to hear their confession in the sacramental way; perhaps the seeker has read or heard about this and feels a need for it. The minister is wise to learn what to do. Information about sacramental confession is included in Appendix 2.

Evangelicals have in the past failed to recognise the value of ritual in expressing contrition. When a seeker confides some sin to a soul friend it is a moment of grace which needs to be honoured. Some seekers may be happy to pass straight on to others things after sharing a sin, with no greater acknowledgement of what they have just done than a simple 'OK', but others need to take time before moving on. A soul friend might suggest a short period of silence, followed by a prayer or a verse from the Bible. Forgiveness and release can be expressed through ritual acts such as washing, lighting a candle, holding a stone, burning written confessions, placing of scent or petals, anointing, silence.

Candles, stones and crayons

A soul friend may wish to have a supply of artefacts for use on a variety of occasions. Sometimes a seeker becomes locked in, and words dry up. Non-verbal forms of expression can unlock the heart. Provide space for reflection. Crayons can be used to paint a picture of something that words cannot express. Clay can be used to express deep feelings of anger or longing. Stones can be held in the hand and can represent significant people, possibilities or problems in the seeker's life; then they can be arranged on a table or in a corner.

Dreams

Sometimes dialogue between soul friend and seeker becomes circular and self-defeating. This may be because things in the unconscious life of the seeker need to be resolved, but the seeker is not aware of what these are. Working with dreams can provide an entrance into the unconscious. Psychologists tell us that the vast majority of dreams are about the dreamer. Some of the dreams in the Bible came to people whose psyche was an uncluttered channel for God, and these conveyed a message for others or for the nation. These are rare, though occasionally a seeker may have a dream that is used by God in such a way. More often a dream can help a seeker discover something they fear, aspire to, need to let go of, or are running away from.

Some soul friends will know nothing about working with dreams, in which case there is no need to use this tool. However, the psychiatrist C.G. Jung pointed out that the best interpreter of dreams is always the dreamer, so a soul friend may simply ask the seeker to describe a dream and to say what they think it means. Their feelings are most important.

There is a glut of books which claim to describe the meaning of symbols that commonly occur in dreams. Much of this material is superficial hype which can leave its readers more confused and self-centred than ever. C.G. Jung's work on dreams offers an altogether more profound treatment.[1]

Some dream symbols connect with symbols in myths that have power in our waking life. For example, a wild horse represents animal energy, a figure in white represents purity, a serpent or spider represents something we fear. It is said that a house represents the self and a motor car represents the ego. According to *The Little Book of Dreams*[2] boats are a symbol of our life journey, flying is a symbol of positive achievement, fish of a life force that is about to emerge. Drowning suggests insecurity, physical attacks may represent spiritual or moral attack, climbing represents ambitions, accidents may be a warning to take preventive action; weight gain in dreams points to the need for praise. Dreaming of people you don't know can be a way of confronting hidden aspects of yourself. Erotic dreams may merely indicate a need for excitement. Red points to passion or sacrifice; green to fertility or envy. Recurring dreams often mean that the message has not been understood. The setting of a dream provides crucial clues to its meaning.

The 'shadow'

The psychiatrist Carl Gustav Jung gave the name 'shadow' to that part of our inner life that is unacceptable to us. It has always existed, of course, under other names. It is the collection of uncivilised desires and feelings which have no place in a cultured society. It is everything we don't want to be; or, perhaps it is what we would wish but do not dare to be. This has damaging results. In his book *Why do Christians break down?* William Miller admits: 'I break down because I am afraid to admit that evil, unacceptable, inappropriate tendencies still exist within me, even though I have committed myself to the way of Christ, and I cannot accept them as being truly part of me.'[3]

There seems to be a law of psychic balance: One quality of our psyche is drawn to the surface and gets attached to the *persona* which interacts with the outside world; whereas the opposite quality can be drawn to the buried part of our inner being. The qualities that interact with the outside world are subtly adapted to ensure that we get the approval of others; we make sure that the desirable qualities come to the top; we behave in a way that enables us to get our way.

The trouble is that the qualities and tendencies that don't gain us quick approval can get buried and lie there unattended. These tend to be qualities that we ourselves do not wish to recognise as part of us. Subconsciously, we don't want to know these parts of ourselves; we may be frightened of them – perhaps they could destroy us or others.

A seeker needs the help of a soul friend to come to terms with their shadow, to cease to deny things they have pushed into darkness, and to work through these places of pain, denial or discovery. Needless to say, to be a soul friend we need to be in dialogue with our own shadow.

A young man named Bruce (not his real name) longed for wholeness, but the conflict between his expressed longing and his other repressed longings racked his soul and body, so a soul friend began to work with his dreams. Bruce had a recurring dream of a man in black who constantly followed him. This man represented his shadow. We encouraged Bruce to visualise himself turning round to hold the man's hand. He could not bring himself to do this. He *was* able to visualise Jesus coming between them as a mediator. Bruce, still with his back to his shadow figure, put one hand in Jesus's hand, while Jesus took the man's hand in his other hand. In this way an impassable gulf between Bruce's shadow and his conscious life began to be bridged, though this came too late to save him from dying at the age of thirty-one.[4] Our relationship with that buried part of inner being that we call our shadow is a life-and-death business.

Often we project our shadow on to others. Jesus became the victim of people who repressed their shadow, and projected it on to him, making him a scapegoat. He called them hypocrites: that means that they were play-actors, they were putting on a *persona*, a face, that was masking their shadow.

A soul friend can help a seeker to recognise their shadow by getting them to focus on the people they dislike or who annoy them. They may be clues to their own shadow.

> *O would some power the giftie gie us*
> *To see ousels as others see us!*
> *It wad frae mony a blunder free us*
> *And foolish notion.*
>
> Robert Burns

Parent-adult-child role-play

Knowledge of tools used in counselling and therapy is too vast a subject to be covered in this book. Some soul friends may do well to remain ignorant of the terms and concepts used in these disciplines; but certain of these tools particularly lend themselves to use in spiritual direction. For example, the 'transactional analysis' approach which encourages a client to dialogue with three personae which they have within themselves: their immature self (child), their responsible self (adult) and their judgmental self (parent). A soul friend may discern when a seeker is being dominated by the first or the last *persona*, and point this out. A soul friend may invite the seeker to talk to or about this *persona*. Then prayers of affirmation, or penitence, or release can be prayed for it. A soul friend might teach a seeker to lay hands on their abdomen and bless their unaffirmed inner child, or lay hands on their forehead and humour their inner parent which dominates other people. And so on.

The worst-case scenario

Suppose the seeker is so dominated by anxiety about a fraught situation that paralysis prevents sensible discussion or action. The soul friend might help the seeker look at the worst possible scenario, then at the whole picture, then at the possibilities. What if the worst happens? It is most unlikely that it will, but if the seeker can embrace and respond to this in imagination, the fear of the unknown is removed. The soul friend then gently leads the seeker to find their way around whatever the future may bring. 'Is God calling you to move out of or to assume responsibilities in this situation? If the latter, what boundaries for yourself should you decide upon?'

A journal

Keeping a journal helps some people to capture the lessons God is teaching them, rather like putting a snapshot in an album. Once it is on paper in front of them they can reflect upon it and come back to it. It helps them to monitor whether they are being truthful with themselves. It helps a soul friend to keep hold of the needs arising out of sessions with a seeker, and to blend these with the inspirations that are given them. Some seekers regularly bring their journal to a soul-friend session, and this can provide the content for the session. Its value is that it enables the seeker to retain the most significant things that have impinged upon their spirit, and to offer these to the soul friend.

Information about referral agencies

Sooner or later it is likely that some seeker will need support from a source other than the soul friend. There are support agencies for almost every form of addiction, abuse, bereavement, trauma, disability, developmental, financial or vocational need. A soul friend is wise to keep a list of such agencies to hand. Libraries or the local Citizens Advice Bureaux often provide lists of local welfare, friendship and counselling agencies. Collecting new information on the grapevine can become an enjoyable hobby. Health centres, pastors, police, telephone directories and the Internet regularly gather new information, which the soul friend can glean.

Exercises
For a soul friend

1. Draw a square on a blank sheet of paper and divide it into four quarters. If you are an adult let the four small squares represent your childhood, your adult life, your present and your future. Write in each square the thing that has been, is, or you believe will be most important for your spiritual journey.

2. Prayerfully think about the present condition of an actual or an imaginary seeker. Now let your mind range over the Scriptures. What Scripture can you share with the seeker that powerfully speaks to their condition?

3. Choose an actual or imaginary seeker, and decide what type of personality they have (using Myers-Briggs, Enneagram or your own commonsense classification). Now think out which method of prayer you would recommend them to try out, and explain this step by step.

4. Become aware of what your inner child is feeling. Talk to it and pray for it.

5. Dream themes relating to stress include death, houses, missing the bus, going to work only partly clothed. Each person has their own stress dream symbols. What are yours?

6. Discovering our shadow: Make a list of everything that is offensive to you in other people. Write in capital letters those things that are *particularly* offensive. Then underline those particularly offensive characteristics that make you angry or that you feel are really despicable.
You have probably drawn a fairly accurate picture of your shadow. Now walk or sit. Invite Jesus to come to the shadow. What does he do?

7. Begin to compile a list of referral agencies.

Further Study
Michael, Chester P. and Norrisey, Marie C., *Prayer and Temperament: Different Prayer Forms for Different Personality Types* (The Open Door Inc., P.O. Box 855, Charlottesville, Virginia 22902, USA, 1984). There is also a cassette learning course by Chester P. Michael, *A Call to Holiness and Wholeness*.

Parker, Russ, *Healing Dreams* (SPCK, 1987). There is also a cassette workshop by Russ Parker, *Praying with Dreams* (Eagle, 1992), which contains a live dream-counselling process.

Harris, Thomas A., *I'm O.K. You're O.K.* (Pan, 1976). An enjoyable introduction to the transactional analysis approach.

England, Edward (ed.), *Keeping a Spiritual Journal* (Highland Books, 1991).

CHAPTER 19

LEARNING TO LISTEN

You have ears, why don't you use them?

Jesus, Luke 8:8

When someone is in a climate of listening they will say things they would not have said before.

Ciceley Saunders, British hospice movement

istening is a key that opens doors to another person's growth. It is a priceless asset. It is an art; with practice it can become a great art, but for most modern people it is a lost art.

A person should not become a soul friend unless they have first learned to listen; but many well-intentioned people are unaware that they fail to listen. The first exercise at the end of this chapter is a simple, well-known way of checking out whether or not someone else perceives you as a good listener. Try it out. If you are not perceived as being a good listener, take a course in listening before you try to be a soul friend. If you pass the test, read on.

Listen to the seeker

In order to help the seeker take the right next steps on their journey you need to know where they are coming from. It may help to build up a simple identikit picture. What are their priorities? What is their temperament? How functional or dysfunctional are their relationships with parents, spouses, children, others? What are their aspirations? What, if any, are their neuroses or dependencies? What makes them angry? What relaxes and reinvigorates them? What particular choices or pressures confront them? How has their Christian faith been formed and what Christian tradition do they come from? What 'language' (way of speaking and thinking) do they use? What are their longings or hurts which are unspoken? What is their world-view?

You can build up this picture in different ways: from what you already know, from casual talk at the beginning of a session; from what you pick up while you listen to them, or occasionally by asking for specific information. Sometimes a seeker might be pleased to send you some information: A report, a reference, or a sample of their poetry, meditations, or art.

Listen to their body

Your body is, in essence, a crowd of different members who work in harmony to make your belonging in the world possible . . .
The inner voices of the body want to speak to us, to inform us of the truths beneath the fixed surface of our external lives.

John O'Donohue

Your body tells you, if you heed it, how your life is; whether you are living from a life-giving flow of water or from a poisoned well of negativity. Body language can tell us more than words. If a seeker avoids eye contact or has head bowed, you know that their spirit is bowed down or bound. While the words flow, you will be asking yourself what they are really saying. A tense or fidgeting body, or hands that are trying to hold something in, also tell us about the needs of a person.

Listen to their feelings

Michael Jacobs likens this aspect of listening to 'trying to spot the bass line of a piece of music, while still concentrating upon the melody on the top line'.[1]

Listen to their mindset

Every person is conditioned by the assumptions, attitudes and beliefs of those who parent, teach or impact them. This conditioning consists of a vast amount of information. Some, perhaps much, of this is misinformation. The soul friend will pick up giveaway words that reveal such misinformation. The soul friend will not be much concerned to deal with misinformation about matters of general knowledge, that is not their sphere; and, in any case, they may be ignorant or misinformed of these things themselves. But the soul friend will take care to pick up from the seeker misinformation about the way human beings are meant to relate to others, to the church, to society, to creation and to God.

Take an obvious example. Many people project their experience of a parent on to God. So one person may perceive of God as a distant Being who is not interested in the personal details of their life. A female who has been abused by men may perceive God as someone who wants to exploit her for purposes that are alien to him. Someone else may see God as non-personal cosmic energy, an expansion of their own (dysfunctional) life-force. To break free from these false perceptions, and to know God as God truly is – total love, total truth – requires the soul friend to identify and correct these misinformations.

Or, in the realm of family relationships, a seeker may perceive the role of a father, a mother, a wife or a husband inappropriately. The soul friend needs to point this out in order that dysfunctional ways of relating may be faced, broken and made whole.

Listen to their past

It can be useful to suggest that a seeker tells their story. This should not be done, however, if for a particular seeker this would be a performance, a fanciful projection of their false self-image. If they are shy or introverted it may take a while for the right moment to come to tell their story.

In some situations a time of reflecting back is helpful, whether from recent experiences or from years before. This is especially suited to the vulnerable seeker who would shrink from answering questions that put them on the spot. For such a seeker, reflection can be a gentle meandering through past memories that – because they, as well as the feelings they bring, are recalled and owned and connected – become a healing influence.

Listen to yourself

Even the most experienced spiritual directors can at times become so overloaded that their own inner needs cry out to be listened to. These cries of one's inner child do not respect other people's boundaries. They have no manners. If this is your situation, it is vital to listen to them, and to what they tell you about your own needs. How might this affect your role as a soul friend?

If you find, during a session with a seeker, that the pressure of your own needs is impairing your ability to be deeply attentive, you can do one of two things, according to the intensity of your problem and the reasonableness of the seeker. You can make an effort to ride it out, but promise yourself that after the session you will plan prime time to deal with your own needs. You may then decide that you need to cancel engagements, or reduce the number of seekers you see. Second, you can be honest, apologise that your concentration has gone, and share with the seeker the fact that you are finding it hard to cope. Unless the seeker is in some distress, this may create a deeper bond between you. There were occasions when I had to do this as a busy parish priest.

229

Sometimes a seeker brings something up about themselves which, consciously or unconsciously, triggers material in your own life that has not been sorted out. It is important to recognise when this happens; otherwise you will project your own experiences and reactions on to the seeker. Although it can be helpful to share and to mutually learn from one another's journeys, a soul friend should beware of projecting their own journey on to that of the seeker. No two people's journeys are ever identical.

Listen to God

I only say what the Father has instructed me to say.

Jesus, John 8:28

When we listen to others we also listen to God whose Presence is in them, but we also hear other voices – fear perhaps, or self-pity, or domination, or resentment. So the soul friend has to learn to distinguish God's voice within the seeker, within themselves and beyond both. Just as some people learn to speak three languages, so a soul friend learns to listen to three 'languages'.

We learn to listen to God through prayer, Scripture, conscience and our senses which can taste goodness, wonder and love. In order to better listen to God in a soul-friending session, a soul friend might become still for a moment before a session begins, relax with palms open in a receiving posture, and offer a prayer such as this: 'I place into your hands my own burdens. Take away all extraneous matter that divides my attention or confuses my spirit. I offer to you the seeker and this session. May I be wholly available to you and to the seeker.'

Through unease

Sometimes God can speak to us through a sense of unease. If you get a sense of unease as the seeker talks, you need to listen to yourself, because it may be the seeker is journeying towards something that you yourself have not faced, so it is unease about yourself which is surfacing. Assuming, however, that you know yourself well enough to be able to discount that, there must be another reason for the unease. This unease may drift away. If it continues, ask the Holy Spirit to bring its cause into the light and give it a name. It may prove to be any one of a myriad things.

Let us take two examples. Perhaps much time has been spent working through genuinely bad ways in which the seeker has been treated, but then the penny drops that there is a spirit of rejection so deep-seated that everybody is viewed by the seeker with a jaundiced eye, whether or not they have mistreated the seeker. Now the focus must switch from the difficult people in the seeker's life to the spirit of rejection within that life.

Or second, suppose the seeker has been frustrated that despite repeated attempts to find creative and fulfilling jobs, they constantly end up in cul-de-sacs. You have worked on ways of moving out of those cul-de-sacs, but this does not seem to make any difference. The frustration seems endemic. You begin to feel uneasy. Then the penny drops. The seeker has such a low self-image that they unconsciously rule out doing any job which they really want to do. They assume that anything they want to do could not possibly be God's will for them. The soul friend's task is to help them see that, once their heart is pure, their heart's desires may very well be pointers to what God has in mind for them. What a release this can be for the seeker.

Through givenness

At times God's voice comes in the form of a gift. Perhaps this and that avenue has been explored in a session, and the exploring has become a striving, driven by human adrenalin. Then a still, small voice whispers, 'You are looking in the wrong places. Accept my Presence in the situation you are in. You will know the place to rest in by the sense of givenness that accompanies it.' That is the cue for a change of focus. Become attentive to the course of least resistance.

Even some of the greatest Christian leaders have fallen into the trap of confusing their own ego with the will of God. A difference between the ego's will and God's will is that that the ego tries to control others, whereas God tries to woo others. Another name for this is the cross. In the cross, God is willing to 'lose' in order to win others. The ego imposes conditions, judges those who refuse to adhere to them. The fruit of the ego is judgmentalism and tension. The fruit of the cross is peace and love. A soul friend looks out for the spirit of control. Is the seeker open to being led in a direction that was not planned, that is not congenial, that requires others to increase in prominence and them to decrease? In other words, to sense the God-givenness in a situation and to embrace it?

Helping the seeker to listen: an exercise

Suppose you agree to be a soul friend, and the seeker arrives for the first session full of stress, bombarded with images and distorted by pressures which have been neither recognised nor addressed. It would be futile to begin by assuming the seeker is in touch with the deeps within. It is necessary to begin further back.

Here are some possible steps that a soul friend might suggest in this situation.

1. Imagine there is a clothes line in front of you. What things on your mind can you, at least for the present, hand over and hang up on that clothes line?
2. Which of the stressful factors in your life do you think you can take in your stride without getting screwed up?
3. Arrange to make a retreat.
4. Build times of silence into your weekly schedule.
5. Consider ways in which you can learn to listen: to music, or to your own body, or to your spouse, or to creation.
6. Focus on yourself. Which of your reactions are driven or defensive? Which are positive convictions? If you are not sure, come back to these over a period of time. The hopes that will not go away may be the true convictions you should heed.

When to speak

As a rule, it is best for the seeker to set the agenda for each session, and to talk about whatever seems important to them. Even silence is not necessarily a cue for a soul friend to talk. Silence may be an essential breathing-space during which something painful or confusing struggles to come to the surface of the seeker. Nothing is worse than for a seeker to be burdened with something deep, which they struggle at first to get out, only to find that the soul friend is babbling on about something that does not touch upon their need. There are, however, some good reasons for a soul friend to take the lead in speaking when appropriate:

To aid concentration

As a rule, don't interrupt a seeker's flow of talk if it is 'real stuff', except for occasional affirming words or to clarify something. If, however, the seeker loses their thread, the soul friend may gently point them to the thread they have lost: 'You were saying that . . .' Or the seeker may rush on from one topic to another, in an unconnected, overheated way. The soul friend might say: 'I can't see the connection between these different topics, and I'm getting confused. May we please stop for a moment's silence, and see which of these stands out as the most important issue you wish us to concentrate upon?'

To challenge

There may come a time when the seeker's talk seems to go round and round in a circle. The soul friend needs, sooner or later, to cut in and point this out: 'What is the point you are trying to make?' Why is the seeker going round in circles? Is it to avoid something? It may be because the seeker has become hooked on a problem. If so, this may be a time to be directive: 'We're getting nowhere. You need to decide what you are going to do about this. Now, let's talk about that . . .'

There are other occasions when the soul friend should be the first to talk: to ask a question in order to understand correctly, or to offer comfort if a seeker becomes distressed. Sometimes it is hard to know whether or how to offer comfort, especially for a shy soul friend. Be attentive to your instincts; do not let any negative conditioning make you hold back. On the other hand, assess whether the seeker wishes for sympathy, and whether it is appropriate.

Finally, there is frequently a place for the word which affirms.

Exercises
For a potential or actual soul friend

1. Find someone you can pair up with. Ask them to talk to you for two minutes about something that matters to them (it could be either a light or a heavy matter). Listen without speaking. After two minutes echo back to them what they said, using their own words as much as possible. Then ask the other person to tell you what you omitted, wrongly assumed, or got wrong, and how this affected their emotions. Discuss your emotions on receiving the other person's reflections on your listening.

2. Make a list of situations in which you think it is appropriate for a soul friend to initiate talk. Imagine a particular episode and what you would say.

3. Look back over the last twenty-four hours. What is the most significant thing God is trying to say to you?

Further reading
Long, Anne, *Listening* (DLT, 1994).

Huggett, Joyce, *Listening to God* (Hodder & Stoughton, 1995).

Huggett, Joyce, *Listening to Others* (Hodder & Stoughton, 1996).

See also the section on discernment and listening in Appendix 2.

STAGES ON LIFE'S JOURNEY

As we have seen, the context of soul friendship in the Celtic tradition is the awareness that each of our lives is a journey. The earthly journey begins at conception and ends at death, which is but a gateway to a journey on a higher plane. To the Celtic mind the sequences of creation's days and seasons are reflected in the human journey. Our lives should have dawns and twilights, springs and autumns, as well as sudden storms. A soul friend should be at home with these stages of the journey, has the privilege of accompanying another along part of their journey, and of helping them to make good transitions.

There is something sun-like within us, and to speak of the morning and Spring, of the evening and Autumn is not mere sentimental jargon ... The afternoon must have a significance of its own. We cannot live the afternoon of life according to the programme of life's morning.

C.G. Jung

here are some stages in life's journey that every person who does not die prematurely will experience, though each in their individual way. There are other 'stages' that seem to come from nowhere, without rhyme or reason, like a sudden squall which deluges some and bypasses others. A soul friend can help a seeker to respond to seasons, squalls and sunshine with integrity and compassion.

A soul friend in the Celtic tradition becomes familiar with these seasons, and helps a seeker to journey through them with acceptance and confidence. Let us look at some of these stages.

Birth

At the heart of life is the eternal womb, as Job says, from which the waters of life have burst forth . . . Do we see with inner sight that each plant, each creature, each human being is born at heart from holy soil?

Philip Newell

Our nine-month journey in our mother's womb shapes the rest of our life. It is the place of well-being or non-being to which we instinctively return. In order to help a seeker, a soul friend needs to know their own birth, to embrace its pain and its wonder, to recognise God in it, to pray about, and to see it as a springboard for the journey that is still unfolding. I have an abiding memory of making an imaginative journey through my own conception and birth following a most beautiful film of sperm, conception and birth. As Dr Frank Lake described the different stages in the conception and birth process, I, and others around me relived our own changing emotions during this first journey of our lives. For some of us there was a period of bliss, such as eternity intends for us; for others there was almost unbearable pain. For all there was a mixture of experiences. It is good to learn what we can from our mothers about our births, and to make our own imaginative birth journey. Then we can work at the process of acceptance of self, parents and God, which is affected in a significant way at birth. God uses 'post-operative prayers', so we can pray for the foetus, and for the transformation of distorted emotional patterns that may have begun at that time.

Adolescence

Adolescence is not intended to be a stable period. It is the period where possibilities and energies burst out and need a process of trial and error which can be checked out with an affirming adult. This stage has gone well if by the early twenties there has been sufficient separation from parents to create a sense of self, an ability to relate to others appropriately, a work identity, a lifestyle and a set of values. A soul friend should expect turbulence, and inconsistency. The primary aim should be to develop trust and good communication of emotions so that gradually the seeker becomes aware of the things that do not belong to them, of patterns that recur, and of eternal things of God.

Dr Frank Lake taught his clinical theology students to think of a four-legged wooden chair as an image of adolescent formation. A chair that is properly put together has the four legs of trust, autonomy, initiative and industry; it has identity as its seat, and intimacy as its backrest. If it is not properly put together the chair collapses when weight is put upon it. The role of a soul friend with a young seeker whose family facilitates these qualities is to enjoy interacting with the seeker's explorations. If a seeker has no such home background, the soul friend's role is to build these qualities both through their own relationship, and by exploring varied relationships through which the seeker can develop these.

Weaning

Just as the umbilical cord must be cut if a newborn infant is to move on into life, or just as an infant has to be physically weaned from its mother's breasts so, as adults, there are cords that need to be cut, and things from which we have to be weaned if we are to begin a new journey. For many the developmental process is fragmented and incomplete. Changes in an adult's circumstances can reveal that their responses remain adolescent in some ways. A soul friend helps us to discern these, and to practice 'weaning'.

A soul friend learns to sense when a seeker is still controlled by the opinions, values or violations of their parents, and is not free to make their own choices. For example: an adult may remain dependent upon a parent to the extent that they do not take responsibility for cooking, cleaning or budgeting; or a spouse may fail to give themself fully in love because their primary emotional attachment is still to their mother or father. The soul friend might talk about this until a seeker becomes clear of the need to separate from such ties that bind. The seeker then has to come to a point of decision. Separation is the condition for finding one's true self. Sometimes this takes time. The soul friend may need to suggest small practice steps. The soul friend might draw out of the seeker an experience that week which reflected this problem, and suggest a more adult way of behaving next time. They might simulate an incident with a parent and discuss how to handle it. Before a fledgling swimmer is willing to jump in at the deep end of a swimming pool, they may need to practise, first wading, then jumping in from the shallow end. Gradually confidence builds up for the big jump.

A soul friend may come to realise that a seeker, who may be any age, has still not separated from false bonding. Perhaps the soul friend becomes increasingly dissatisfied with their sessions with a seeker, because every time they meet it feels as if an old CD is being replayed that does not ring true, and nothing the soul friend suggests makes any difference.

It is important to try and find out the cause of this feeling. Is it because the seeker has not yet found their true self? Are they bonded to a peer figure in a way that imprisons and blinds them? If so, what can a soul friend do? To begin with, perhaps, the soul friend can only point out that the seeker's path is leading away from fulfilment, and that they should seriously consider the possibility that they may be following someone else's *persona*, not their true self. The soul friend may have to wait until the consequences of following this false trail become so painful that the pain of facing the truth becomes bearable. Then what?

In her novel *Mystical Paths*[1] Susan Howatch describes how a son, whose mother's death devastated both him and his father, coped by believing that he was some sort of replica of his father.

> 'My fundamental problem is that I hate being me and I want to be someone else' Nicholas Darrow told a spiritual director. 'No, your fundamental problem is that you hate being someone else and you want to be you' his spiritual director informed him.

Nicholas's false self-image, which his father colluded with, led to one disaster after another before he was willing to face the reality. Once that time had come, the director asked father and son to face each other across a table, with himself seated between them at the end of the table. The time had come for 'the operation' when they would be separated psychically. The director prayed in the name of Father, Son and Holy Spirit that each would be aligned with the divine will. Then he asked them to grip each other's forearms, and he took a daffodil from a vase and placed it across their forearms. He asked them to reflect upon how confined they were by their present positions; their joined forearms deterred all spontaneous movement; how narrow and distorted their lives would be if they were always joined like that. For five minutes of silence they contemplated the full horror of that picture of the lives they had been leading. Then he asked them to relax their fingers, while still holding each other's arms, and to think about words from St John's Gospel: 'Whoever follows me shall have light . . . I have come that you may have life . . . Whoever believes in me, even though he was dead, shall live.' God's power broke through the false bond. Warm feelings towards his mother flooded into the son. Light shone. They both relaxed, moved back, and the daffodil, free now to be itself on the table, seemed to glow brilliantly. They began to live their true lives.

Immaturity, which is natural in the early stages of life, can cling even to wrinkled frames if their owners have missed out on the developmental process. A soul friend learns to read the signs of immaturity. Is there a restlessness? A denial of where one is at? A refusal to grow up, or to take responsibility? A refusal to accept loss, or to let go in order to take different kinds of responsibility? Time spent in deciding what are the next steps the seeker needs to be responsible for is time well spent.

Wading out

With the inner journey, as with physical voyages, it is best to start in the shallows, and to have stopping places en route. Tease out all the no-go areas that, sooner or later, the seeker might wish to visit, but start with the easier ones.

In the ancient world, journeys could be dangerous and it was easy to get lost; but cairns, standing stones, hills, stars, shorelines, rivers – all these formed landmarks to guide the traveller. Modern travellers have more, not fewer, signs to guide them along the routes of the world

We, seeker and soul friend alike, need landmarks no less on our inner journey. These landmarks, however, are reference points which we can refer to when the time is right, for no two people make identical spiritual journeys. As seeker and soul friend together sense the time is right, they can move on and check out the journey against one of the landmarks.

A soul friend desires that a seeker 'wades out' into the fulness of their manhood or womanhood. A soul friend will not stereotype people, but neither will they pretend that men and women are the same. A soul friend will seek, among other things, to draw out the 'mother' that is in every woman and the 'father' that is in every man.

The physical phase

In the first third of life the body tends to be dominant. Energy expresses itself in physical activity, including sex, but also, for a sincere seeker, in mental dedication and in passion for God.

Early in life we gradually become aware of new energies and emotions in our bodies, and of physical and emotional attractions to other people. Our journeying takes the form of putting a name to these and moulding them. That in turn requires us to work out our values and priorities. The seeker needs a vision of what fulness of body–mind–spirit means, and to develop clarity about boundaries and priorities.

Sometimes the natural release of energy that should come at this stage of life gets blocked or perverted. Then the soul friend has to help a seeker to identify and disown negativity. Once this has been done, creativity has to be released. That is a good time to explore longings, dreams and imaginings. The soul friend should introduce the seeker to exercises of mind and body which bring a balance between the physical and the spiritual impulses, and between the yin and yang. Prayer exercises which use bodily postures or dance may help some seekers, perhaps using recorded music or meditation. These can be done in one's room or as open-air prayer walking. A Christian soul friend should not fear to draw on methods used, for example, in t'ai chi, so long as they serve to build up a mind immersed in the Trinity.

The mental phase

In the middle phase of life we become aware that 'there are more things in heaven and earth than are dreamed of', as William Shakespeare wrote. We become multidimensional but, because the pressure to succeed is so strong, unacceptable tendencies – such as ambition, lust, envy or rage – get pushed down, only to resurface, perhaps in some form of midlife crisis. Now these emerge into consciousness and threaten the self-image we built up in early life. A soul friend, who begins to develop the eye of an eagle, can give us feedback which helps us get to know this important part of our being.

The soul friend may accompany the seeker up hill and down dale, through valleys of shadow, into vistas yet to be explored. During this mid stage of life the soul friend may perhaps encourage the seeker to learn about personality, or gifts, or danger points, and to develop mind and spirit in balance.

It is during the mental phase of life that there is the greatest danger of a seeker being overtaken by ambition. A soul friend will help the seeker become attentive to ways we manipulate by tone of voice, unspoken assumptions, lack of hospitality and the making of conditions. The soul friend will be alongside as the seeker struggles with questions of justice and integrity. They can usefully spend time reflecting upon value choices.

The spiritual phase

In the later years of life, physical powers and restless activity tend to recede. The very fact of having survived the vicissitudes of life creates a certain security. There is space to become more aware of the spiritual side of life, and to contemplate eternal perspectives. A key question each person in the third phase of life needs to face is this: 'Will I be responsible for cradling life in others or will I retire and live only for myself?' At this age we develop a need for both community and solitude.

The wisdom of old age is the wisdom of letting go.

> The value of what he did and believed was rooted not in any outward status or claim but in the simple practice of being still. It was his commitment to being empty before God that gave him his inner certainty of strength and security.
>
> *Philip Newell, writing of an aged monk*

Unfortunately, many people who are old in years are not old in wisdom. One reason may be that they are too full of hidden anger to be able to grow in wisdom. This kind of anger can at times well up in most of us. The worst advice we can give anyone is to ignore it, or to forgive the person who caused it before owning up to the anger.

Prayer is the seed of gentleness in the absence of anger.
Sayings of the Desert Fathers

If a seeker comes to you festering with anger, your role as a soul friend might be to encourage the seeker to pour it out. Invite the seeker to talk about it, to shout, or weep, or swear. Occasionally, violence may need to be expressed. If you feel that you cannot cope with this, it is important that you make this clear. In that case, you might suggest that the seeker works through this anger with someone else, perhaps with a counsellor. But maybe you feel able to provide, say, a cushion for the seeker to punch. Or you might ask if the seeker would like to speak out their feelings against the person who has angered them by imagining that person is sitting in an empty chair which is placed opposite. Perhaps one of the 'hate' psalms can be read aloud (e.g. Psalm 137); this can be a way of bringing anger out but at the same time bringing it to God.

Bede relates how the elderly monk Egbert was stubbornly set upon going to Germany. He was operating as if he was in an earlier phase of life. The dreams of a brother whom he pressed to accompany him told him to do a deeper work closer to home. In this brother's dreams, Boisil, the former Abbot of Melrose, directed Egbert to the Iona Community which, generations after Columba, 'was cutting a crooked furrow'. Egbert refused to heed these deeper voices, and set sail for Germany. A prevailing storm prevented them from sailing and capsized the boat. Only then did Egbert accept that he should work as befitted the spirit phase of his life. This story serves as a parable for us. We must stop trying to be what we are not, and go with the ebb as well as the flow of life.

Autumn

The autumn of life is a time for harvesting the fruits of your experience. You come to see aging, not as the dissolution of your body, but as the harvest of your soul.

Old age, as the harvest of life, is a time where your times and their
fragments gather. In this way you unify yourself, achieve a new
strength, poise and belonging that was never available to you
when you were distractedly rushing through your days. Old age is
a time of coming home to your deeper nature ... One of the
places where inner harvesting is most vital is the abandoned areas
within your life. Areas of inner neglect and abandonment cry out
to you ... You can undo the damage that you did to yourself early
on in your life.

John O'Donohue

Retirement

Twilight makes the night welcome.

John O'Donohue

A male seeker has retired and now feels redundant. His feeling of
worth had come from being known and being asked to do things.
Now he has to fit in with his wife, who is ten years younger, and who
takes the car for her work. Dark depression threatens. The seeker
fears falling into a swamp, being useless, losing his cutting edge.

A soul friend will explore with him the question 'What is life for?'
and help him to grasp that relationship is the essence of life. Aidan,
ailing and dying at Bamburgh, perhaps feeling that his life's work
was a failure, nevertheless had with him those with whom he had an
organic relationship. Not for him the superficiality of job contracts
and golden handshakes. So the soul friend will help the seeker
discern who are the people with whom he is meant to build
relationships.

Retirement is the time when the seeker should be encouraged to
think of the saints who were greeted and escorted to heaven. Aidan
may have died feeling a failure, but a vision of him being escorted to
heaven by angels moved Cuthbert to dedicate his life to God. A soul
friend will encourage a seeker to think about their 'place of
resurrection' (see Chapter 14). That is, the physical place and the

surroundings in which they wish to leave the physical body for the resurrection body, in the belief that this will have a distinctive influence upon those who remain in that place. The soul friend and seeker should explore the reality of heaven, saints and the heavenly career.

Soul friendship in the Celtic tradition is sensitive to the seasons of life and creation, yet many 'townees' have become distant from creation. A soul friend will bear in mind the need of the seeker to develop an abiding awareness of the Presence of God in all things, to grow in the wisdom of nature, and in the rhythms of time and eternity. For example, I often try to extend summer, and to avoid being fully present to colder, darker days. By learning to accept the loss of summer days and to embrace the 'death' of winter, I become aware of good things only winter can bring, birds arriving from colder parts, thoughts within that I have had no time to ingest during hectic summer activity. In such ways I acquire a habit of preparing for my final passing from this world. A soul friend can usefully discuss with a seeker how a changing season will change their mode of life.

When the journey comes to a halt

'For ten years I stopped the journey,' an explorer with the Community of Aidan and Hilda told me. This can be a person's experience in any of the three phases of life. It may take some time for either the seeker or the soul friend to realise that a pause has become a halt. Once a soul friend is aware of this, the causes need to be looked for. For one person, the entrapment of dreary or demeaning duties can lead first to weariness, then to resignation and bitterness. No longer is love new every morning; it lies sodden and deadening on the soul. For another person, the walk with God may be mixed with unacknowledged ambitions which have come to nothing. They feel let down by God. Without even acknowledging it, they turn upon God. Their spirit dries up. Or perhaps a keen and passionate pilgrim for God falls into a sin of passion, in mind or in deed. The pleasures of God fade beside the pleasures of erotic, financial or leisure quick-fixes. A barrier has been erected between the pilgrim and God.

A soul friend helps the seeker to acknowledge what is actually happening. 'Do you want to stay where you are?' 'What options can we explore in order to move forward?' If a specific sin lies at the root of the impasse it should be confessed and the assurance of Christ's forgiveness be given. If someone is simply tired out, the soul friend will explore with them how to have a break, a change, a stimulus or affirmation.

Summary

A soul friend helps a seeker to be aware of the season of life they have presently reached; to grieve for, vicariously make up for, and let go of past seasons they have not fully savoured, and to become fully present to whatever the incoming season brings.

Exercises
For soul friends and seekers

1. If possible, read an illustrated book or leaflet about the process of conception and birth, or look at a picture of an unborn child. Go on an imaginative journey of your own conception and birth. Write down your emotions and thoughts.

2. Draw a clock face without hands but fill in the numbers. Look at this and ask, 'What time is it in my life?' Wait until you feel the right time has suggested itself to you, and then fill in the two missing hands on the clock face to represent the time.

If you are a soul friend with a seeker who seems unaware of their stage in life, look out for a timely moment to invite your seeker to do this exercise.

3. Draw in pencil a four-legged 'chair of identity'. Reflect on the

development in yourself of the six attributes which make up the legs, seat and back (trust, autonomy, initiative, industry, identity, intimacy). Recall an experience which reveals you have gained each attribute in a measure. As you do this, fill in the chair parts with ink, and write by each part its attribute and a keyword to denote the experience. If you have a seeker, do this exercise with them, or on your own, imagining that you are the seeker.

4. Draw a line across a blank page to represent your life journey. Put a circle for the most significant stages you have been through. Describe each in one word, and write this in the circle. What lesson can you learn from your experience of each stage?

5. Suppose your seeker tells you, 'I can't do what is in my heart because it would upset my parents,' what advice might you give the seeker?

6. Reflect upon your own inner journey, and make a list of landmarks which have been there for you.

Further reading
Newell, Philip, *One Foot in Eden: A Celtic View of the Stages of Life* (SPCK, 1998).

CHAPTER 21

PITFALLS

No one can for long act as a soul friend without meeting pitfalls. That is in the nature of human beings. Here are a few of the most common ones.

Pride comes before a fall

Proverbs 16:18

Remaining problem-centred

If the seeker has real problems and seeks help in overcoming them, that is good and necessary. However, if after a length of time every session is still dominated by personal problems, then the soul friend needs to challenge the seeker to look outwards as well as inwards.

A surgeon needs to wash his hands before operating, not for the hands' sake but for the sake of the patient. We noted in Chapter 1 that soul friendship is different to counselling: whereas the purpose of counselling is often to solve a client's particular problems, the purpose of soul friendship is to help a seeker grow in the love and calling of God. A true seeker journeys away from being self-centred to being other-centred. If the seeker does not wish to do this, but wishes to remain problem-centred, they should seek a counsellor or therapist. A soul friend needs to be able to make this clear, and to terminate the meetings if necessary.

Dependency and the 'hysterical' personality

A widespread virus that infects Christians who have sought counsel and made some progress in their journey is that of dependency, either upon the person from whom they seek support, or upon something they have developed, such as a godly habit or virtue. Selwyn Hughes, the veteran evangelical Christian counsellor, claims that the root problem in the human heart is misplaced dependency upon persons or things.

Dr Frank Lake[1] examines the 'hysterical personality' which, more than any other type, craves a false dependency. This does not refer to someone who is in hysterics, though it may include them; it refers to the person who is so overwhelmed by desire for an object of intimate sustenance that they are unable to bear aloneness, and constantly grab at a person to make them a substitute source of nourishment. Because for one reason or another they failed to receive sexual or emotional satisfaction in the womb, from mother's breasts, or from early mothering or fathering, they become discontented, wandering in every direction, clutching at persons who might provide the missing source of wellbeing. In some there is an infantile agenda of attention-seeking, in others a compulsion to have sex with anyone regardless of their situation. Since no person can make up for the lack of love in early years, they accumulate failed relationships, which makes the problem worse. In their despair of making deep relationships they tend to think of all social opportunities in terms of superficial skin sensations. The seeker uses emotional blackmail: 'Why don't you love me any more?' The soul friend should make clear at once that the seeker is making illegitimate demands which cannot be met, and should explain why this is so.

Some hysterical women do not trust other women, so they will press a man to be their soul friend. But any soul friendship that does not lead her to engage with women again will be fruitless. Some hysterical types will press the soul friend to be a substitute mother; and she or he may trigger the frightened child within the soul friend. A soul friend who tries to help such a person may end up being destroyed themselves. Rev. Ichabod Spencer, who wrote in the middle of the nineteenth century, discovered that one may learn more about one's weaknesses from a thwarted hysteric in ten minutes than one does from one's usual friends in ten years! It is essential not to try to handle a situation like this on one's own.

It may well be better to place a hysterical seeker with a mature married couple. This allows the suffering seeker a measure of security and the possibility of a gradual transference of trust from one spouse to the other, which can later be distributed in a mature fashion to a number of people. The couple need to be able to come closely alongside the seeker in deep empathy, allowing the seeker to unfold every aspect of their lives and feelings; yet they must be able at the same time to be detached, and free from the spider's web of emotional entanglements that come from the unhealed places in the seeker. The aim must be to help the hysterical seeker to accept the buried pain and loneliness of early experiences, and to accept that their lives are driven to compensate for these in inappropriate ways. Once the seeker learns to live 'in the desert' of nothing, then relationships of 'gift', that will not be destroyed by clutching, become possible.

The healing of this condition calls for the church as a whole to play a part. The seeker should be encouraged to draw deeply from the word of God in Scripture and in sacrament, to enjoy the fellowship of a group or household church (a group of mature Christians, with no single person who could be easily subverted within it), and to engage in outgoing service with others. Yet something must also be done to fill those moments when the seeker is alone; perhaps contemplation of an ikon of Christ on the cross, or the repetition of a hymn which affirms the seeker in Christ. The aim is 'Christ-realisation', and the example of Jesus's relationship with Mary Magdalene has much that can help to bring this about. Tradition suggests Jesus may have cured her of prostitution by offering her unconditional love, and the Bible notes that Jesus discouraged her from clinging to physical contact with him when she met him on the first day of his resurrection (John 20:17).

Getting stuck

Sometimes our lives can be like a record or CD that gets stuck, and goes round and round repeating the same tune. As we have already seen, the sessions of a soul friend and a seeker may get stuck like that. They seem to talk about the same issues and the same responses each time they meet. The seeker is not moving on. The relationship has become stale. The soul friend needs then to take the initiative. First, by praying and reflecting upon why this is. The soul friend may be given insight that enables the seeker to break out of the vicious circle. Or the soul friend may conclude that another soul friend with different experience or skills will be better placed to help the seeker move on. If the soul friend fails to take the initiative, the seeker should talk through the impasse with the soul friend and, if nothing changes, in due course suggest a change.

Is the seeker evading something? Questions which challenge should be open-ended. There may be occasions, if the seeker persistently colludes with an inner 'renegade', when this should be pointed out.

Perhaps there are repeated moral lapses? Try and get to the bottom of these, and bring them to God. Perhaps the soul friend wonders if they are wasting their time? If the seeker does not care about the relationship, by all means end it; but if the seeker is struggling, the soul friend's help is still needed.

Smothering

Each person has to travel alone into their deep places of pain or despair or emptiness. The soul friend must avoid the temptation to deflect the seeker from doing this because they themselves wish to avoid reminders of such pain. They can kill by kindness, for offering palliative comfort at the time when a seeker needs to walk alone is really to let them down.

Fear of silence

Occasionally a seeker's emotions are touched so deeply that no words can suffice. Time is needed to let this dawning realisation sink in, to own and embrace a part of self that has hitherto been hidden. If either soul friend or seeker, through fear of silence, sabotages that precious and pregnant moment by talk that distracts, they may never get another such opportunity. A soul friend who senses that this is the situation may need to say something such as 'I sense we have touched something too important for words. Feel OK about being silent for as long as you like. If you feel it appropriate, just leave and we will resume when we next meet.' One seeker spent half an hour in silence with their soul friend, and then walked quietly out to spend the rest of the day continuing the inner dialogue.

Copying

It can happen that, as friendship increases, one person tends to imitate the other, or even to re-image herself in the image of the other. John O'Donohue tells of an old Irish man who used to collect photographs of newly married couples. He would then obtain a photograph of that couple some ten years later. From that photograph he would begin to demonstrate that one of the couple was beginning to resemble the other. There can be a subtle copying process which is destructive. If a soul friend and a seeker develop deep bonds of friendship it is well to remember that one of the most precious things to preserve in a friendship is our own distinctiveness. It is often that which attracts.

Losing heart

'When a seeker is knocked off their prayer perch, how do you get them back on track?' one soul friend asked me. She meant that after a defeat, depression or deviation a seeker can lose both the habit of prayer and the desire to recover it. If this is caused by actions which have put up a barrier between the seeker and God, agree on ways of letting out anger, or repenting of sin. But if it is caused by a need to move on to a different plane of prayer, explore how to move on.

Exercise
For a soul friend

1. Add to this list of pitfalls. Write down your suggestions for avoiding or surmounting these.

CHAPTER 22

WORKING WITH A RULE OF LIFE

Early Celtic soul friends lived within the framework of a Rule of Life which their community espoused, or which they kept as wandering hermits or anchorites. Some of the seekers they befriended would keep or be influenced by the Rule of their local monastic community. Growing numbers today find it helpful to adopt a Rule of Life, and try to apply it with the help of a soul friend.

In a single day we make so many decisions we cannot possibly weigh up the good and evil consequences of each decision. We are liable to make foolish and wrong decisions.

For this reason we need a rule, a simple set of moral principles that we can apply to each decision we make. This will not be foolproof, but with a good rule, our decision will for more often be right than wrong.

St Morgan

I n the days of the Celtic monastery, members of the surrounding population who came for confession and guidance had not promised to keep the celibate monks' Rule, but they were expected to keep to its spirit. A Rule sets out the values and goals of a community or an individual, and a checklist of practices which help them to live these. In recent centuries, a Rule has not been thought of as 'mainstream' by the majority of Western Christians. They realised that monks, nuns and friars kept a Rule. They were perhaps only dimly aware that many ordinary Christians, who related to these communities as friends, oblates, or members of a third order, also kept a form of the Rule suited to people in ordinary occupations. They assumed that a Rule pertained only to a minority drawn from one stream of Christianity.

That is now changing. Rules of Life may become mainstream again, though in an imaginative, adaptable way suited to a plural society. In 1973 a little book was published entitled *Rule for a New Brother*.[1] This has inspired people in all walks of life and has been reprinted many times. New networks are emerging which draw Christians from diverse streams to commit themselves to some form of Rule.[2] Christians who wish to join certain evangelical or charismatic churches are now invited to subscribe to the church's mission statement, or to its statement of values. These diverse modern Christians find that a Rule of Life helps them to focus better on the path God calls them to follow, and to avoid getting sidetracked into useless ways.

The value of a Rule of Life was far from obvious to some university students who told me: 'We've too many rules and regulations already – that's what we want to get away from.' Reading between the lines they seemed to be saying: 'We are only just starting out on life, so we want to keep our options open as we explore; we dislike the idea of any hierarchical body imposing restrictions on us.' Some Christians argue that, since no two situations are alike, a Rule is unnecessary; instead all they need is the Holy Spirit to guide them.

The advice of Morgan (Pelagius), quoted at the head of this chapter, is therefore worth pondering. Morgan continues:

> Another reason for a rule is this: Jesus tells us to pray always; yet sometimes we love to devote much time to prayer whereas at other times we are dry or feel far too busy to pray. A rule prevents us

from making excuses; it spurs us to pray at a particular time even when our heart is cold towards God.

The teaching of Jesus must be the primary general guide for any disciple, but Jesus himself did not give rules. The source of a rule is inside your own heart. What we call conscience is a kind of rule which God has written in your heart. If you wish to formulate a rule you must listen to your conscience and write down on paper what God has written on the heart.[3]

In making a Rule of Life we try to discern what God desires our lifestyle, values, priorities and schedules to be. By discerning and committing ourselves to these, we are better able to process the huge number of influences, expectations and decisions with which we are confronted.

A way of life

The Community of Aidan and Hilda took to heart the students' criticism of rules that don't fit the evolving life of a young person, even though their criticism shows a misunderstanding of the nature of a Rule. The community use the term 'Way of Life', and invites each person who wishes to explore it to evolve their own distinctive application with a soul friend.

Discerning my Way of Life with the help of a soul friend then becomes a way of discovering my true, God-given calling. In this understanding, a Way of Life is a means to identify and cherish the things that help me to follow my true way, and to keep false things from obscuring this. It is a way of appraising progress; it is the opposite of legalism.

Explorers with their soul friend will not ask, 'How many times have I broken a rule?' Rather, they will ask, 'How is God leading me, and nurturing a deeper and wider love and wisdom?' A Way of Life enables us to focus on different areas where change and growth are needed; it enables us to set short-term and long-term objectives, to find patterns and a lifestyle that suit us. It enables us to be better stewards of time, energy and money; to be more efficient. And the knowledge that others have a similar dedication can be a source of encouragement. The term 'Way of Life' reminds us that the first Christians were known as belonging to 'the Way'; they were not perceived as people who were aimless.

Christ Church, Epsom, has over one hundred people who follow a 'pattern for living'. This term for a Rule reminds us that God has designed the universe to have patterns. God calls us to live in harmony with the rhythms and patterns implanted in the genetic stream which, though in danger of being distorted and pulled into chaos by sin, Jesus wants to be embraced.

The term 'Rule of Life' does contain one element that these other terms lack. A Rule provides something against which we can measure our performance. This may not attract at a superficial level, but without some such yardstick we may sink into a morass.

In his helpful Grove Booklet *Finding a Personal Rule of Life*[4] Harold Miller explains how Rules of Life ought to differ according to the temperament a person has. For example, the type of person he describes as 'the desert Christian', who perhaps may be more of an introvert, sees separation from the world as the essence of true spirituality. Whereas another type, whom he describes as 'the marketplace Christian', is the opposite. For him 'eating spaghetti is prayer'. A Rule, says Miller, should focus on what, for you, is the heart of spirituality, but it should also try and keep a balance between the two extremes.

Making a Rule practical

Most Rules of Life set out a number of principles which their adherents have felt called to follow. A seeker who adheres to a Rule of Life will pray about it, and work out a home-made schedule for putting these principles into practice. This is provisional. It has to be tested in the actual conditions of the seeker's life. These may change, and so may the needs of the seeker.

What is the role of a soul friend in enabling a seeker to make a Rule of Life work well?

> If anybody enters the path of repentance, it is sufficient to advance
> step by step. Do not wish to be like a charioteer.
>
> *From the Rule of St Comgall*

Other needs may, of course, clamour for attention when a soul friend and seeker meet, but if they do not, it is best 'to advance step by step'. One or two areas of a Rule may be explored in any one session.

We shall now look at some areas that are commonly included in Rules of Life, and suggest some questions that a soul friend may ask in order to facilitate a schedule that is truly of God, that truly fits the seeker's soul and circumstances, and that brings growth in wholeness.

Study

❋ In what ways do you read or study the Bible?
❋ Is this satisfactory for you?
❋ If not, shall we explore others ways to read, study, memorise or apply Scripture?
❋ What do you know about spiritual classics? About Celtic spirituality?
❋ Would you like suggestions for reading?
❋ Have you considered setting aside a period each week or each month for study?
❋ If study seems out of reach in your home situation, shall we explore the idea of a study day, in a quiet place with a library, or with a group?
❋ If you are not a book person, what can we provide on cassettes for you to listen to?

Spiritual journey

* Where have you got to on your journey?
* Where is God leading you?
* Since we last met, how have you grown?
* What has frustrated growth?
* What came out of your last retreat?
* What plans can be made for a retreat? Or a pilgrimage?
* If family responsibilities prevent this, shall we consider the use of Lent or Advent, or ways of getting free even for a day?
* Is there a nearby caravan, shed, a quiet house you could get away to?

Prayer and worship

* What is your daily or weekly pattern of private prayer, family prayer, corporate prayer?
* What are the ingredients in these times of prayer? What is helpful in these?
* What is missing? Are you stuck?
* Shall we explore other styles or options for prayer?
* What do you understand by spiritual warfare?
* Shall we explore imaginative ways of interceding? Prayer walking?

Work and rest

* How do you express a rhythm of prayer, work and recreation in your family context? In your marriage? Alone? In groups?
* What bits of your work cannot be done to God's glory?
* What about stopping points during the day? The use of your talents?
* How do you express the principle of rest daily? On Sundays? According to the seasons?

❊ What about hobbies? Physical exercise? Planned spaces? Social occasions?

❊ Holidays?

Lifestyle

❊ What is the simplest way you can order your office, work, mind, home, family, schedules, holidays, dress?

❊ Do you tithe your income and assets or do you give your surplus away?

❊ Have you prayed through what proportion of this should be covenanted or given to your church and to other needs?

❊ Have you made a will that reflects in your death your Way of Life?

❊ What ecofriendly products and habits do you adopt?

❊ Shall we explore further possibilities? Purchases? Gardens? Travel habits? Eating habits? Ways of blessing and appreciating nature? Animals?

❊ What action do you take to cherish creation? What about rest days for cars?

❊ Remembering that the Western world has a split mind, shall we check out if you still split off the sacred from the secular, money from morality, the created world from the Creator, healing from the land, prayer from work, churches from their neighbourhoods, signs and wonders from everyday life, the past from the present, heaven from earth, death from life?

How do you make unity and community with your home?

❊ With your church? With different ethnic or social groups?

Mission

* Have you been able to share something of Jesus with anyone since we last met?
* To invite someone to a Christian gathering? To offer hospitality?
* To create friendship? To provide a Christian context for a life experience that is significant to someone? To stand up for justice?
* To offer prayer, healing, a listening ear?
* To offer a supportive presence during a birth, anniversary, death, sport, art, work?
* To be part of a celebration of talent, an act of witness or action for social justice?

Ultimately, any person, even if they live by the M25, can find a pattern by learning to live out of the deep rhythm of their heart. A seeker should be encouraged to take time to write out their personal Rule of Life in the light of each session, and to bring a revised version to the next session. This keeps it a living, evolving, spiritually renewing enterprise.

Social awareness and the clash of world-views

A seeker who has no conception of faith as other than an intensely personal, private matter might begin work with a soul friend who has a different world-view, for example, one which sees the struggle for world justice as a primary aspect of spirituality. The soul friend must not impose this world-view on the seeker, but might ask the seeker if they are willing to explore values. This is like working with a Rule of Life, except that no Rule has been formalised at this stage. Of course, it could be that the seeker has a commitment to justice which the soul friend does not share. This may be a sign that the seeker should seek another soul friend, but not necessarily. I think it was Teresa of Avila who said that if a person has to choose between an intelligent and a holy spiritual director, it is better to choose the intelligent one. An intelligent soul friend can help a seeker clarify their choices even if they do not adopt those choices for themselves.[5]

Working out a personal pattern of life from scratch

Sooner or later a soul friend who relates to a variety of seekers may sense that one of them needs, above all else, to sort out a pattern to live by. Their lives are all over the place, and they need to sort out priorities, values and routine structure. This pattern will reflect the goals, values, weaknesses, circumstances and stage in life of the seeker. The following is an example of a possible pattern of life which I drafted for a seeker to consider after we had clarified those things.

Aim
That the glory of God be seen through my human life lived to the full.

Goals
That my personality, talents, energy flow in their fulness with God.
    That all of life (work, rest, recreation and relationships) become prayer.

Preparation
Strip myself of words, activities, possessions and mindsets which are surplus to this aim.
    Punctuate the day, week and year with natural 'pattern developing habits'.

First Steps
1. *On waking*, repeat memorised words of appreciation of and offering to God (e.g. 'Shine on me Lord, like the sun

that lights up day, chase away the dark and all shadow of sin. May I wake eager to hear your word. As day follows night may I be bathed in your glory.' 'All that I am, all that I do, all whom I'll meet today I offer now to you.' Take time to soak in the meaning of these words.

2. *Midday*, memorise a brief midday prayer that can be said anywhere.[6]

3. *Before food or physical exercise*, offer appreciation of food and the body, and offer the body as a reflector of God's glory.

4. *Some time during the day either* explicitly praising God through creation *or* an imaginative meditation on a passage of Scripture or a theme which speaks to you.

5. *Before sleep*, offer back the day and offer any persons on your heart and your sleeping to God.

I then encouraged the seeker to delete what did not fit and add things that did.

Exercises

1. Make your own list of questions to explore that relate to a Rule of Life. Add to or revise the above list.

2. Think of someone whose personality and circumstances you know quite well, and imagine they asked you to help them sort out a structure for their lives. What would you suggest for their consideration?

Further reading

Miller, Harold, *Finding a Personal Rule of Life* (Grove Books, 1987).

A FINAL WORD

The best Celtic soul friendships flowed with wisdom and were graced with affection. This was often expressed through the giving of gifts. Brigid gave Finnian a ring, David gave Findbarr a horse. Samthann gave her neighbours her badger skin, Ciaran gave Kevin his bell. Each of us, too, has a gift to offer, a gift above all gifts, the gift of ourselves.

God gives all to us. God is friendship, unfathomably deep, endlessly fecund, three eternally flowing loves. God is soul of my soul. So soul friendship is the essence of God, the heart of life, the secret of endless possibility.

This book has revealed to us that friendship is the secret law of life, the golden thread that gives meaning to the universe. Love is the continuous birth of creativity between us. When it awakens in a life it is like a dawn bursting.

The danger of portraying this ideal is that readers who are potential soul friends feel this is unattainable, and dismiss the idea of becoming a soul friend. That would be a mistake. This book has also explored a broad spectrum of soul friendships. Just because one end of the spectrum is out of reach is no reason not to begin at the other end of the spectrum, which might be to offer a listening ear to someone four times a year.

Moreover, in reality few, even among the Celtic saints, were blessed with the ideal soul friendship. And some poor soul who milked cows up a muddy track miles from a monastery might have had as his soul friend a cantankerous old monk who was quite out of touch with that person's world!

Love is a many splendoured thing, and as it showers its fragments upon us, we do well to pick up a fragment near to us and let it work as it wills.

A FORM OF COMMISSIONING
OF A SOUL FRIEND

A soul friend may be commissioned in their local church by the priest or pastor as part of public worship. It would be good for Christian denominations to do this on a wider scale. For example, in a diocese that offers training in spiritual direction the commissioning might take place in a cathedral or minster church. Religious communities, orders and networks who provide training or have some form of accreditation might commission soul friends in the context of a communal gathering. In certain cases – for example, if a soul friend cannot travel – they may be commissioned in their home by a representative appointed by their church or community. The soul friend of the person to be commissioned should be present if possible, and friends and family may be invited. If the soul friend wishes the commissioning to be private, it is important that a card or letter of reference is provided by the commissioning person, and that the fact of their commissioning is made known. If the newly commissioned person is willing to be approached by other seekers, their name could be forwarded for inclusion in any local registers.

1. *There may be a call to worship, singing, prayers of adoration, confession and an assurance of forgiveness.*

2. *A prayer such as the following may be used:*

Father, you give us many gifts that we may share them in the work of building up your people. Help us to receive deeply, and to give ourselves generously, that in the work to which you call us we may know the wonder of your presence in another human life.

3. *The commissioning minister says:*

In the name of the Lord Jesus Christ, the king and head of the Church, who has ascended on high, and given gifts for the building up of his body, we today commission N... to be a soul friend, recognised by this community/church/fellowship of... (*state name*)

4. *Scripture readings such as the following may be interspersed with singing:* Proverbs 18:24; Proverbs 27:6; Isaiah 54:4–5; 61:1–3; Ecclesiasticus 6:16; John 15:9–17; Romans 15:1–7; 1 Corinthians 13; Galatians 6:1–2; 1 Thessalonians 5:11–24; James 5:16–20.

5. *There may be a talk.*

6. *Those to be commissioned make an act of dedication such as:*

I offer myself
  humbly, prayerfully and responsibly, as a soul friend to be
  used or laid aside as God wills.

I dedicate myself
  to find and follow my own true path,
  to draw deeply from the wells of Scripture and Christian tradition,
  to learn from the wise and good among our people,
  to be transparent with my own soul friend.

I commit myself
>   to respect friendship as a gift never to be clutched at,
>   to seek integrity in all relationships,
>   to build up those who confide in me,
>   to listen to the depths as well as to the surface of others,
>   to remain vulnerable and open to pain,
>   to make love my golden rule.

7. *A minister of the church or community to which the soul friend belongs commissions them in these or similar words*:

N ... I know that you have followed the way of Christ over the years, and that you have sought to set aside your own will for a higher will in open sharing with a soul friend (*or* spiritual director). You have committed yourself to practise disciplines and prayer that aid discernment and human growth, and to flee sins that distract from that path.

We believe God has called you to be be available for the work of soul friendship, in his way and in his time. We now therefore commission you as a soul friend.

8. *The soul friend may kneel, and be signed (or anointed*) on the forehead with the cross. The commissioning minister lays hands on the candidate and says:*

May the Creator who nurtures, the Christ who succours, and the Spirit who counsels grant you gifts of gentleness and discretion, integrity and compassion, faithfulness and understanding.

* *Some traditions reserve anointing with oil for ordination, healing and preparing for death. Those traditions which also use it for commissioning to a new form of ministry may anoint the candidates with oil.*

9. *There may be singing, testimony, informal words of encouragement, or prayer.*

10. *Those present may encircle the soul friend with hands stretched out in prayer. All, or a representative may say:*

When the journey as a soul friend is easy and when it is hard may you be encouraged by the great cloud of witnesses who urge you on:

> *Christ the great soul Friend of the world*
> *Beloved John, and Mother Mary at his side*
> *Desert fathers and mothers*
> *Brigid the fosterer of saints*
> *Aidan of the gentle heart*
> *Columba of the eagle eye*
> *St Francis*
> *St Teresa*
> *St Ignatius*
> *François Fenelon . . .*
> *A noble procession which now you join.*

> *The Blessing of the Three of limitless love be upon you*
> *The Father who affirms*
> *The Son who accompanies*
> *The Spirit who reveals*
> *That a well shall you be in the desert*
> *An island shall you be in the sea*
> *A light shall you be in the dark.*

RESOURCES FOR SOUL FRIENDS

Training

The range and availability of training courses vary widely in different countries. The USA is ahead of the field. In many countries an increasing number of Roman Catholic and Anglican dioceses offer training or advice for soul friends or prayer guides. An enquiry to a local office should ascertain what is available.

The Spiritual Directors International can be contacted at 1329 Seventh Avenue, San Francisco, California, CA94122–2507, USA.

Below are some training resources available in the UK at the time of publication.

The National Retreat Association keeps a list of contact people in each region who will meet an enquirer and may be able to link them up with a suitable spiritual director. It also publishes a leaflet, '*Choosing a Spiritual Guide*'. In its annual magazine *Retreats*, it includes information about retreats for soul friends. The NRA maintains a list of courses in spiritual direction run by the different denominations in the UK. For details send a C5 s.a.e. to: The National

Retreat Association, The Central Hall, 256 Bermondsey Street, London SE1 3UJ. Tel: 0171 357 7736. Fax: 0171 357 7724.

SPIDIR is a spiritual direction network which provides courses in various Anglican dioceses with aims such as 'to help participants to deepen their own spiritual experiences and awareness as a base from which they can begin to help others'. Initial contact through Ms Paddy Lane, 51 Lime Tree Grove, Shirley, Croydon CRO 8AZ.

The London Diocesan Centre for Spiritual Direction offers a two-year ecumenical course 'The Art of Spiritual Direction' to all who feel God is calling them to this much needed ministry. For information send a C5 s.a.e. to: The Administrator, LDCSD, S. Mary Woolnoth Vestry, Lombard Street, London EC3V 9AN.

The Scottish Churches Open College offer two courses, 'Training in Faith Accompaniment', and 'Training in Spiritual Direction', at either Craighead Spirituality Centre, Bothwell, Glasgow G71 8AU (Tel: 01698 285 300. Fax: 01698 891 014); or at House of Prayer, 8 Nile Grove, Edinburgh.

The Ministry of Spiritual Direction is a two-year course to test vocation and to develop skills as a spiritual director in the 'classical' form. It is led by an ecumenical team based in the west of England. The Course Administrator, Bristol Baptist College, The Promenade, Clifton, Bristol BS8 3NF. Tel: 0117 946 7050.

Craighead Spirituality Centre specialises in training courses, individually guided retreats and spiritual direction. These explore the senses, personality types, story, etc. The Retreat and Course Secretary, Craighead Spirituality Centre, Bothwell, Glasgow G71 8AU. Tel: 01698 285 300. Fax: 01698 891 014.

St Beuno's Ignatian Spirituality Centre offers courses in spiritual direction, as well as retreats. The Secretary, St Beuno's, St Asaph,

Denbighshire, North Wales LL17 OAS. Tel: 01745 583 444. Fax: 01745 584 151. <StBeunos@aol.com>

Acorn Christian Healing Trust sponsors *Christian Listeners*, a nationwide training programme in listening skills. Those who complete the training are used in listening ministries sponsored by churches and other groups. Acorn Christian Healing Trust, Whitehill Chase, High Street, Bordon GU35 OAP. Tel: 01420 478 121. Fax: 01420 478 122.

Mary Potter Centre offers short courses in the Myers-Briggs Personality Types and the Enneagram. Sr. Josephine Bugeja, 33 Mattock Lane, Ealing, London W5 5BH.

The Clinical Theology Association offers training in Christian pastoral counselling using insights from psychiatry, theology and primal work. Clinical Theology Association, St Mary's House, Church Westcote, Chipping Norton. OX7 6SF. Tel: 01993 830 209.

For those interested in caring and counselling from a biblical Christian perspective it is possible to subscribe to a quarterly periodical, *Carer and Counsellor*, published by CWR, Waverley Abbey House, Waverley Lane, Farnham, Surrey GU9 8EP.

Those who wish to explore the relationship between depth psychology and religion from the perspective of C.G. Jung may find out about lectures and local groups from: *The Guild of Pastoral Psychology*, P.O. Box 1107, London W3 6ZP. Tel: 0181 993 8366.

The author is not in a position to affirm everything that is offered by these agencies, but he believes that something of value can be received from them. Remember, however, that

> The neon consciousness of much modern psychology and spirituality will always leave us in soul poverty.
>
> *John O'Donohue*

Books and cassettes

(Only the UK publisher is given for books that are published both in the UK and in other countries.)

On soul friendship and spiritual direction
Allen, Joseph J., *Inner Way: Toward a Rebirth of Eastern Christian Spiritual Direction* (Eerdmans, 1994).

Barry, William A. and Connolly, William J. *The Practice of Spiritual Direction* (Harper & Row, 1991).

Barry, William, *Spiritual Direction and the Encounter with God* (Paulist Press, 1992).

Byrne, Lavinia (ed.), *Traditions of Spiritual Guidance* (Geoffrey Chapman, 1990).

Clutterbuck, David, *Everyone Needs a Mentor* (Institute of Personnel Management, 1990). Secular, but includes useful skills.

Conroy, Maureen, RSM, *Looking into the Well: Supervision of Spiritual Directors* (Loyola Press, Chicago, 1995).

Culligan, Kevin, *Spiritual Direction: Contemporary Readings* (Flame Press, New York, 1983).

Edwards, Tilden, *Spiritual Friend* (Paulist Press, New York, 1980).

Gratton, Carolyn, *The Art of Spiritual Guidance* (Crossroad, New York, 1995).

Guenther, Margaret, *Holy Listening* (DLT, 1994).

Guenther, Margaret, *Toward Holy Ground: Spiritual Directions for the Second Half of Life* (DLT, 1996).

Jeff, Gordon, *Spiritual Direction for Every Christian* (SPCK, 1987).

Kelsey, Morton, *Companions on the Inner Way* (Crossroad, 1984).

Leech, Kenneth, *Soul Friend* (DLT, 1994).

Liebert, Elizabeth, *Changing Life Patterns*: *Adult Development in Spiritual Direction* (Paulist Press, New York/Mahwah, 1992).

Long, Anne, *Approaches to Spiritual Direction* (Grove Spirituality, 9, 1984).

Neunfelder, J. and Coelho, M. *Writings on Spiritual Direction by Great Christian Masters* (Seabury Press, 1982).

Rakiczy, Susan, IHM (ed.), *Common Journey, Different Paths: Spiritual Direction in Cross Cultural Perspective* (Orbis Books, 1992).

Thornton, Martin, *Spiritual Direction* (SPCK, 1984).

Sellner, Edward C., *Mentoring: The Ministry of Spiritual Kinship* (Ave Maria Press; Notre Dame, IN, 1990).

Yungblut, John R., *The Gentle Art of Spiritual Guidance* (Element, 1991).

Zuercher, Suzanne, *Enneagram Companions: Growing in Relationships and Spiritual Direction* (Ave Maria Press, Notre Dame, IN, 1993).

Some classic letters of spiritual direction
Baird-Smith, Robin (ed.), *Living Water: An Anthology of Letters of Direction* (Fount, 1987).

Beausobore, Julia de (ed.), *Macarius: Russian Letters of Direction* (London, 1944).

Chitty, Derwas J., *The Letters of Saint Antony the Great* (SLG Press, Oxford, 1995).

Waterfield, Robin (trans.) *Streams of Grace: A Selection from the Letters of the Abbé de Tourville* (Fount, 1985).

Van der Weyer, Robert, *The Letters of Pelagius: Celtic Soul Friend* (Arthur James, 1995).

Useful introductions to Celtic spirituality
Mitton, Michael, *Restoring the Woven Cord* (DLT, 1995).

Newell, Philip, *Listening for the Heartbeat of God* (SPCK, 1997).

O'Donohue, John, *Anam Cara: Spiritual Wisdom from the Celtic World* (Bantam, 1997).

Sellner, Edward, *Soul-Making* (Twenty-Third Publications, Mystic Connecticut, 1991).

Sellner, Edward, *Wisdom of the Celtic Saints* (Ave Maria Press, 1993).

Simpson, Ray, *Celtic Daily Light* (Hodder & Stoughton, 1997).

Simpson, Ray, *Exploring Celtic Spirituality* (Hodder & Stoughton, 1995).

Waal, Esther de, *The Celtic Way of Prayer* (Hodder & Stoughton, 1996).

The Community of Aidan and Hilda publishes *A Classified Guide to Christian Celtic Books* for those who wish to make a deeper study of Celtic spirituality.

Useful books on discernment and listening
Aveyard, Ian and Muir, David *Fit for the Purpose: The Meaning of Christian Vocation How to Respond when God Calls* (St John's College Extension Studies, 1997).

Green, Thomas H., *Weeds Among the Wheat – Discernment: Where Prayer and Action Meet* (Ave Maria Press, Notre Dame, IN, 1994).

Huggett, Joyce, *Listening to Others* (Hodder & Stoughton, 1996).

Huggett, Joyce, *Listening to God* (Hodder & Stoughton, 1995).

Jacobs, Michael, *Swift to Hear* (SPCK, 1985).

Long, Anne, *Listening* (DLT, 1994).

Parker, Russ, *The Wild Spirit* (SPCK, 1996).

Useful books on prayer and spiritual disciplines
Companions for the Journey series published by SPCK includes:
    Praying with Francis of Assisi
    Praying with Ignatius Loyola
    Praying with Teresa of Avila
    Praying with Hildegaard of Bingen
    Praying with Julian of Norwich

Aelred of Rievaulx, *Spiritual Friendship*, trans. Mary Eugenia Laker SSND (Cistercian Publications, Kalamazoo, MI, 1977).

England, Edward (ed.), *Keeping a Spiritual Journal* (Highland Books, 1991).

Foster, Richard, *Celebration of Discipline* (Hodder & Stoughton, 1980).

Miller, Harold, *Finding a Personal Rule of Life* (Grove Books, 1987).

Brother Ramon SSF, *The Heart of Prayer* (Marshall Pickering, 1995).

Useful introductions to good and evil
Carter, T.T, *The Treasury of Devotion* (Longmans, 1960).

Parker, Russ, *The Occult: Deliverance from Evil* (Inter-Varsity Press, 1989).

Richards, John, *But Deliver Us from Evil* (DLT, 1978).

Useful introductions to desert wisdom
Bondi, Roberta, *To Pray and to Live: Conversations on Prayer with the Desert Fathers* (Burns & Oates, 1991).

Merton, Thomas, *The Wisdom of the Desert* (Sheldon Press, 1973).

Steward, Columba OSB (trans.), *The World of the Desert Fathers* (SLG Press, Oxford, 1995).

Waddell, Helen (trans.), *The Desert Fathers* (Collins, 1996).

Ward, Sister Benedicta (trans.), *The Wisdom of the Desert Fathers* (SLG Press, Oxford, 1995).

Useful introductions to self-knowledge
Goldsmith, Malcolm and Wharton, Martin *Knowing Me Knowing You* (SPCK, 1993).

Hanger, Joan, *The Little Book of Dreams* (Penguin, 1998).

Harris, Thomas A., *I'm O.K. You're O.K.* (Pan, 1976).

Miller, William, *Why do Christians Break Down?* (Augsberg, 1981).

Parker, Russ, *Healing Dreams* (SPCK, 1987).

Parker, Russ, *Praying with Dreams* (Cassette, Eagle, 1992).

Peck, M. Scott, *The Road Less Travelled* (Arrow Books, 1990).

Rayner, Claire, *Lifeguide: A Commonsense Approach to all Your Problems* (NEL, 1980).

Sheldrake, Philip, *Befriending our Desires* (DLT, 1994).

Useful introductions to personal or sexual wholeness
Michael, Chester P., *A Call to Holiness and Wholeness* (a cassette learning course).

Payne, Leanne, *The Broken Image* (Kingsway, 1994).

Payne, Leanne, *Crisis in Masculinity* (Kingsway, 1996).

Payne, Leanne, *The Healing Presence* (Kingsway, 1995).

Payne, Leanne, *Restoring the Christian Soul through Healing Prayer* (Kingsway, 1996).

Rumford, Douglas J., *Soul Shaping* (Tyndale, 1996). This includes questions for reflection and exercises.

Useful books about sacramental confession
In the Roman Catholic Church a booklet *Simple Penance* may be purchased from the Catholic Truth Society, 40–46 Harleyford Road, London SE11 5AY.

In the Church of England a card for the traditional Confession and Absolution and a card for the modern Rite of Penance may be purchased from the Additional Curates Society, Gordon Browning House, 8 Spitfire Road, Birmingham B24 9PB.

Two books which explore sacramental confession are

Ross, Kenneth, *Hearing Confession* (SPCK, 1974).

Speyr, Adrian von, *Confession: The Encounter with Christ in Penance* (Nelson, 1964).

Guidance on retreats and pilgrimages
The annual magazine of the National Retreat Association lists retreat centres in the UK: *Retreats* (£3.75 in 1998), The Central Hall, 256 Bermondsey Street, London SE1 3UJ.

The Irish Missionary Union, Orwell Park, Dublin 6; Tel: 00353 14965433; will send information on Irish Retreat Centres (enclose £1.50).

Pilgrim Adventure, 120 Bromley Heath Road, Downend, Bristol BS16 6JJ; Tel: 0117 957 3997; organise pilgrimages in Celtic lands.

Leighton, Adrian, *In the Footsteps of Our Native Saints*, is available from the Community of Aidan and Hilda.

O'Malley, Brendan, *A Pilgrim's Manual: St David's* (Paulinus Press, 1985).

Robinson, Martin, *Sacred Places, Pilgrim Paths: An Anthology of Pilgrimage* (Marshall Pickering, 1997), contains guidance about the meaning and method of making pilgrimages.

Toulson, Shirley, *Celtic Journeys* (Fount, 1995), outlines pilgrimages in Scotland and Northumbria.

Notes

Introduction

1. 'A soul friend is like' © Heulwen Carrier, 1998. Printed with permission.

1 Why the revived interest in soul friendship?

1. Clutterbuck, David, *Everyone Needs a Mentor* (Institute of Personnel Management, 1990).
2. Quoted in *For a Change* magazine, December/January 1997/8.
3. Cassian, John, *Institutes* and *Conferences*, trans. E.C.S. Gibson in *Nicene and Post Nicence Christian Fathers* (London, 1899–1900).
4. *Book of Leinster*.
5. Aelred of Rievaulx, *Spiritual Friendship* (Mowbray, 1982).
6. I have no published statistics, but Roman Catholic colleagues without exception report that the numbers who come for formal confession are a small fraction of what they used to be.
7. Simpson, Ray, *Exploring Celtic Spirituality: Historic Roots for Our Future* (Hodder & Stoughton, 1995).

2 Becoming a soul friend – A new calling?

1. Schumacher, E.F., *A Guide for the Perplexed* (Harper & Row, New York, 1977).

2. *The Week*, 20 June 1998.
3. Wakefield, Gordon S. (ed.), *A Dictionary of Christian Spirituality* (SCM, 1983).
4. Merton, Thomas, *Spiritual Direction and Meditation* (Anthony Clarke, 1975), provides insight into Merton's spiritual direction of contemplative nuns.
5. Cassian, John, *Conferences*, trans. E.C.S. Gibson in *Nicene and Post Nicene Christian Fathers* (London, 1895–1900).
6. Brother Ramon SSF, *The Heart of Prayer* (Marshall Pickering, 1995).

3 Rapport – John and biblical insights into soul friendship

1. In *Liber Ardmachanus*: *The Book of Armagh*, ed. with Introduction by J. Gwynn (Dublin, 1913).
2. The Greek word *antileipsis* is often translated as 'helper', but the first meaning given in Liddell and Scott's Greek-English Lexicon is 'a receiving in turn or exchange'.
3. Goldingay, John, *St John's Nottingham Newsletter*, December 1996.

4 Detachment – Desert insights into soul friendship

1. Ward, Benedicta (trans.), *Institutes* and *Conferences*, Cassian 16.
2. The word for soul friend in the Greek Orthodox Church, *syncellus*, 'one who shares a cell', still expresses this.
3. *The Sayings of the Fathers*, Anonymous Series, no. 17.
4. This story is based on Jerome's *The Life of St. Paul the First Hermit*. There is an English translation in Waddell, Helen, *The Desert Fathers* (Collins, 1996).
5. Ward, Benedicta (trans.), *Institutes* and *Conferences*, Cassian 11.10.
6. The sayings, anecdotes and short stories of the fourth-century desert fathers and mothers were handed down and collected in

the fifth century. One collection was arranged alphabetically under the name of each monk; another collection was arranged under themes. In addition, groups of monks would preserve the sayings of their founder. These were also collected together and published in Latin as *The Lives of the Fathers*. Other early writers such as Athanasius, Jerome, John Cassian, Evagrius and St John Climacus also wrote about some of the desert fathers and mothers. The two small books referred to under *Further Reading* at the end of Chapter 4 give information about translations and selections in English.

7. *The Lives of the Fathers*.
8. These are explored in Chapter 11.
9. Seven letters of spiritual guidance which Antony wrote to his disciples have been translated by Derwas Chitty as *The Letters of St Antony the Great* and are published by SLG Press, Fairacres, Oxford (1995).
10. Merton, Thomas, *Seeds of Contemplation* (Anthony Clarke, 1972).

5 Envisioning – Pre-Christian insights into soul friendship

1. Chadwick, Norah, *The Druids* (University of Wales Press, 1966).
2. See Piggott, Stuart, *The Druids* (Thames & Hudson, 1994); and Kendrick, T., *The Druids* (Senate, Random House, 1996).
3. In Hull, Eleanor, *The Poem Book of the Gael* (Chatto & Windus, 1912).
4. See Matthews, John and Caitlin, *The Little Book of Celtic Wisdom* (Element, 1993).
5. See Squires, Charles, *Mythology of the Celtic People* (Bracken Books, 1996).
6. See Piggot, *Druids*; and Kendrick, *Druids* (Senate).
7. Craig, Mary, *Man from a Far Country* (Hodder & Stoughton, 1983).

8. Polanyi, Michael, *Personal Knowledge: Towards a Post-Critical Philosophy* (Routledge, 1998).

9. Bryant, Christopher, *Jung and the Christian Way* (DLT, 1983); and *The River Within* (DLT, 1978).

10. Jung, Carl Gustav, *Modern Man in Search of a Soul* (Routledge & Kegan Paul, 1978).

11. Satinova, Jeffrey M.D., Chapter 16, 'The Pagan Revolution', in *Homosexuality and the Politics of Truth* (Baker Books, USA, 1996).

12. This is explored in an essay by Sellner, Edward C., *A Common Dwelling: Soul Friendship in Early Celtic Monasticism* (Cistercian Publications, College of Saint Catherine, 2004 Randolph Avenue, Saint Paul, Minnesota, 55104).

13. See Gants, Geoffrey (trans.), *Early Irish Myths and Sagas* (Penguin, 1981).

14. Madden, Eric, *A Teacher's Guide to Storytelling at Historic Sites* (English Heritage, 1992).

6 Discernment – St Morgan's insights into soul friendship

1. Augustine and other figures in the Western Church attacked Pelagius for his criticisms of their writings. He was accused of heresy and twice cleared of this charge at church synods. A pope declared him innocent of these charges but retracted this under pressure. A synod in Africa declared him to be heretical. Synods at this time were influenced by worldly politics of the sort that Pelagius wanted to clean up. No council representing the universal Church condemned him, and Pelagius reaffirmed his allegiance to all the teachings of the Holy Catholic Church at one of these synods. As the universal Church weighs these things, there is growing conviction that Augustine himself may have been heretical in teaching that the material and human creation (including sex) were inherently evil, and that Pelagius may have

been misrepresented. For a full treatment of this issue see Rees, B.R., *Pelagius: A Reluctant Heretic* (Boydell Press, 1991).

2. See Rees, B.R., *The Letters of Pelagius and His Followers* (Boydell Press, 1991); also a popular edited paraphrase of his letters, Van der Weyer, Robert, *The Letters of Pelagius, Celtic Soul Friend* (Arthur James, 1995).

3. I decided to follow this up, and discovered that, before the time of Christ, the Celts mingled with the Iberian people, who might be called the Aborigines of Europe. This people then spread outwards, and some people think that the Basque people have inherited their language. That seems doubtful, since research into the Basque and Celtic languages fails to uncover obvious connections. What seems more likely is that that the Basques are a parallel people and that both they and the Celts have retained certain primal qualities in common. Certainly the Basques are a remnant of prehistoric populations, and are as distinct from the continental peoples as are the Celts. See Hubert, Henri, *The History of the Celtic People* (Bracken Books, 1993), p. 77.

4. Puhl, Louis J. (trans.), *The Spiritual Exercises of St Ignatius* (Loyola University Press, Chicago, 1951).

5. Israel, Martin, *The Spirit of Counsel: Spiritual Perspectives in the Counselling Process* (Hodder & Stoughton, 1983).

7 Fostering – Irish insights into soul friendship

1. Ryan, John, *Irish Monasticism: Origins and Early Development* (Four Courts Press, 1992), gives extensive treatment of the training of monks and their roles within monasteries.

2. The sources for these stories in English translation are Stokes, Whitley (trans.), *Lives of Saints from the Book of Lismore* (Llanerch, 1995); Plummer, Charles (ed.), *Lives of Irish Saints* (Oxford University Press, 1922).

8 Faithfulness – insights into soul friendship in Britain

1. Ninian and David were Britons; Brother Aidan and St Aidan of Lindisfarne were Irish who lived in Britain; Cuthbert, Herbert, Hilda, Oswald and Oswin were Saxons, and Boisil might have been any of these.
2. Rhigyfarch, *Life of St David*, trans. J.W. James (University of Wales Press, 1967), ch. 15.
3. Bede, *The Ecclesiastical History of the English People*, trans. B. Colgrave (Oxford University Press, 1994), 1V 23.
4. The four sources of the life of Cuthbert are *The Life of St Cuthbert* by an anonymous monk of Lindisfarne available in *Two Lives of St Cuthbert*, ed. and trans. B. Colgrave (Cambridge University Press, 1985); Bede's prose *Life of St Cuthbert* now available in the above and in *The Age of Bede*, trans. J.F. Webb and D.H. Farmer (Penguin, 1985); Bede's *Metrical Life of St Cuthbert* now available in *Cuthbert, His Cult and Community*, ed. G. Bonner et al. (Woodbridge, 1989); Bede's *Ecclesiastical History of the English People*, ed. and trans. B. Colgrave and R.A.B. Mynors (Oxford University Press, 1994).

9 Wildness – Hermits' insights into soul friendship

1. See Marsden, John, *Sea-Road of the Saints: Celtic Holy Men in the Hebrides* (Floris, 1995).
2. Bowen, E.G., *Saints Seaways and Settlements in the Celtic Lands* (University of Wales Press, 1977).
3. Jung, C.G., *Modern Man in Search of a Soul* (Routledge & Kegan Paul, 1978), p. 248.
4. Rodgers, Michael and Losack, Marcus *Glendalough: A Celtic Pilgrimage* (Columba Press, 1996).
5. *The First Voyage of the Coracle* with *The Way of Life*, Community of Aidan and Hilda, Lindisfarne Retreat, Holy Island, Berwick-upon-Tweed TD15 2SD.

6. Rohr, Richard and Martos, Joseph *The Wild Man's Journey: Reflections on Male Spirituality* (St Anthony Messenger Press, 1991), ch. 16.

10 Prophecy – Columba's insights into soul friendship

1. Adamnan, *Life of St Columba*, trans. Richard Sharpe, (Penguin, 1991).
2. Leech, Kenneth, *Soul Friend* (Sheldon Press, 1979).

11 Fitness training – Columbanus's insights into soul friendship

1. Epistles 1:6 in Walker, G.S.M. (ed.), *Sancti Columbani Opera* (The Dublin Institute for Advanced Studies, 1970). This contains the complete writings of Columbanus in English.
2. Lapidge, Michael (ed.), *Columbanus: Studies on the Latin Writings* (Boydell Press, 1997).
3. Carothers, Merlin, *From Prison to Praise* (Hodder & Stoughton, 1996).
4. Comiskey, Andrew, *Pursuing Sexual Wholeness: How Jesus Heals the Homosexual*, Workbook (Lake Mary Creation House, 1989).
5. This paragraph draws from Yungblut, John R., *The Gentle Art of Spiritual Guidance* (Element, 1991).
6. See Vonholdt, Christl Ruth (ed.), *Striving for Gender Identity: Homosexuality and Christian Counselling: A Workbook for the Church* (German Institute for Youth and Society, Schloß Reichenberg, D-64385, Reichelsheim, Germany).
7. For information on the Celtic soul friend's influence on the evolution of the sacrament of penance in the West, see Watkins, O.D.A., *History of Penance* (Longmans Green, 1920), vol. 2 on *The Keltic System*. Also Dallen, James, *The Reconciling Community: The Rite of Penance* (Pueblo, New York, 1986).

8. Tommasini, Anselmo M., *Irish Saints in Italy* (Sands, 1937), quoting extensive notes by Mrs. Concannon in *The Life of St Columban* (Dublin C.T.S., 1915).
9. Stuttaford, Dr Thomas, *The Times*, 1 January 1998.

12 Order – Later monastic insights into soul friendship

1. These Rules are printed in English in Maidin, Uinseann O. (trans.), *The Celtic Monk: Rules and Writings of Early Irish Monks* (Cistercian Publications, Massachusetts, 1996). I have adopted the scholarly consensus as to the dating of the Rules that this book records. Most of the Rules other than Tallaght were written some two centuries after the death of the saint in whose name they were composed. In some cases this attribution may have been simply a dedication to the founder of the monastery concerned.

13 An art – Aelred's insights into soul friendship

1. Cicero, *On Friendship*, in *On the Good Life* (Penguin Classics, 1971).
2. Aelred of Rievaulx, *Spiritual Friendship*, trans. Mary Eugenia Laker SSND (Cistercian Publications, Kalamazoo, MI, 1977).
3. *The Life of St Ninian* by Aelred is included in *Two Celtic Saints: The Lives of Ninian and Kentigern* (Llanerch, 1989).

14 Dying – soul friends at heaven's door

1. Wilcock, Penelope, *Spiritual Care of Dying and Bereaved People* (SPCK, 1996).
2. Kennedy-Fraser, Marjory and Kenneth Macleod (eds.), *Songs of the Hebrides and Other Celtic Songs from the Highlands of Scotland* (Boosey, 1909).

3. Carmichael, Alexander, *The Carmina Gadelica* (Floris Rooks, 1992), Note on prayer no. 51, p. 578.
4. *The Martyrdom of Ignatius, Ante-Nicene Fathers* (Eerdmans, 1981), vol. 1, p. 131.
5. From 'The Life of St Davevca, or Moninna, the Abbess', in De Paor, Liam (ed.), *Saint Patrick's World* (Four Courts Press, 1993).
6. Sellner, Edward, *Soulmaking: The Telling of a Spiritual Journey* (Twenty-Third Publications, Mystic Connecticut, 1991).

15 Choosing and changing a soul friend

1. See Appendix 2.
2. Athanasius, *The Life of Antony*, trans. R.C. Gregg (Classic of Western Spirituality, New York, 1980).
3. *The Sayings of the Desert Fathers: The Alphabetical Collection, Poeman 189 Sayings*, trans. Benedicta Ward (Mowbray, 1981).
4. Maidin, Uinseann O. (trans.), *The Celtic Monk: Rules and Writings of Early Irish Monks* (Cistercian Publications, Massachusetts, 1996).

16 Qualities and disciplines of a soul friend

1. Michael, Chester P. and Norrisey, Marie C. *Prayer and Temperament Different Prayer Forms for Different Personality Types* (The Open Door Inc., P.O. Box 8, Virginia 22902, Kalamazoo, 1984). See also Goldsmith, Martin and Wharton, Malcolm *Knowing Me Knowing You* (SPCK, 1993).
2. See, for example, Rayner, Claire, *Lifeguide: A Commonsense Approach to all Your Problems* (New English Library, 1980).

17 Principles and ground rules for accompanying others

1. Quoted in *Honest to Goddess* by Geraint ap Iorwerth, which, despite its misleading title, is an interesting study of the eternal feminine and wisdom within God.
2. Quoted in *Wellspring* sponsored by Francis Dewar and the Journey Inward Journey Outward Project.
3. *The Tablet*, 18 October 1997.

18 Some tools for the soul friend

1. See, for example, Jung, C.G. *Dreams* (Ark, Routledge, 1985).
2. Hanger, Joan, *The Little Book of Dreams* (Penguin, 1998).
3. Miller, William, *Why do Christians break down?* (Augsberg, 1981).
4. The story is told in Simpson, Sally, *Bruce: Patience Please, I Think I'm Melting* (New Millennium, 292 Kennington Road, London SE11 4LD, 1997)

19 Learning to listen

1. Quoted in Monk Kidd, Sue, *God's Joyful Surprise* (Hodder & Stoughton, 1990).

20 Stages on life's journey

1. Howatch, Susan, *Mystical Paths* (HarperCollins, 1996), pp. 538–44.

21 Pitfalls

1. Lake, Frank, *Clinical Theology: A Theological and Psychiatric Basis to Clinical Pastoral Care* (DLT, 1973).

22 Working with a rule of life

1. *Rule for a New Brother*, foreword by Henri J. Nouwen (DLT, 1973).
2. For example, the Community of Aidan and Hilda, the Iona Community, the Northumbria Community.
3. Van der Weyer, Robert, *The Letters of Pelagius, Celtic Soul Friend* (Arthur James, 1995).
4. Miller, Harold, *Finding a Personal Rule of Life* (Grove Books, 1987).
5. See Shea, Elinor, 'Spiritual Direction and Social Consciousness', in Byrne, Lavinia et al., *Approaches to Spiritual Direction, The Way Supplement* (The Way Publications, no. 54, Autumn 1985), p. 30.
6. See 'Midday Prayer', in Simpson, Ray, *Celtic Worship through the Year* (Hodder & Stoughton, 1997).

INDEX

Other books by Ray Simpson published by Hodder & Stoughton

Exploring Celtic Spirituality: Historic Roots for our Future

"Ray Simpson has provided us with a glimpse of a spirituality which is now re-emerging from the mists of time. He helps us to get beyond nostalgia, and challenges us to learn from our Celtic saints a way of being renewed in Christ."

Russ Parker

In each chapter a feature of original Celtic Christianity is highlighted, such as cherishing the earth, contemplative prayer, triumphant dying and the healing of society. The book has a practical emphasis with prayers and responses at the end of each chapter, providing material for all churches and individuals to enrich and deepen their faith.
ISBN 0 340 64203 3

Celtic Daily Light: A Spiritual Journey Through the Year

In the standard 'daily light format' but sourced from the great wealth of Celtic literature, including the author's own work, this book has been highly acclaimed:

"These words affirm that tradition is not dead, it is very much alive and has power to penetrate our being and to transform us. These readings will have profound relevance for all who read them."

David Fitzgerald

"It's biblical with a Celtic edge. This is the time to soak in the Scriptures and our rich heritage. This publication will help us do both."

Gerald Coates, speaker, author and broadcaster
ISBN 0 340 69488 2

Celtic Worship Through the Year

Preface by Ian Bradley

"The book is rich in worship rites for days of the week and the various seasons of the church calendar as well as settings for Celtic Saints Days and special celebrations in the Celtic way of being the church without doors. Although we have virtually no records of the forms of liturgy in the ancient church of these islands, many of their hallmarks – simplicity, freshness, directness of imagery, reythm and brevity in a poetic quality – have survived, and they are characteristic of the style and content of this excellent collection I recommend this book as a wonderful resource for both understanding and enjoying something of the worshipping heart of our Celtic ancestors."

Russ Parker

ISBN 0 340 68667 7

Celtic Blessings For Everyday Life: Prayers for Every Occasion

Our forbears, the Celts, had blessings for just about everything, from getting dressed to milking the cow. Home life, work life, travel, birth and death and everything in between got blessed.

Sleep
Sleep in peace
Sleep soundly
Sleep in love
Weaver of dreams
Weave well in you as you sleep

ISBN 0 340 71421 2